Consciousness Lost and Found

Consciousness Lost and Found

A Neuropsychological Exploration

Lawrence Weiskrantz
University of Oxford

Oxford New York Tokyo

OXFORD UNIVERSITY PRESS

1997

Oxford University Press, Great Clarendon Street, Oxford OX2 6DP
Oxford New York
Athens Auckland Bangkok Bogota Bombay Buenos Aires
Calcutta Cape Town Dar es Salaam Delhi Florence Hong Kong
Istanbul Karachi Kuala Lumpur Madras Madrid Melbourne
Mexico City Nairobi Paris Singapore Taipei Tokyo Toronto
and associated companies in
Berlin Ibadan

Oxford is a trade mark of Oxford University Press

Published in the United States
by Oxford University Press Inc., New York

A catalogue record for this book is available from the British Library

Library of Congress Cataloging in Publication Data
Weiskrantz, Lawrence
Consciousness lost and found: a neuropsychological exploration / L. Weiskrantz
Includes bibliographical references and index.
1. Consciousness.   2. Neuropsychology.   3. Brain damage.
4. Amnesia.   I. Title.
QP411.W45   1997   612.8–dc21   96-52109

ISBN 0 19 852301 7

Typeset by Hewer Text Composition Services, Edinburgh
Printed in Great Britain by Bookcraft (Bath) Ltd
Midsomer Norton, Avon

Acknowledgements

A stay at the Rockefeller Study Center, Bellagio, Italy during March, 1992, offered a marvellous opportunity and perfect environment in which to prepare an early draft of this book, which then remained more or less dormant until after my retirement late in 1993, except for invaluable comments from Jimmy Schwartz, who was a Visiting Fellow at Magdalen College, Oxford in 1992–3. A Leverhulme Foundation Emeritus Fellowship for the academic year 1994–5 provided welcome secretarial support. A stay at the University of Arizona in January, 1995, allowed me to take the matter farther in a lovely, sheltered, and stimulating environment, and finally, during a visit later that year to the Salk Institute and the University of California, San Diego, I was able to benefit from a number of stimulating discussions with Francis Crick and some of his colleagues there and also at the California Institute of Technology. I have had helpful exchanges about specific points in the book with Paul Azzopardi, John Barbur, Alan Cowey, Bea DeGelder, Harvey Karten, Brenda Milner, Mortimer Mishkin, Dick Passingham, David Rosenthal, Keith Ruddock, Petra Stoerig, Endel Tulving, and Bill Verplenck, to all of whom I am grateful. I owe a special vote of thanks to Arash Sahraie, who has been not only a skilled and dedicated post-doctoral research colleague, but has also helped with many of the diagrams in the book.

Academics are privileged to be able to attend a variety of specialized conferences, and I owe a very large debt to many persons, too many to list, who have both stimulated my interest and have informed it. I am truly pleased to express my gratitude to so many, at least collectively.

More particularly and more concretely, two referees of this manuscript both made many helpful suggestions, dropping their cloak of anonymity to me. I do not reveal who they are because—seeing the finished product—they may well not want to be known publicly! But I owe them a very special thanks. My wife, Barbara, during her own busy life, has shown her usual forbearance, support, and help—including preparation of the indices.

Recognizable variants of passages in this book will be found in 'The problem of animal consciousness in relation to neuropsychology' (*Behavioural brain research*, 1995, **71**, 171–5), 'Fragments of memory' (to appear in

Neuropsychologia), Chapter 1 of *Animal Intelligence*, a Royal Society Discussion Meeting publication (Oxford University Press, 1985), and in *Blindsight* (Oxford University Press, 1986).

Oxford, May 1996   L. W.

Contents

Introduction

The starting point for this book is the study of brain-damaged subjects who retain the very capacities they think they have lost. The form in which each of these capacities is demonstrated may be different, but in some sense it is the same capacity. And so a 'blindsight' patient may claim not to 'see' the very visual stimuli that he or she can be shown to be able to discriminate by 'guessing', and without the patient's having knowledge of such success. The amnesic patient can be shown to learn and retain information that he or she does not realize is 'memory'—nor can be made to realize. For that patient, there is no experience of 'remembering' an event beyond a minute or so. In fact, in every major class of defect in which patients apparently lose some particular cognitive ability through brain damage, examples of preserved capacities can be found of which the patient is unaware. This range extends from perception, to meaning, to memory, and to language, with several different subtypes within each of the categories.

These facts are well known to neuropsychologists, but not so well known to a wider public. But quite aside from their intrinsic interest, they seem to offer both a challenge and an opportunity to consider the brain mechanisms of conscious awareness, and what its functional status might be in patients' lives. It also presses us to ask whether animals who share much the same brain anatomy as humans also share awareness. To tackle such a question requires that we ask of animals the same types of questions we ask of people when we try to decide whether they are aware.

There is something of an epidemic of interest these days in consciousness, and especially in trying to understand how the brain manages it—whatever 'it' may be, and for that matter, whatever 'manages' means. Philosophers, psychologists, cognitive scientists, physicists, and neuroscientists have been addressing the issues in surprisingly large numbers over the past 5 years, and this is to be warmly welcomed. The development, in itself, is remarkable because the subject, at least for scientists, traditionally was dismissed pejoratively as metaphysics, outside the scope of their subject and impossible to pursue empirically. No doubt some aspects still are, but several are not. And many philosophers of mind considered it to be unnecessary for their arguments to turn to, or be based upon, scientific facts; their task as regards science, if there was one, was to clear up the muddle in the utterances of the scientists. Some, of neo-Wittgensteinian ilk, attack these with self-congratulatory zealotry. Personally, at any rate, had it not been for patients actually forcing me to admit that not only was there a problem, but a fascinating and important one, I probably should have stayed clear of what scientists used to think of as metaphysics, and what philosophers relished as a muddle. I find it mildly amusing that for some 26 years I held the Chair of Psychology in a department at Oxford that was dedicated to teaching undergraduates in the School of P.P.P.—Psychology, Philosophy, and Physiology. The majority of students combined psychology with philosophy (only 2 of the 3 P's were studied), but during my tenure these two disciplines, for most tutors, with a few exceptions (one of them a noteworthy Wilde Reader of Mental Philosophy), and for most students, remained quite disparate. The P.P.P. students could well have been reading Greek and not philosophy as far as the psychologists were concerned, and the same separation, perhaps even greater, was maintained by the philosophers regarding psychology. By the time I was about to retire in 1993, forces from both within and outside Oxford had moved to bring the psychological and philosophical interests closer together, and today, throughout universities in the West there is a heavy barrage of joint seminars and lectures on related aspects of psychology and philosophy of mind, together with new allied subjects, such as cognitive science. And there are academic societies devoted to their union, or at least their disputation, both in America and in Europe. I have benefited enormously from attendance at many of these meetings, and from discussions with a wide spectrum of interesting contributors. Admittedly, some Oxford philosophers have remained resolutely and disdainfully aloof from this development. (I can recall trying to introduce two of the leading and well-known investigators of 'sign language' in chimpanzees to a distinguished Oxford philosopher in the Senior Common Room of an Oxford college. The topic and my guests' findings at the time were innovative, provocative, intrinsically fascinating, and deeply controversial. I failed—no flicker of interest could be evoked in him.) There are so many philosophers in Oxford that there is room for non-standard deviations, but I have no doubt that the liaison is here to stay. We may even graduate soon to joint examination questions!

This book will not review the manifold offerings of others. This will be interpreted by some as arrogance on my part, or as ignorance, or as laziness, attributes that are not mutually exclusive, and I am willing to admit some culpability in at least two of these regards. In part, I am unable to do justice to some of those offerings, even though I have read or attempted to read much of what is available, and have found many reviews useful. But I simply do not understand the intricacies and mysteries of arguments from quantum mechanics (Penrose, 1989; Hameroff and Penrose, 1995) and wave collapse (Burns, 1990), nor what specific investigations, if any, must be truncated by Gödel's theorem. And what I do understand only serves to puzzle me as to the form in which some of the arguments are constructed and how one would forge links with the empirical evidence that sits at quite a different level. As regards philosophers of mind, they are a very heterogeneous group and I have been stimulated and provoked by many. Those who actually address empirical findings are close to my heart, but philosophers do not usually actually *start* from that position. And by and large the philosophers' knowledge of the empirical findings in the field that I wish to examine is understandably patchy, with certain notable exceptions, and is sometimes just wrong. In other cases they seize upon a single interesting phenomenon, like 'split-brain' patients, and expand it into a universe of speculations, gedanken experiments or even gedanken fantasies, without fussing over whether the original details were correct. Finally, I am wary of some philosophers who wish to solve the problems from the armchair by verbal boot-strapping, no matter how clever they are, and some are very clever. It is curious how some attacks on folk psychology emanate from that folksy piece of philosophical equipment, from which it is simply not possible to generate new *domains* of knowledge. I have found the scientists writing on the topic, especially Crick (1994) and Edelman (1989), not to mention some of my own colleagues and coworkers, to be the most helpful to me, and am grateful that they do not let philosophical niceties get in the way of speculation about real brains. In any event, to write such a treatise that reviewed this wealth of opinion would simply detract from my main purpose. Aside from *The neuropsychology of consciousness* (Milner and Rugg, 1992), an excellent but varied collection of reviews by different authors, and the valuable edited volume by Marcel and Bisiach (1988), *Consciousness in contemporary science*, which includes some neuropsychological material but also ranges more widely, there are few books that systematically derive their arguments from the varieties of consciousness that are lost in brain damage, and that pursue the implications for how the brain might operate when they are present, both in people and in animals. It seemed worth trying to concentrate on that as the main project.

But first of all, some explanation of the oddity of the title is required. As the book concerns patients who, in one sense or another, have *lost* awareness, there is no puzzle over 'Lost' in the title. By 'Found' I mean 'retained' and 'established' (*The concise Oxford dictionary*). To convey that sense, strictly speaking, it should be 'founded', but that would be infelicitous. I wish to contrast my position with any other that explains consciousness by explaining it away, or substitutes as yet unknown computer software for it. I think, instead, one should try to elevate one's explanations to the level where they actually give full credence to the importance of awareness. Any patient who has lost his sense of 'seeing' or of 'touch' will understand that: what he has lost is his awareness, not his concept, nor a draft, nor the key to allow him to escape from a Theatre, Cartesian or otherwise. This is in no sense to diminish the great complexity of the issues and of allied human cognitive capacities generally, nor to deny the vagueness with which the terms like consciousness and awareness are used, nor to fail to acknowledge the illuminating treatment of these terms by skilful dissectors, but notwithstanding all that, there is a hard nub that requires explanation—not only for such patients (some of the blindsight subjects I have studied are avid readers of the topic!) and anyone else interested in them—but also because perhaps it offers a starting point, from where the matter might be pursued further. It would be pretentious in the extreme to suggest that I have 'Found' the solution to the thorny problem of conscious awareness and its neurological basis. I have had a go. The character of what is 'Lost' in the syndromes under consideration offers a challenge, as well as suggesting a possible route towards a solution, or at least to a step in that direction. Moreover, it is one that maps onto both philosophical and a neuroscientific landscapes. If this particular enterprise fails, it will be in part because at least some aspects of the exploration are empirically testable. Whatever the outcome, I hope it may nevertheless tempt others to also have a go.

When I first embarked on this project, I teasingly put it forward to the relevant editor at Oxford University Press as a proposed book on the 'What, Whether, How, and Why of Consciousness'. I thought the mock pretentiousness might amuse some of my fellow Delegates of the Press. Embarrassingly, this was actually preserved as the title of the proposal that was forwarded to the Delegates of the Press by the editor, and it was actually endorsed by the Delegates as such—but with a wry note that perhaps a simpler title might be preferable! Indeed, it would be. But I do seriously think the neuropsychological facts are pertinent to all four of these questions, and all four are, in one way or another, addressed in the book. There are even four chapters that contain these words in their titles. I am not wholly satisfied with my efforts, but they are starting points, for me at least.

I have tried to make each chapter intelligible in its own right, and the book as a whole readable to the non-specialist. As a result, there is a measure of redundancy between some of the chapters to make it unnecessary for the reader to skip backwards or forwards, although the figures are only reproduced once. Addressing the non-specialist will annoy some, but hopefully will be a relief to others. I know that I would be very annoyed in reading this book as a specialist. There are many pertinent facts and counter-arguments that the expert will accuse me of omitting and, even more serious, many authors whose work deserves to have been included will note the absence, the more so as I might actually be ignorant of it. This is especially so in the areas in which I have not personally worked, or worked to a much lesser extent than with the phenomena of blindsight and amnesia, with which in total I have spent some 30 years. Nothing offends the active scientist more than for his or her work to be passed over, and nothing more titillates an author who wishes to irritate a competing adversary than knowingly to fail to quote their work. I can only plead that I have not deliberately discriminated, nor have I been tempted by or enjoyed any such titillations here. I am sorry for admissions and over-simplifications; I have no doubt these will be pointed out to me.

There is another difficulty with which an author in this area must contend, namely that the field is moving so quickly that he is bound to be out of date. Some of the speculations found in the chapter on brain mechanisms, (How?) may well have already been put to the test by the time this goes to press, especially as non-invasive methods of examining function are evolving apace. Especially in the area of blindsight, memory, and brain imaging, I resolutely hope that current research will have made some of the speculations redundant!

The book starts with a review of some of the conditions in which brain-damaged patients can be said to have lost an awareness of a retained capacity, followed by a discussion of some of the general issues that are pertinent to neuropsychological analysis. There are aspects of these general issues and matters of terminology that are not necessary for the argument, but an Appendix is devoted to taking some of these a bit farther. There follow chapters on blindsight and amnesia, but the former deliberately focuses on neural pathways and visual attributes, and the latter more on the nature of the psychological disorder and patients' commentaries. Given the importance of commentaries in making decisions about another person's awareness, the next chapter addresses the question of awareness by animals, the possible homologous role of commentaries for them, and how the question might be addressed in practical terms. The chapter on 'How?' grapples with the question of how the brain deals with the problem in its normal intact state, and I also take the opportunity to expose my own general strategic proclivities.

Finally, except for a brief summary chapter, there is a treatment of the question of the evolutionary value of awareness. Here, too, as is true throughout, the emphasis is derived from the patients: if you want to know what something might be good for, examine the situation where it is no longer present.

The summary chapter tries to bring some of these disparate strands together. If many other readers are like me, they will jump to that chapter first, but although there are mysteries about consciousness, the final chapter is not quite like the final chapter of a mystery thriller. I hope it will not discourage them from going back to the evidence and the arguments.

1

The unseen and the unknown

The very phrase, 'brain-damaged' conjures up terrible images of lives blighted or destroyed. Those types of damage which do cause serious loss of mental and physical capacities are what most people associate with brain damage, and I do not want to trivialize these cases in any way. However, there are many different types of damage, resulting in a whole spectrum of effects. At the less serious end of the spectrum lie those phenomena which impact on everyday life in relatively minor ways, and can be accommodated through changes in habits and routines. It is possible to sustain damage to the brain which affects only your ability to remember strings of numbers longer than one or two, or your memory for names—which plagues practically everyone sooner or later, with or without brain damage. Or a part of the visual field might be made insensitive as a result of damage to the visual cortex. But in that case the subject simply uses the remaining intact visual field for everyday purposes, and may scarcely notice the 'missing' part of the field. Indeed, we all have a small region of absolute blindness in each eye, the optic disc, of which we remain unaware in everyday life.

To the scientist brain-damaged patients have been a source of highly specific knowledge and fascinating, illuminating insights. Through the cooperation of patients, neuropsychologists have made significant progress in understanding what the damaged brain tells us about the normal brain. Those cases of specific impairments restricted to relatively isolated capacities that occur with damage in limited regions of the brain have been especially useful. They can tell us not only what capacities can be disturbed in relative isolation from others, but also which anatomical systems of the brain are important for their processing, especially in conjunction with modern imaging methods that reveal the functioning of both the normal and the damaged living brain.

There is another aspect of brain damage that is really the major focus of the book. It turns out, surprisingly, that in virtually all of the major cognitive categories that are disturbed by brain damage, there can be remarkably preserved functioning without the patients themselves being aware of this (cf. Schacter *et al.*, 1988; Weiskrantz, 1991a). In some cases the patient is unaware *that* the capacity remains, in others the patient is actually unaware *of* the events that he or she can be demonstrated to be able to detect and discriminate.

It took quite a long time for these phenomena to be recognized, even in neuropsychology. The best and most thoroughly studied example of this 'performance without awareness' is the severe memory disorder known as the amnesic syndrome, for which experimentally proven evidence of residual function after damage emerged some 30 years ago. But the evidence was so counter-intuitive in nature that it inevitably led to some resistance among researchers during the ensuing 5 to 10 years, although the study of residual memory function is now something of an industry. Another is the phenomenon of blindsight, in which patients can make visual discriminations even though they are 'blind' as a result of damage to the visual cortex of the brain. Gradually, however, evidence has been generated for a whole range of capacities, which I will briefly review here. My object is not to be absolutely encyclopedic, as there is no shortage of reviews and studies in each of the areas of interest. Instead it is to give an indication, a flavour, of the type of evidence that exists for residual, so-called implicit, processing. I will concentrate mainly on amnesia and blindsight, as these are problems on which I have worked myself, but will also briefly review evidence from other types of brain damage.

Because many of the examples of performance without awareness are so counter-intuitive and surprising, it is worth citing a classical, much older example of such a disconnexion familiar to neurologists. If the spinal cord is severed there is loss of feeling and motor control below the level of the cut. Yet it is well known that the spinal cord isolated from the brain still shows some intact function—indeed, some adaptive features of the 'spinal frog' (i.e., in which the spine is isolated from the brain) reported by physiologists in the last century so impressed William James that he concluded that the spinal cord isolated from the brain of the frog shows 'conscious intelligence', but on an argument that we would certainly reject today, namely that if one limb normally used to scratch at the source of an irritating stimulus is blocked, the spinal frog will substitute another limb directed at the same source of irritation. James generously interpreted this as an example of 'the pursuance of future ends and the choice of means for their attainment.' Even given such generosity, a variety of cybernetic devices show the same capacity, and assuredly not the cyberneticists, nor anyone else, would call these devices conscious. In any event, the residual function of the spinal cord in humans *also* shows a striking dissociation, because the 'paralysed' limbs withdraw from stimuli that normally would be painful, for example, the thrust of a sharp pin. To quote Sherrington (1957, p. 227), the Nobel Laureate whose classical work brilliantly illuminated the organization and functions of the spinal cord, 'A needle-prick causes invariably the drawing up of the limb. . . . It is those stimuli which are most fitted to excite pain which are prepotent. . . . The nervous arcs of pain-nerves, broadly speaking, dominate the spinal centres . . . *where pain is, of course, non-existent.*' (italics added).

The pain is 'non-existent' because, as we know—or think we know—it is necessary for the information from the spinal cord to reach the brain to be *experienced*. What we have is a disconnexion, literally, between an intact response to normally painful stimuli and the resulting experience of pain. Such a disconnexion has occurred between an input to the brain and the brain itself. The dissociations we are now about to consider involve disconnexions *within* the brain itself, but these, too, lead to intact functioning in the absence of experience.

As mentioned, the *amnesic syndrome* is historically probably the oldest, and certainly the most thoroughly worked-up, example of this phenomenon. A somewhat fuller account is presented in a later chapter (Chapter 5). Amnesic syndrome patients, who suffer from damage to particular, restricted parts of the brain, are grossly impaired in remembering recent experiences even after an interval as short as a minute. If the person with whom they have been conversing leaves the room and then returns soon afterwards, the patient does not recognize him; they cannot recall a story or information related to them a short time earlier. The brain damage typically affects structures in the medial temporal lobe and/or in the medial thalamus. Within the medial temporal lobe lies a structure, the hippocampus (so named because it looks like a sea-horse in cross-section), damage to which is thought to be of special importance, although there is still considerable uncertainty about what brain structures are absolutely critically involved in the amnesic syndrome. The syndrome can be caused by encephalitis, chronic alcohol toxicity, stroke, head injury, and other insults. (For reviews see Squire and Cohen, 1984; Schacter, 1992.) The patients need have no impairment of short-term memory, for example in reciting back strings of digits, nor need they have any perceptual or intellectual impairments, but they have grave difficulty in acquiring and holding new information (anterograde amnesia). Memory for events from before the onset of the injury or brain disease (retrograde amnesia) is also typically affected, especially for those events that occurred a few years before the brain damage. Older *knowledge* can be retained— patients retain their vocabulary and acquired language skills, they know who they are, they may know where they went to school, although in some of the severe and densely amnesic cases patients may be vague even about such early knowledge. They may not know, for example, how many children they have, or whether their spouse is alive or dead. The same memory problems are also seen in the Alzheimer patient, but such a patient also has a whole variety of other impairments. The striking aspect of the amnesic syndrome is its relative purity and its isolation from other cognitive, motor, and perceptual difficulties.

It is not surprising that the disorder is severely crippling, and such patients typically need constant custodial care. They cannot be left to roam freely because they cannot find their way back; they cannot remember what time it is, or what has been told to them a few minutes before, even if told repeatedly, and so forth. And yet—and here is the surprise—there is good evidence of storage of experiences. Indeed, some of the anecdotal evidence is more than 100 years old. Thus, Korsakoff describes an amnesic patient who openly exhibited fear of a shock apparatus—justifiably, as he had been shocked by it! But there was denial of having seen the apparatus nor was there any overt acknowledgement of the experience as such (cf. Delay and Brion, 1969). The anecdote told by Claparède (1911) is now often cited: it describes the amnesic subject whose hand was stuck with a pin by Clarapède during an examination, and who thereafter vigorously withdrew her hand whenever she saw him. On questioning she denied having any idea of why she did so. Claparède persisted relentlessly with his questioning and, eventually, after much pressing, she said, 'well, you never know who might have a pin in his hand!'

More experimentally robust evidence was reported in the 1950s of the famous patient H.M., who became, and still remains, severely amnesic after bilateral surgery to structures in the medial portions of his temporal lobes for the relief of intractable epilepsy. Because part or all of the hippocampus was certainly included in the lesion, it tended to capture most of the interpretative attention, although the lesion also included other structures. H.M.'s epilepsy was significantly relieved, but he paid an unexpected and heavy penalty: he displayed a severe amnesic syndrome. But it soon became apparent that he was able to learn various perceptual and motor skills, such as mastering a pursuit rotor in which one must learn to keep a stylus on a narrow track on a moving drum. He was also able to learn mirror drawing, that is, learning to copy from the reversed image of a pattern seen in a mirror. He was able to retain such skills excellently from session to session. But he demonstrated *no* awareness of having remembered the experimental situations nor could he recognize them; he claimed he had never seen them before (Corkin, 1968). That type of demonstration of excellent acquisition and retention of motor skills, as well as classical conditioning, without explicit recognition or recall, has been confirmed in a variety of situations by various authors (cf. Schacter, 1993; Schacter *et al.*, 1988). For example, Fig. 1.1 shows normal learning by amnesic subjects of a pursuit rotor, with excellent retention after an interval of a week, but without any recognition of the apparatus by the subjects (Brooks and Baddeley, 1976). Results with classical conditioning can be seen in Fig. 1.2. The subject, a highly intelligent school teacher who suffered from Korsakoff's psychosis, was severely amnesic. He was subjected to a classical conditioning procedure in which an air puff to the eye followed 1/2 second after a neutral light + tone conditioning stimulus (Weiskrantz and Warrington, 1979). As can be seen, he produced an increasing number of anticipatory eyelid closures as conditioning trials proceeded, and showed

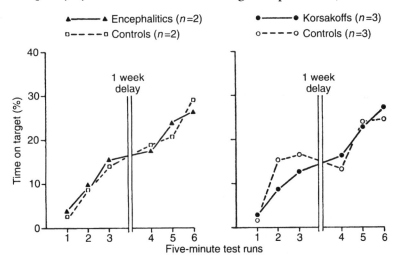

Figure 1.1. Learning of a pursuit rotor task by two groups of amnesic patients, showing gradual and sustained improvement with increasing practice, equivalent to that of normal control subjects. (Severe amnesia can be caused by a number of conditions, among them encephalitis and chronic alcoholism leading to Korsakoff's psychosis, plotted separately in the figure. See text.) Learning of such a skilled task depends upon the specific visual details of the actual rotor display. Amnesic subjects show no acknowledged recognition of the apparatus or their past experience with it. (Reprinted from Brooks and Baddeley, 1976, with kind permission from Elsevier Science, Ltd, The Boulevard, Langford Lane, Kidlington OX5 1GB, UK.)

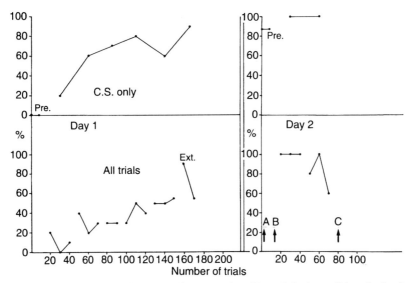

Figure 1.2. Classical conditioning of an amnesic subject, A.S. A conditioned stimulus (C.S.), consisting of a light plus a tone, appeared 1/2 second before an air puff to the eye. Each daily session started with control trials in which the C.S. was presented without the air puff (PRE). With repeated conditioning trials, a conditioned response emerged (partial closure of the eyelid prior to the air puff, a 'bracing of the eyelid') after the C.S. but before the air puff. In the upper graph only the C.S. was presented, and in the lower graph both the C.S. and the air puff were presented. There was good conditioning, which was perfectly retained over a 24 hour period. In the rest periods indicated by the breaks in the lower curve, the subject was questioned about his experience, as reported in the text, and recordings were made at A, B, and C (arrows). EXT refers to a brief 'extinction' session in which the C.S. was presented without the air puff. (Reprinted from Weiskrantz and Warrington, 1979, with kind permission from Elsevier Science, Ltd, The Boulevard, Langford Lane, Kidlington OX5 1GB, UK.)

perfect retention the following day. In the rest-breaks that occurred between blocks of trials, when his comments were recorded, the subject denied having had any experience of the normally strongly memorable air puffs, even though he remained seated in front of the apparatus throughout the whole session. For example, he was asked, 'Can you remember what was happening with this equipment here—what were you doing?'

Subject A.S.: 'I've forgotten for the moment; it's at the back of my mind.'
Q.:   'Yes, well just have a guess.'
A.S.:   'I was telling where the position of certain things were in relation to others?'
Q.:   'I see. And where was your head?'

A.S.: 'My head was on the ledge [the chin rest used during testing].'

Q.: 'Yes, and what happened when your head was on that ledge? Can you remember?'

A.S.: 'Well, I looked—I kept my attention on that point there and then I answered several questions. Then, no, no; I kept my attention on there and watched the picture, as it were, and this flashed and I gave an answer.'

Q.: 'I see.'

A.S.: 'Which, was a form, I think, of some Eastern language.' [A.S. was fluent in several languages.]

Immediately after such a failure of recall, when the conditioned stimulus was presented, out came the conditioned eye blink.

The examples of perceptual–motor skill learning and possibly even of classical conditioning did not unduly stretch credulity about cognitive capacities because such skills can become more or less automatic. Indeed, it was originally argued that the hippocampus need not be concerned with such servile perceptual or motor matters. But counter-intuitive results were much more obvious when it was shown that amnesic subjects could also retain information about verbal material, but again without recognition. The use of verbal material also allowed one to make direct quantitative comparisons between retention of the words using various indirect tests of retention, on the one hand, and explicit recognition or recall of the words, on the other.

The demonstration depended on showing the patients lists of pictures or words and, after an interval of some minutes, testing for recognition in a standard yes/no test, that is, asking them to say whether they did or did not recognize having seen the previously exposed words or pictures (together with new items that had not been exposed). Not surprisingly, the patients performed at the level of chance. But when asked to *guess* the *identity* of pictures or words from difficult fragmented drawings, however, they were much better able to do so for those items to which they had been exposed. For example, if they had first been exposed to drawings of complete words or objects, they were much better able to guess the identity of their fragmented, degraded versions, examples of which are shown in Fig. 1.3. (If the reader has difficulty in identifying the object or the word, turn to Chapter 5 and Fig. 5.1; after that has been done, never again is there likely to be any difficulty in identifying them in Fig. 1.3!)

Figure 1.3. Fragmented pictures of an object and a word (see text).

Another way of demonstrating this phenomenon was to present just some of the letters of the previously exposed word, for example, the initial pair or triplet of letters (Weiskrantz and Warrington, 1970). For example, after exposing words such as COTTON, KITCHEN, MARKET, etc., they were asked for the identity of words starting COT. . . , KIT. . . , MAR. . . . Here, too, the patients showed enhanced ability for finding the correct words to which they had been exposed earlier compared to control items to which they had not been exposed. This is a procedure that now is called priming—which means the increased facilitation of retention induced by previous exposure. Presenting some of the letters, for example, the initial triplets, of a word and asking the subject to identify the complete word has come to be called 'stem completion'.

Frank disbelief was our own first response to this result: it surely could not be true that a patient, whose memory for important events was so shot, could actually show normal and robust retention of material when tested indirectly with partial cues or fragmented pictures, while having no recognition or recall at all with direct testing. It must have been a fluke; it would not hold up if repeated. But it did. This type of demonstration of retention by amnesic patients has been repeatedly confirmed, and retention intervals can be as long as several months: in H.M., successful retention was reported after an interval of 4 months (Milner *et al.*, 1968). Priming is said to reveal 'implicit memory' or 'implicit processing' in the absence of explicit memory.

It has turned out that such patients, in fact, can learn a variety of new types of tasks and information, such as new words, new meanings, new rules. We will focus on this topic in more detail in Chapter 5, in an effort to analyse and characterize such learning by amnesic patients, and also to put the findings in the context of 'commentary' responses. There also has been intense interest in discovering which brain structures are necessary for explicit as well as for implicit memory. At this stage, however, our object is to record the fact that, when tested indirectly, amnesic patients can store and access information for which they have no acknowledged recognition.

The first response by some memory researchers to the reports of positive memory retention by subjects who could not 'remember' was that such subjects might be just like normal people but with 'weak' memory. This was a natural interpretation of the evidence at hand. But when dissociations started to appear for other specific forms of memory disorders that were different from the amnesic syndrome, it gradually became clear that there are a number of different memory systems in the brain operating in parallel, although, of course, normally in interaction with each other. (Further reference will be made to dissociations in neuropsychology in the next chapter, and a discussion of the power and limitations of dissociations can be found in the Appendix.) For example, it was found that lesions well removed from the medial temporal lobes produced loss of such skills as learning a pursuit-rotor route, or riding a bicycle, and yet another lesion far removed from the temporal lobe (in the cerebellum) could interfere selectively with conditioned eyelid responses, in neither case causing any loss of recognition. Yet other subjects sustained damage which caused them to lose the meanings of words, but without behaving like amnesic subjects; that is, they could remember having been shown a word before, and that on that occasion they also did not know its *meaning*! Other brain-damaged subjects could have very impoverished short-term memory—being able to repeat back only 1 or 2 digits from a list—and yet were otherwise normal for remembering events and recognizing facts.

These sets of double and multiple dissociations thus demonstrated that 'memory' is not a term to be used as a singular concept. The brain apparently has a variety of systems that deal with types of material according to their different demands and, at the very least, has a variety of independent processing modes. Depending on the situation and the material to be stored (or not to be stored) or recovered, different processes will be entailed, with different time constants and different matching operations. It is necessary for some material to be 'recognized' on subsequent occasions, but for others it is not—in fact, it can be deleterious. Who would want to 'recognize' the meaning of a red traffic light on every occasion? Who wants to recall learning how to catch a ball as it comes hurtling towards one? Indeed, who would find it useful to recall how one learned the meanings of each word, or recognize each word as being 'familiar' in the course of uttering a sentence? To do so would be a terrible handicap.

Alexander Luria (1968) described the extraordinary subject, 'S', a professional mnemonist, who simply could not forget even trivial items of information, nor inhibit the great variety of colours and other images that were elicited by them. Even tables of random numbers were recorded faithfully. The man's life was a very disturbed one, and his inability to forget became a torment to him. Some years ago, after appearing on a television programme about memory, I received a telephone call seeking help from an anguished parent whose child was suffering from apparently the same difficulty as Luria's subject. I could not offer any good advice on how to forget! Nor could Luria in the course of following his subject for some 15 to 20 years. His subject apparently *did* eventually discover a way of forgetting, by somehow inhibiting the vivid images that invariably accompanied his memories. But Luria was at a loss to explain the process, or even to describe it. 'It seems pointless to conjecture', he remarked ruefully, 'about a phenomenon that has remained inexplicable.' (p. 72). I have wondered whether it was the fact that S was ageing that actually released him!

The experimental evidence about residual function after damage to the *visual cortex*, a condition that has been dubbed *blindsight*, is more recent (but, as always, there are fascinating and important historical antecedents, e.g. Bard, 1905; Riddoch, 1917; Poppelreuter, 1917; Holmes, 1918). In its way the evidence is more dramatic and counter-intuitive than for amnesia, or, in fact, for any other syndrome. The major target of the eye in its connexion to the brain lies at the back of the brain in the occipital lobe, in a region of cortex known as 'striate cortex' (because of its microscopic striped appearance) or 'V1' or Brodmann's area 17 by anatomists. (Chapters 6 and 8 will go into more detail.) The connexion is not direct—the largest portion of the optic nerve first terminates in a sub-cortical structure (the lateral geniculate nucleus, LGN), from which a relay is sent to striate cortex. But while this is the largest pathway originating in the eye destined for targets in the brain, it is not the only pathway. In fact, the eye connects in parallel to 9 other targets in the brain aside from V1, although of course these pathways interact with each other via other connexions (see Chapter 6). Thus when V1 is damaged or blocked in the primate brain, information from the eye can still readily reach the brain via these other routes. It is not surprising, therefore, that monkeys can still carry out visual discriminations even in the absence of V1. Their ability is altered in some ways, but it is still quite creditable. One of the main demonstrations came from years of observation by Nicholas Humphrey (1970, 1974) of a monkey, 'Helen', who had bilateral lesions of V1. She could locate and retrieve visual objects, even quite small specks of dust, with considerable ease. The evidence is quite similar to that reported much earlier by Luciani in 1884 (cf. Weiskrantz, 1986). The vision of monkeys without V1 is altered in various ways, the details of which need not concern us here—some of them will be dealt with more fully, in relation to human patients, in Chapter 6. The main point here is that there is considerable residual visual capacity through multiple pathways in the absence of the major input to cortex in the monkey's brain, Brodmann's area 17, (striate cortex, V1). But here is the paradox: human patients in whom the occipital lobe is damaged say that they are blind in that part of the visual field that maps onto the damaged V1. (Typically, such patients are blind in only one-half of their visual fields, because the left halves of the visual fields of *both* eyes project to V1 in the right cerebral hemisphere, and the right halves of the visual fields to the left hemisphere. Of course, with damage to the both V1s, they would be blind across the whole of the visual field, but fortunately for the patients such cases are very rare.)

As the anatomy of the visual pathways is thought to be the same in monkeys and humans, why are the human patients apparently unable to make use of the parallel visual pathways from the retina that remain after damage to the occipital cortex and to V1? Why are they blind? Or are they *really* blind? The answer to the question gradually emerged when such patients were tested in the way that one is forced to test animals. One cannot ask an animal, alas, to describe what it sees, or to read a list of letters on an eye chart. One must provide the animal with a choice of alternatives, and reward it for choosing one or the other. Or one trains the animal to retrieve a reward at one or another position at which one places a cue. In short, you do not ask the animal directly about what it 'sees', but only test what it can discriminate.

The first clue about residual vision in people with visual cortex damage came from a study at M.I.T. in 1973 (Pöppel *et al.*) in which brain damaged U.S. war veterans were asked simply to move their eyes to the position of a brief spot of light shone into their blind fields. The position of the light was varied from trial to trial in a random order. As they could not 'see', the subjects thought the instruction odd, but it emerged that their eyes did, in fact, move to the correct position (of course, as the light was only briefly presented, it was no longer there when the eyes moved). The effect was not strong, and it only held for positions within 20° or so from the centre of gaze (perhaps because the subjects were not allowed to move their heads—we normally use both head and eye movements together for targets off the centre of gaze), but it was statistically reliable. The 'unseen' light was having some control over the subjects' visual responses.

Soon afterwards, a subject was found in London with a visual field defect caused by surgical removal of a small non-malignant tumour that had invaded V1. That subject, D.B., was seen by Elizabeth Warrington, other colleagues, and me, and given a variety of tests that extended, in fact, over some 10 years. The M.I.T. results on eye gaze were confirmed, but a range of 'monkey-type' tests were also administered in which D.B. had either to reach out to locate a stimulus, or to guess which of two alternative stimuli had been shown. In the latter case, he was told what the two choices were and shown them in his intact half-field of vision before the tests in the blind half-field were started. The result was that D.B. could succeed in a variety of discriminations by 'guesswork' in his blind field, even though he said he did not 'see' the stimuli. He could, for example, tell whether a circular patch of lines was oriented in one or another direction (Fig. 1.4), or whether a stimulus was moving or stationary. His visual acuity could be measured by varying the spacing of a grating (Fig. 1.5). His ability to locate the position of stimuli in his blind field was not absolutely normal, but remarkably good (Fig. 1.6). In fact, his ability matched reasonably well that of a monkey without V1.

Figure 1.4. Stimuli used to measure orientation discrimination by a blindsight subject, D.B., in his blind field by forced-choice guessing. He was asked to guess whether a stimulus to be flashed briefly was orientated horizontally (left figure) or non-horizontally. He was virtually perfect in guessing that the grating shown at the right was non-horizontal, and that the left figure was horizontal. The task was made more difficult by decreasing the angle between the horizontal and non-horizontal gratings, to measure his threshold (the limit of his ability). The figure in the centre, which is 10° off horizontal, was his threshold. In his task the subject reported that he saw nothing, not even the brief flash when the grating was presented. (Data in Weiskrantz, 1986, Oxford University Press.)

After all of these tests he was questioned as to how well he thought he had done, and the answers recorded and published with the summary of results (Weiskrantz, 1986). In many cases he said he was just guessing, and thought he was not performing better than chance. When he was shown his results (this never took place until the end of testing sessions, which typically lasted 2 or 3 days), he expressed open astonishment in the early days. There were conditions under which D.B. did have *some* kind of awareness. With some stimuli, he 'knew' that something had moved in his blind field, for example, and with very rapidly moving stimuli

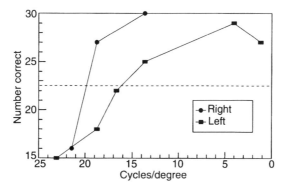

Figure 1.5. Determination of visual acuity in the blind (left) vs. the intact hemifield of subject D.B. The subject was presented (whilst maintaining fixation on a central spot) with either a sine-wave grating stimulus or a homogeneous stimulus equal in energy and size to the grating. He was asked to guess whether or not there were 'lines' in the stimulus. The spacing of the bars in the grating was varied to make the task more or less difficult. Dashed line indicates threshold performance, defined as the value half-way between chance performance (15 out of 30) and performance perfect (30 out of 30). His capacity to discriminate 'lines' from 'no lines' was better in the intact hemifield, but he still had a measurable visual acuity in his blind hemifield. (Adapted from Weiskrantz *et al.*, 1974, and Weiskrantz, 1986, Oxford University Press.)

of high luminance contrast, he reported 'seeing' some peculiar waves. That he had such experiences under certain conditions turned out, in fact, to be quite fortunate for further investigations, in two ways. The first was that these experiences were distracting to him, and actually misled him in making his choices—the 'waves' did not represent the stimuli accurately. And so we deliberately arranged conditions to eliminate the experiences by adjusting the contrast and other stimulus conditions appropriately, although at first by trial and error. The bulk of the reports on D.B. were of good visual discrimination capacity in the absence of any acknowledged experience. The phenomenon, in a passing moment, was dubbed 'blindsight', and the term has stuck. (In fact, it was an off-the-cuff response to an urgent request for a title of a seminar in 1973 that I was asked to give to local neurologists. I chose 'blindsight and hindsight'— hindsight because of the putative role of midbrain visual pathways in residual visual function.)

The second sense in which it was fortunate that D.B. reported some kind of experience, a feeling or knowing, is that it later became clear that it was possible to specify the parameters that defined the feeling mode (good discrimination with some awareness) as distinct from those that applied to the blindsight mode (good discrimination without *any* awareness) for the

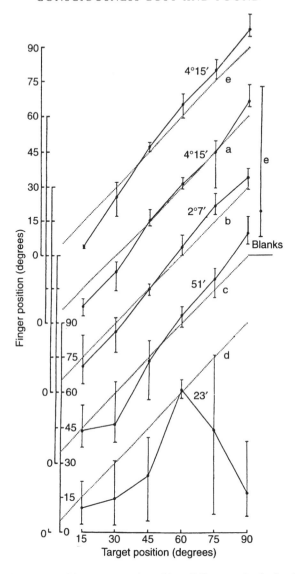

Figure 1.6. Average reaching responses by subject D.B. to a visual stimulus presented randomly at different positions in the impaired hemifield, whilst maintaining fixation on a spot at position zero throughout. The series was conducted in the order **a** through **e**, in which the size of the visual stimulus was fixed at different values. The vertical bars indicate the ranges of the reaches. In condition **e**, blank trials were randomly interspersed without the knowledge of the subject, and responses to these are shown separately. The dotted lines indicate the values to be expected if he responded perfectly. Note that his performance broke down when the stimulus size was smaller than about 1/4 of a degree. (Reprinted with permission from Weiskrantz *et al.*, 1974, Oxford University Press.)

same type of visual discriminations. From this it follows that it might be possible to use brain imaging techniques in each of the two modes, for the same type of discrimination and with equivalent levels of performance, and thus determine whether any structures are involved uniquely for visual awareness. The matter will be discussed further in Chapters 3, 6, and 8.

That the gap between monkey and man should be narrowed was no surprise to us, but the manner in which it happened was deeply counter-intuitive and surprising (Weiskrantz, 1977). How could anyone discriminate visually events they could not see? A number of possible objections were raised, as is the healthy response in science. Perhaps, it was suggested, light could spread from the blind field into the intact field. Or perhaps blindsight subjects just became more cautious about admitting that they saw something. Or perhaps there were small rogue bits of V1, still lurking in the brain despite the lesion, that were responsible for any residual capacity to be demonstrated. The matter of rogue bits of V1 will be discussed in Chapter 6. The questions of stray light and subjects' caution have been dealt with experimentally and formally elsewhere (Stoerig *et al.*, 1985; Werth, 1983; Weiskrantz, 1986). Briefly, stray light has been controlled in a variety of ways, for example, by flooding the intact visual hemifield with high levels of illumination so that if there were any stray light it could not be detected. Also, the stray light function has been determined experimentally (Barbur *et al.*, 1994a). Perhaps the most demanding method of ensuring that no effective stray light reaches intact parts of the field is to use the *genuinely* blind part of the eye as a control. Every eye has such a blind spot, the optic disc, caused by the penetration of the optic nerve fibres between the rear and the front of the retina. There are, of course, no receptors in the optic disc, but we do not usually notice this in our everyday lives. As the size of this natural absolutely blind area is fixed and known ($5° \times 7°$), we can be certain that if a small target light projected onto it cannot be detected by the subject, there can be no diffusion of light beyond the edge of the disc, and hence maximum diffusion would be no more than half of the size of the disc. This tells us what size and intensity of light to use. The critical test comes in requiring the subject to guess whether or not a light has been projected into his blind hemifield. Sometimes the light is shone onto the disc, and in random order, sometimes in neighbouring blind regions. As far as the subject is concerned, all of them are unseen. But when it is on the receptorless disc the subject's performance is at chance, and when it is on the neighbouring region it is significantly above chance (Fig. 1.7). The question of the subjects' caution (known formally as the response criterion) can be tackled by deliberately changing it by adjusting the proportion of stimuli to blank trials, as has been done by Petra Stoerig in a number of studies (cf. Stoerig *et al.*, 1985). The patients' capacity to detect stimuli in the blind hemifield remained more or less impervious to such variations in the response criterion. Aside from this, response criterion still does not account for the difference in the commentaries offered by the subjects for stimuli in their blind hemifields as contrasted with their intact hemifields when the thresholds for the two are equated (cf. discussion in Weiskrantz, 1986, and also Werth, 1983).

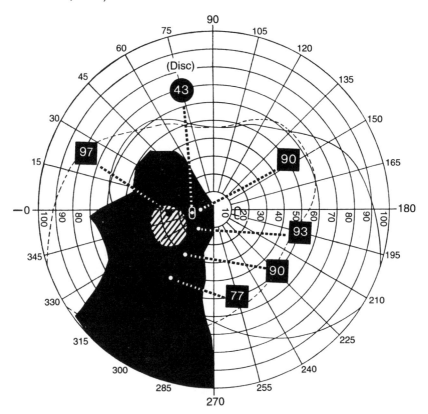

Figure 1.7. Results with subject D.B. when small lights were presented either in his blind field or on the genuinely blind optic disc. Numbers in the insets show the per cent correct in 30 trials when the subject was required to guess whether a light had been presented (chance = 50%). The hatching indicates an area in which D.B. had a feeling that something had been presented. He was well above chance when the light fell in the blind field, but at chance when it fell on the disc. The results provide clear evidence against his good performance being based on stray light or diffusion within the eye. (Reproduced with permission from Weiskrantz, 1986, Oxford University Press, as adapted from Weiskrantz, 1983, Cambridge University Press.)

The results on the studies of D.B. were among the first to be documented. Other subjects have been tested by a number of researchers. As in the early days of memory research, much work depended, and still depends (for reasons discussed in Chapter 6), upon small numbers of subjects who agree to be tested intensively, with sessions lasting several days or even longer. One of the subjects in this category, still being tested in several different research centres, is G.Y., about whom more will be written in later chapters. The question of just what proportion of patients with occipital damage show blindsight is a taxing one. But taken together, subjects with V1 damage have been reported who are able, in their blind hemifields, to detect the presence of stimuli, to locate them in space, to discriminate direction of movement, to discriminate the orientation of lines, to be able to judge whether stimuli in the blind hemifield match or mismatch those in the intact hemifield, and to discriminate between different wavelengths of light, that is, to tell colours apart (cf. reviews by Weiskrantz, 1986, 1995, in press 1996; Cowey and Stoerig, 1991a; Blythe et al., 1987). The latter capacity—discrimination of colour—presses credulity to the limit, because in those tests—which by their nature were very time-consuming and lasted for several days—the subjects uniformly and consistently denied seeing colour at all, and yet performed reliably above chance, even between wavelengths falling relatively close together. Moreover, the fine-grained features of the spectral sensitivity curves of these subjects (carried out, again, by forced-choice guessing) suggested that wavelength opponency, that is, colour contrast, was intact (Stoerig and Cowey, 1989, 1991, 1992). The subjects seemed to be able to respond to the stimuli that would normally generate the philosophers' favourite species of 'qualia', namely colours, but in the absence of the very qualia themselves! But this is, in principle, no more striking or mysterious than being able to discriminate any kind of visual event in the absence of awareness.

There have been claims of residual function even with removal of all cortex in one hemisphere of human subjects—hemispherectomy (more strictly, hemi-decortication), carried out for relief of otherwise intractable epilepsy (Perenin, 1978; 1991; Perenin and Jeannerod, 1978; Ptito et al., 1987, 1991). The evidence is important for deciding whether sub-cortical pathways alone (assuming they are undamaged by the drastic surgery) can sustain residual visual function. Recently the positive evidence has been called into question (King et al., 1996), and we must withhold judgment about whether the original evidence can be replicated in other cases.

It is not only in the visual mode that examples of 'unaware' discrimination capacity have been reported. There are reports of 'blind touch' and also a report of 'deaf hearing'. The first case of blind touch (Paillard *et al.*, 1983) was closely similar to the early accounts of blindsight. The patient had a severe right tactile anaesthesia caused by a left parietal lobe lesion. She did not respond to touch on her right arm, even with 'the strongest pressure'. But when asked to point (blindfolded) to where she was touched with the pressure instrument, she was able to point, 'to her own considerable surprise', to the approximate locus of stimulus. The patient's comment was 'but I do not understand that! You put something here. I don't feel anything and I go there with my finger. . . . How does that happen?' But, again in parallel with some blindsight phenomena, she did react positively to a moving tactile stimulus and could judge its direction. A more recent case (Rossetti *et al.*, 1995) has been dubbed 'numbsense'—a splendid new oxymoron—in an Abstract by Rossetti *et al.* (1996), who also report that the ability to localize on the insensate forearm of a brain damaged subject decays after a delay of about 2.5 s following the tactile stimulus.

The example of deaf hearing is only briefly presented (Michel and Peronnet, 1980) in a case of 'cortical deafness' caused by lesions in the supratemporal region of both temporal lobes (the region of the brain that is strongly associated with the capacity for speech comprehension). The subject was no longer able to recognize speech or environmental sounds, in spite of relatively normal pure tone audiograms with intact speech, reading, and writing. But, 'he may indeed recognize some words given orally if he has read these words together with incorrect ones in a task of double choice.'

Other examples of residual function following brain damage can be found across virtually the whole spectrum of neuropsychological defects. *Unilateral neglect* is associated with lesions of the parietal lobe in humans, typically the right parietal lobe, resulting from stroke or other causes. The patients behave as though the left half of their visual (and sometimes also their tactile) world is missing. If shown a picture of a butterfly and asked to copy it, they draw only its right half. This striking syndrome is the subject of quite intense experimental research and attracts a number of theories, which need not concern us here. The point is that, even though the subjects neglect the left half of their visual world, it can be shown in some cases that 'missing' information is being processed by the brain. In an experiment by John Marshall and Peter Halligan (1988) such a subject was shown two pictures of houses that were identical on their right halves, but different on the left. In one picture a fire was vigorously projecting from a window, and in the other no fire was shown (Fig. 1.8). Because the subject neglected the left halves of the pictures, she repeatedly judged them as being identical and scored at chance in discriminating between them. But when asked which house she would prefer to live in she retorted that it was a silly question, because they were the *same*, but nevertheless she reliably chose the house not on fire. Edoardo Bisiach (1992) has carried out some variations on this theme. Other studies have asked whether an

Figure 1.8. Figure used to investigate covert processing in a patient with hemi-neglect of the left half of visual space. The two figures looked identical to the subject because only their right halves were reported as seen. Nevertheless, when required to indicate which house she would prefer to live in, she chose the bottom one, although she said she was guessing. In the original, the fire in the top figure was coloured red. (J. Marshall and P. Halligan, personal communication.)

'unseen' stimulus in the neglected left field can 'prime' a response by the subject to a stimulus in the right half-field. Thus, Ladavas *et al.* (1993) have shown that a word presented in the right visual field was processed faster when the word was preceded by a brief presentation of an associated word in the neglected left field. When the subject was actually forced to respond directly to the word on the left, for example, by reading it aloud, he was not able to do so—it was genuinely neglected. A similar demonstration was made by Berti and Rizzolatti (1992) using pictures of animals and fruit in the left neglected field as primes for pictures in the right which their patients had to classify as quickly as possible, either as animals or fruit, by pressing the appropriate key. The unseen picture shown on the left generated faster reaction times when it matched the category of the picture on the right. And so material, both pictorial and verbal, of which the subject has no awareness in the left visual field, and to which he or she cannot respond explicitly, nevertheless gets processed, at least in some patients. The subject may not 'know' it, but some part of the brain does.

There is a type of memory disorder that is socially awkward for the patient, but intriguing to the scientist. *Prosopagnosia* is an impairment in the ability to recognize and identify familiar faces. The problem is not one of knowing that a face is a face, that is, it is not a perceptual difficulty, but one of facial *memory*. The condition is associated with damage to the inferior, posterior temporal lobe, especially in the right hemisphere. It usually occurs with other types of visual recognition problems (e.g., in identifying animals or household tools), but there are cases in which recognition of familiar faces is the principal or even the only difficulty. The condition can be so severe that patients do not recognize the faces of members of their own family. But it has been demonstrated clearly that the autonomic nervous system can tell the difference between familiar and unfamiliar faces. In one study, Bauer (1984) measured the skin conductance responses (SCRs) of prosopagnosic patients when they were asked to read names when shown an individual face of a famous person or a family member. (Changes in skin conductance occur commonly in subjects with stimuli that are meaningful, especially emotionally so.) Some names were correct matches for the face, others were not. When the correct name was read, SCRs were much larger than those to the incorrect names. Tranel and Damasio (1985) carried out a similar study in which patients were required to pick out familiar from unfamiliar faces. They scored at chance, but notwithstanding their SCRs were reliably larger for the familiar faces as against the unfamiliar faces. And so the patients do not 'know' the faces, but some part of their autonomic nervous system obviously does.

It is not only the autonomic system that can respond differentially to familiar faces in the absence of explicit recognition by the patient. Andy Young and his colleagues have used techniques from experimental psychology to demonstrate intact processing of faces of which the patients are unaware (Young, 1988, 1994; Young and De Haan, 1992). Thus, a patient showed faster matching of familiar faces than of unfamiliar faces even though he was at chance when asked to select familiar from unfamiliar ones. It was also shown that recognition of target names of familiar people was helped by priming them with a picture of a face that the subject does not recognize. Further, it was demonstrated that a patient learns the 'true' pairings of faces and names more rapidly than 'incorrect' pairings, a result also shown by Diamond *et al.* (1994). Thus, some part of the brain, presumably involving cortex, 'knows' the correct identification of the face, but this is covert; the subject himself does not demonstrate or acknowledge recognition in a task that explicitly demands it.

Even in that uniquely human cognitive achievement, the skilled use of language, which can be severely disturbed by brain damage, there is evidence of residual processing of which subjects remain unaware. One example comes from the patients who cannot read whole words, although they can painfully extract the word by reading it letter by letter. This form of *acquired dyslexia* is associated with damage to the left occipital lobe. In a study by Shallice and Saffran (1986) one such patient was tested with written words that he could not identify—he could neither read them aloud nor report their meanings. Nevertheless, he performed reliably above chance on a lexical decision task, that is, he could guess correctly the difference between real words and nonsense words. Moreover, he could correctly categorize words at above chance levels according to their meanings, using forced-choice responding to one of two alternatives. For example, he could say whether the written name of a country belonged inside or outside of Europe, whether the name of a person was that of an author or politician, or whether the name of an object was living or non-living. All this, despite his not being able to read or identify the word aloud or explicitly give its meaning.

An even more striking outcome emerges from the study of some patients with severe loss of linguistic comprehension and production, *aphasia*. So-called Broca's aphasics suffer from poor control of speech output and have difficulty in appreciating the grammatical structure of sentences. Yet there is evidence that there can be sensitivity to grammatical structure in so-called agrammatic aphasics, when forced to make judgments about grammatical rule violations (Frederici, 1982; Linebarger *et al.*,

1983). A contrasting type of aphasia, Wernicke's aphasia, is characterized by poor comprehension of language. Here, too, sensitivity to semantic information can be retained even though the patients are impaired in their explicit comprehension or use of this information. An informative study that tackled both grammatical and semantic aspects of comprehension in a severely impaired patient is that of Lotty Tyler (1988, 1992). She presented the subject with sentences that were degraded either semantically or syntactically. The subject succeeded in being able to follow the instruction to respond as quickly as possible whenever a particular target word was uttered, for example the word 'guitar' in the following cases :

A.   The crowd was waiting eagerly. The young man grabbed the *guitar* and . . .

B.   The crowd was waiting eagerly. The young man drank the *guitar* and . . .

C.   The crowd was waiting eagerly. The young man slept the *guitar* and . . .

D.   The crowd was waiting eagerly. The young man buried the *guitar* and . . .

Sentence A is a normal and un–degraded. Sentence B is semantically anomalous because it violates the meaning of a guitar. Sentence C is syntactically anomalous because 'slept' is an intransitive verb. Finally D is what Tyler calls 'pragmatically' anomalous: burying a guitar is a possible act, but a silly one.

It is known that normal subjects are slower to respond to the target word when it is in a degraded context than when in a normal sentence. Even though Tyler's aphasic patient was severely impaired in his ability even to judge overtly when a sentence was anomalous or normal, his pattern of reaction times to target words in a degraded context showed the same slowing as is characteristic of normal control subjects. Over-all the patient was slower, but the same pattern emerged. In other words, it was demonstrated that the patient retained an intact capacity to respond both to the semantic and grammatical structure of the sentences. But he could not use such a capacity, either in his comprehending of speech or his use of it. Tyler distinguishes between the 'on-line' use of linguistic information, which was preserved in her patient, and its exploitation 'off-line'. The subject could 'develop the appropriate representations of an utterance; his problem lies in being unable to gain access to them for the purpose of making explicit decisions about them.' (Tyler, 1992, p. 170.)

In all of the examples so far there has been, in some sense, a retained capacity in the absence of an acknowledged awareness—either of the information content itself or of the knowledge of the residual existence of the capacity. But there is a more subtle way in which perception can be shown to be *fractionated* in patients, such that they can be said not to perceive in one sense, but to perceive very well in another. In evidence garnered impressively by David Milner and Mel Goodale (1995) patients are described who are agnosic for judging the shape of objects, or even the orientation of simple lines. Yet such a patient might be able, without difficulty, to slot cards into a 'mail box', the orientation of which is set to various different angles. They discuss a lovely experiment in which it was shown that the patient still had the capacity for the orientation of a stimulus to make itself 'seen' indirectly. Advantage was taken of the fact that the patient showed the 'McCollough After-Effect'. This phenomenon occurs in normal subjects when they view two gratings which are flashed briefly and in alternation. One grating has its lines oriented in one direction and is coloured, say, red. In the other grating the lines are at right angles to the lines in the first grating, and it is coloured, say, green. After the two gratings are alternated every few seconds over a period of several minutes, an after-effect can be demonstrated when a black-and-white grating is shown: subjects then see that grating, depending on its orientation, tinged with the complementary colour of the one originally associated with the orientation of the lines. The 'orientation-blind' subject was able to see the orientation-linked complementary *colours*, although she could not see the difference in the orientations of the lines in the gratings as such.

These authors distinguish sharply between perception for making explicit judgments, and perception for action. The two modes can be dissociated in different types of patients. That there are patients who can perceive stimuli but not use the information for action is no surprise— Parkinson's patients and Huntington's chorea patients fit the bill. More surprising is the opposite, where visually guided action is preserved but perception is impaired, as Milner and Goodale have shown. They argue that perception for action is dependent upon the so-called 'dorsal stream', the neural pathway emerging from the striate cortex and projecting into the parietal lobe. Such perceptually governed action, they argue, typically is not accompanied by acknowledged perceptual awareness. In contrast, for perceptual *judgments*, in which the subject makes an explicit and conscious identification of what it is he or she is perceiving, there is a dependence on the 'ventral stream', the neural pathway that projects from the striate cortex in the direction of the temporal lobe.

A recent study by Goodale *et al.* (1994) bears directly on the question of awareness and imagery, and is closely relevant to the question of perceptual awareness. They studied the differences between natural grasping movements by normal subjects in reaching towards a real object, on the one hand (no pun intended), and in reaching towards objects, on the other, that were removed from view a short time before the trial; that is, 'remembered' objects, 'pantomimed' objects. They argue that 'pantomimed reaches were being driven by stored perceptual information about the object', and as such the subjects' reaches did not use the normal visuomotor control system. And, although subjects continued to adjust their hand opening for object size when pantomiming, their grip formation and other hand and arm adjustments were different from those seen in reaching for *real*, currently present targets. In other words, responding on the basis of a memory entails visual imagery, and this is cast in the normal perceptual mode. But in reaching for a real object, control can be taken over by the system that controls visual *action*. This interpretation received strong support from their observations with an agnosic patient who was unable to discriminate between objects *perceptually* on the basis of size, but who did nevertheless adjust the size of her grasp when reaching for a real object, as discussed in the previous paragraph. When she was required, however, to reach on the basis of the remembered object, her performance was severely disrupted because the perceptual mode was damaged in her. The relevance of this proposed difference between 'percepts' and 'targets for action', and their suggested link with the ventral and dorsal outputs from the striate cortex, will be taken up in Chapters 6 and 8.

Another example of a fractionation of perception has been analysed in some detail by Heywood *et al.* (1991, 1994). They studied a patient suffering from *achromatopsia*, that is, the loss of perceived colour caused by brain damage to the ventral and posterior temporal–occipital region. Their subject, like other achromatopsic patients, saw the world only in different shades of grey, devoid of colour (although he had possessed normal colour vision prior to the brain damage). But he demonstrated an excellent capacity for 'colour discrimination' even though he could not *see* colour under the very same conditions in which he discriminated. This occurred when stimuli of different wavelengths were made contiguous to each other. He said that he then could detect edges between them, and indeed could discriminate different shapes when the contiguous patches were arranged in that way, but nevertheless without the *colour* of boundaries that made these discriminations possible. Heywood *et al.* show clearly that the information *must* have arisen from intact colour processing mechanisms, even though the subject had lost the colour qualia.

Neuropsychology is replete with specific deficits, such as the one just mentioned, where the patient lost the perception of colour (but nevertheless showed residual colour processing ability). Another neuropsychological patient (L.M.) has attracted much attention because she has apparently lost the ability to see movement, at least within wide limits of speed (Zihl *et al.*, 1983). She sees a moving bus, for example, as advancing in a series of discrete 'stills'. The spout of tea emerging from an urn is seen as a solid curved cylinder. Her perceptual life is not at all comfortable! Nevertheless, my colleague Peter McLeod (personal communication) finds that she catches a ball thrown straight at her with the skill that one would expect of a normal middle-aged woman! She also has no difficulty in identifying the 'natural' movements of 'Johansson' figures, which are films of persons moving in the dark with small lamps fixed at the ankle, knee, hip, elbow, and shoulder joints. They were filmed walking, running, jumping, crawling, etc. Normal persons can recognize and name these different 'biological' movements. And so can L.M. (McLeod *et al.*, 1996.)

As a slight digression, it is not surprising that such clear-cut and relatively isolated deficits as loss of colour or movement perception should lend support to the attractive idea that the brain processes information in highly specialized separate modules, one each for colour, orientation, movement, objects, spatial position, etc., and such a view has devoted advocates, especially as different regions of the brain also show some specialization in terms of their electrical responsiveness for different categories of visual information (Zeki, 1978, 1981, 1993). But a certain degree of caution may be in order: the deficits, while relatively specific, are rarely confined to just one isolated perceptual category—to colour or movement, alone, for example—and the lesions that cause them are not necessarily located where the electrical sensitivities would suggest they should be found. (Thus, monkeys with lesions of the electrophysiological V4 colour area do not have a significant problem with colour discriminations, whereas a lesion (in the inferotemporal cortex) that does cause colour discrimination problems is far away from V4, Heywood *et al.*, 1992, 1995.) And even if there were isolated modules for specific categories of visual processing, these in isolation, it will be argued later (Chapter 6 and 8), cannot be sufficient for perception as such.

Perhaps the most celebrated and dramatic evidence of function without awareness has come from the study of commissurotimized patients, colloquially known as *split-brain* patients. These, like H.M., suffered from epilepsy (the history of neuroscience owes a great debt to epilepsy sufferers), but the surgical treatment was different. Because epileptic electrical outbursts in the brain tend to spread from one cerebral hemisphere to another (and, in fact, thereafter to become autonomous), surgeons have cut the massive connections, the corpus callosum, between the hemispheres in an effort to contain the electrical conflagration. Thus, at least at the level of cortical–cortical connexions, the two hemispheres are rendered independent, although the lower connecting structures of the midbrain still remain intact. Many workers, among them Roger Sperry and colleagues (1960), and Ron Myers (1956), had shown that cats or monkeys in whom the hemispheres were disconnected in this manner behaved as though each hemisphere learned and remembered visual discriminations and other visual habits quite independently of the other hemisphere. In humans the brain systems that are critical for language are located (in most people) in the left hemisphere, whereas the right hemisphere is more apt to be specialized for perceptual skills. (There is some evidence for hemispheric inequality in monkeys (Jason *et al.*, 1984), but obviously this does not include any specialized capacity for language.)

When commissurotomized patients are observed going about their normal everyday lives, they appear reasonably normal—only a skilled observer in particular situations may notice some occasional 'conflict' between the hemispheres, for example the left hand may try to button up a coat, while the right hand tries to undo it. But for the most part, because both hemispheres are being engaged, patients cope quite well—in fact, one surgeon staked his claim to enduring fame by concluding that the quite massive corpus callosum (it consists of some 200 million nerve fibres) serves no important function. Roger Sperry (1974) and colleagues, having shown the critical importance of the commissure in animals in learning, took pains to ensure that visual information directed to their human patients only went to one hemisphere (at least at the first stage—a roundabout route is available via midbrain circuits). This is easily accomplished because, as already mentioned, each *half*-field of vision projects to the opposite cerebral hemisphere. Therefore, if the subject maintained his or her visual fixation on a central spot, visual information flashed on the left side of the spot would travel to the right hemisphere, and vice versa for information flashed on the right side of the fixation spot.

What Sperry and coworkers found was that when they projected visual stimuli to the left, 'speaking' hemisphere, of split-brain subjects, the subjects reported seeing the stimuli quite normally and could identify them. But when they were projected to the 'silent, non-speaking' right hemisphere, the subjects said they saw nothing at all. Nevertheless, they could be shown, by indirect means, to have identified the 'unseen' visual events. For example, as shown in Fig. 1.9, they correctly retrieved with their left hand (which is controlled by the right hemisphere) the object that had been shown to the right hemisphere, even though it was reported as not seen by the subject (Sperry, 1974). Several other demonstrations of 'covert' perception were made. In one, less formal experiment, a woman patient was shown a picture of a nude figure. When projected to the right hemisphere she claimed that no visual stimulus had been presented, but she nevertheless blushed and exhibited other very obvious signs of embarrass-ment. These were recorded on a video tape. (When I tested this same lady some years later, she told me that she had known all along that the experimenters had shown her a nude, but said she was too embarrassed to admit it. I recounted this to Roger Sperry and colleagues who insisted,

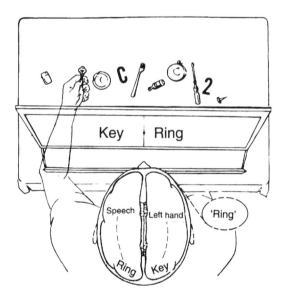

Figure 1.9. Schematic of results with a split-brain patient, in whom the commissures connecting the two cerebral cortices have been cut. The subject maintains fixation on the centre of the screen. A word flashed to the right of the fixation (ring) projects to the left hemisphere, in which speech is processed. When asked to report what words he sees, he readily reports a word that projects to the left hemisphere, and, in this instance, says 'ring'. But when a word is shown on the left of the screen, projecting to the 'silent' right hemisphere, the subject denies that there is a word there. Nevertheless, when required to select an object with his left hand (which is controlled by the right hemisphere), the subject reaches correctly for the object indicated by the 'unseen' word. (From Sperry, 1974, M.I.T. Press, with permission.)

convincingly, that this was a reconstruction *after* the lady had seen the video tape of the experiment!) Numerous other experiments with more mundane stimuli demonstrated dramatically how information that reached the 'silent' hemisphere could be processed even though the subject denied seeing them at all. For his work on split-brain subjects, which has become classical, Sperry was awarded the Nobel Prize in 1981. This event gave great pleasure to neuropsychologists around the world, who were surprised nevertheless that Sperry had not already received the Prize for his earlier brilliant work on mechanisms of neural growth and development.

There was a superficial similarity in the early results of blindsight and the split-brain findings, namely, both denied 'seeing' visual stimuli which they nevertheless gave good evidence of processing. In 1975 Sperry kindly allowed me to test the split-brain patients with the types of stimuli Warrington and I had used with D.B. (Weiskrantz *et al.*, 1974). Our patient had a surgical removal of visual cortex (in the right hemisphere, resulting in blindness in his left visual hemifield) and it seemed possible, even if very unlikely, that the posterior portion of the corpus callosum had been damaged in the surgical procedure (this posterior portion is known to be especially important for *visual* transfer of information between the two hemispheres). Information travelling over remaining pathways serving his blind left hemifield (either through sub-cortical routes that might bypass the striate cortex, or because the striate cortex might not have been completely damaged) might project to the right hemisphere, but be unable to gain access to the left hemisphere. That is, information might not be 'seen' for the same reasons as with the split-brain patients—because it was disconnected from the 'seeing' left hemisphere. The results showed that D.B. was quite different from Sperry's patients, and that no such explanation would hold. Indeed, those split-brain patients that I later studied no longer denied seeing stimuli projecting to the right hemisphere—they could give accurate descriptions and approximate dimensions of them. D.B., of course, could not see the stimuli that Sperry's patients could. In discussions with Sperry's group it appeared that there are long-term longitudinal changes in the commissurotomized patients, who have been willing subjects in a large range of experiments over several years. It is to be hoped that these longitudinal changes, given their obvious importance for plasticity as well as possible 'indirect' bodily signalling stratagems, will some day be documented.

To summarize, neuropsychology has exposed a large variety of examples in which, in some sense, awareness is disconnected from a capacity to discriminate. There is nothing surprising in our performing without awareness—it could even be said that most of our bodily activity is unconscious, and that many of our interactions with the outside world are carried on 'automatically' and, in a sense, thoughtlessly. What is surprising about these examples from neuropsychology is that in all these cases the patients are unaware in precisely the situations in which we would normally expect someone to be very much aware! These patients might help to reveal to us not only something about the capacities which can operate in the absence of awareness, but also the consequential penalties. Perhaps, more tantalizingly, they may open some routes to a characterization of awareness that derives from empirical dissociations rather than from philosophical ruminations, or might complement, support, amend, or even conflict with such ruminations. Beyond that, as particular experimental methods have evolved for studying performance in human patients with and without awareness, do they offer any possibilities for studying animals with similar methods to address age-old questions of awareness in non-verbal creatures? And, finally, as all of the material derives from patients with known or potentially knowable brain dysfunction, do any suggestions emerge about the *neural organization* underlying acknowledged awareness?

2

Deficits, degradation, and dissociations

The discovery—the uncovering—of covert residual functions by now extends, we have seen, to all of the major syndromes in cognitive neuropsychology—and even to some not normally considered to be 'cognitive'. In every major realm of cognitive achievement—perception, memory, language, problem solving, meaning, motor skill learning—there are robust hidden processes that survive the neurological insults that appear to destroy them.

Frank disbelief was the initial response to the two syndromes that were first analysed in the 1960s and 1970s: amnesia and blindsight. The epidemiology is such that the more recent examples have escaped such concerted overt scepticism. Indeed, having been involved in both of these bodies of research, disbelief was an early attitude that Elizabeth Warrington and I had upon retesting patients on each occasion anew: it could not really be the case, could it, that a patient, whose memory for important events was so shot, could actually show normal and robust retention of material when tested indirectly with partial cues or fragmented pictures, or with a conditioned stimulus, even though recognition or recall was totally absent with direct testing? Similarly, could a blindsight subject really discriminate visual stimuli virtually perfectly with forced-choice guessing and yet firmly deny seeing the stimuli being discriminated? Surely these results were flukes, and would not be repeated on retest. It was for this reason that in both areas we often invited colleagues to view the testing, not only to detect and prevent any 'Clever Hans' trickery, but to share our surprise and indirectly give reassurance (and in at least one or two cases, to tempt distinguished onlookers into similar research).

The sceptical attitude at the outset led to various forms of suggested degradation. In both the amnesic syndrome and blindsight, the first response was to deny the data on methodological grounds: to suggest that in amnesia, for example, there might have been a possible mismatching of initial performance scores between patients and controls; and in blindsight, protest on multiple fronts, for example diffusion of light into intact visual fields, incomplete lesions, differential response criteria. These were healthy responses, given the counter-intuitive nature of the phenomena, although they were pursued in some instances with unseemly zeal and persistence beyond the point of positive relevance.

But the next level of degradation historically was in terms of comparisons with normal capacity. The data underlying the residual phenomena might be (eventually were conceded to be) sound, but it was argued that these phenomena were just weak versions of normal function, qualitatively unaltered. It would not be surprising if brain damage caused a general weakening of a capacity or a raising of thresholds. In amnesia research this led to comparisons of 'strong' with 'weakened' memory in normal subjects, supposedly weakened, typically, by using long delays between initial and test sessions, with the conclusion—given particular critical delays—that 'covert' function could still be intact in the weakened case when tested *indirectly* (e.g. by priming) even though absent in *direct* tests of recognition or recall. That is, it was argued that the amnesic patient could be simulated in normal subjects. This general line of attack on the amnesic syndrome has almost completely dissipated as a self-sufficient explanation and the research has advanced farther than in blindsight, although in fact theoretically, as we shall see, some of the same issues remain at the heart of the analysis of dissociations. But in other domains this type of interpretation is still being pursued: for example, in blindsight, by the finding in one patient of small islands of intact vision within the blind field putatively due to tags of striate cortex (Fendrich *et al.*, 1992; Gazzaniga *et al.*, 1994), and in prosopagnosia by finding covert function in weakened face-name learning tasks induced by long delays between initial presentation and test (Wallace and Farah, personal communication). Related arguments are advanced in Farah (1990), Farah *et al.* (1993), and Feinberg *et al.* (1995).

One positive benefit of this line of comparative enquiry was, however, to arouse an interest by experimental psychologists in implicit processing in normal subjects, and that is now an active field in the fields of visual processing (Milner and Goodale, 1995), memory (Jacoby and Hollingshead, 1990; Jacoby and Kelley, 1992; Roediger and McDermott, 1993; Shanks and St. John, 1994), decision-making (Berry and Dienes, 1993), and learning of syntax (Reber, 1993). It is becoming widely appreciated that much of our behaviour is not accessible to conscious control or awareness, and that implicit phenomena such as priming, so powerful a factor in the memory of amnesic patients, also has a counterpart in normal learning and retention.

It will remain an empirical issue as to what extent residual function will be successfully and comprehensively cast in qualitatively different forms from normal function. Even if, with a careful adjustment of parameters in normal subjects, a simulation of the residual function found in patients might sometimes be manufactured in normals, this general approach will always be at risk of a practical failure to get the parameters just right, even though in principle it might be achievable. But the approach withers away, not logically, but pragmatically, when there are demonstrations of double dissociations between normal and residual function.

The history of the research on memory disorders provides a useful guide. The early rejoinders after the discovery of good retention of verbal material by amnesic patients, as revealed by priming and related methods, as we have just recounted, were precisely in terms of degraded normal function; that is, it was argued that amnesic patients were just like normal people with 'weak' memories. And, indeed, in some respects normal subjects tested after very long delays are like amnesic subjects after just a minute or two—they may sometimes show priming in the absence of recognition. It was argued that the amnesic patient either had a very narrow bottle-neck in getting information from short-term to long-term storage, or alternatively failed to 'consolidate' the information completely in a long-term store.

What cut through this approach was, in the first place, a cascade of double dissociations. It was shown that there were patients with impaired short-term memory who could retain information normally after long intervals, and so the simple model assuming direct transfer from short-term memory to long-term would not do. Moreover, a double dissociation could be demonstrated between them and amnesic patients, who are not impaired on short-term memory tasks (see Appendix for a discussion of the pragmatics and logic of dissociations). Subsequently it was realized that some of the residual functions shown by amnesic patients, for example tasks involving perceptual or motor skill learning or classical conditioning, *could* be impaired in other patients who, in no sense of the word, were like amnesic patients in failing to recognize or recall material. Secondly, similar distinctions emerged from animal research, which also reinforced the evidence from human neuropathology that *where* in the brain the damage occurred was of paramount importance. Thirdly, as post-mortem examinations of human patients gradually appeared, it became clear that amnesia could be caused by relatively tiny, but crucially placed, lesions. In no sense did this mimic a 'graceful degradation' in a computer simulation based on parallel distributed processing (PDP), in which performance falls off as a function of increasing damage to the system. This is not to say that PDP simulation, more carefully constructed, cannot be made to simulate functional dissociations, although it may be doubted whether a pure and absolute double dissociation could be so simulated (Shallice, 1988). As far as I can judge, nowadays no one believes that the amnesic syndrome can be explained by an appeal to generalized degraded normal function. Instead, there is an acceptance of the conclusion that the system damaged in amnesia, usually called the episodic memory system, is but one of a number of memory systems that can operate independently, albeit in many situations interactively and conjointly. Our brain contains multiple memory systems, one of which is damaged in the amnesic syndrome, and the different memory systems have distinctive functions to perform.

The appeal to degradation is more tempting in blindsight and related disorders like unilateral neglect, in which it can be argued that patients' sensory information is too weak to 'reach the sensorium', in the language of the nineteenth century, but is nevertheless capable of having a covert effect on some parts of the nervous system. One reason for the natural inclination to treat this is as a raised threshold problem is that there are claims from the 'subception' domain with normal subjects that information below a 'threshold for awareness' can sometimes be detected better than expected by chance. If the strength of the signal is increased, of course, then the threshold for awareness is exceeded. But while this may not be an uncommon occurrence in psychophysics, typically the levels of performance achieved, while statistically better than chance, are still quite weak. In contrast, blindsight performance can reach and remain at high levels, 90 to 100% correct, well outside the range of performance in the shadowy domain of near-threshold levels of psychophysics with normal subjects. Even that will not satisfy everyone, because there *are* occasional reports of high levels of discrimination in experiments with stimuli below the threshold for awareness, for example by Tony Marcel (1983a, b). His studies used a backward masking procedure in which a patterned visual stimulus was flashed immediately after the visual stimulus to be discriminated. If the interval between the stimulus and the flash is short enough, the target stimulus is not 'seen'. But Marcel reported that it could nevertheless be discriminated by guessing. As a matter of fact, I think this particular backward masking procedure might literally be a functional equivalent of striate cortex inactivation, and so Marcel's experiment should not work in a blindsight patient in whom visual cortex is already damaged; cf. Weiskrantz, 1986. A second reason for thinking in terms of degradation of normal function is that the total capacity of the parallel pathways that remain after V1 damage is, indeed, much smaller than the pathway to V1, which contains about 85% of all optic nerve fibres. And so it may be natural to think of a visual system that is literally degraded in total capacity, and perhaps, therefore, in signal strength of optical events.

But, while it is premature to judge the outcome of 'weakened normal' function explanations in blindsight and related syndromes, I confess that I feel uneasy with such a simplistic view as a general account of dissociations of awareness. For one thing, I do not know why awareness should emerge once a given level of strength has been reached, nor does it help me understand what it *is* that actually emerges. What governs the properties and proclivities of the 'sensorium'? In everyday life awareness of events seems to relate much more to what one is attending to than to signal strength alone, and when one is 'aware' certain acts can be carried out that are not possible when attention is not focused. Nor can I understand just how to set the 'threshold' for awareness, or why there should be one. Admittedly, a loud and sudden signal can certainly bounce one into awareness, but so can the quiet whimpering of a baby. In case 'sensorium' is thought to be a relic of nineteenth-century language, note that it appears in one pristine twentieth-century physiological treatise: Giles Brindley's (1960) well-known and influential visual monograph. If one does not like the term (and I don't), in what way is 'threshold for awareness' an improvement? How do events above the threshold differ from those below?

But there are some more empirically based reasons to question the degradation interpretation of blindsight. Firstly, as already mentioned, using one of the favourite methods of neuropsychologists, Warrington and I found a double dissociation between the blind hemifield of a patient (D.B.) and his intact hemifield. We found that the blind hemifield was much poorer than his intact hemifield in discriminating visual shape by forced-choice guessing, but there were conditions in which it was better than the intact hemifield in actually detecting a visual stimulus, again, by guessing (Weiskrantz, 1986). Thus the intact field seems to be biased towards object identification, and the blindsight field towards stimulus detection; it is hard to explain this on a simple degradation basis. The difference in motion discrimination when D.B. was aware of the motion, as opposed to when he was not (but could still discriminate) did not shake down to a simple difference in stimulus thresholds (Weiskrantz, 1986), as will be shown in the next chapter, but more studies of this kind are needed. Secondly, there are several kinds of ganglion cells in the primate retina (the ganglion cells give rise to the optic nerve fibres themselves). These cells have different morphologies, different electrical properties, and project differentially to targets in the brain. Strikingly, there are anatomical changes in the retina itself following V1 damage (because of a phenomenon known as retrograde transneuronal degeneration), with a heavy shift away from a predominance of beta ganglion cells, with alpha and gamma cells being more protected. Beta ganglion cells are smaller, have colour opponency properties, and project only to the thalamus and thence to visual cortex. Gamma cells project only to the midbrain, and alpha cells project to both the thalamus and the midbrain. Thus, the structure, distribution, properties, and pathways of these cells of origin of the optic nerve are themselves different from the pattern in the normal visual system. One is not just a weak or degraded version of the other. Finally, although this appeals to an a priori argument, given that there are 10 separate and parallel pathways originating in the eye with different targets in the brain, it seems more parsimonious to assume that they have remained segregated, and have survived in evolution for a good functional reason (the two largest divisions in the primate visual pathways are present in reptiles and birds), rather than to assume they are all pouring into a common functional bucket. As in the case of memory, it is reasonable to assume that we are dealing with multiple systems carrying out different operations upon inputs from the eye. But I am expressing a preferential view. Only further research will decide.

Fortunately, it may be possible and practicable to decide relatively directly. This line of argument will be expanded in later chapters, but briefly: some blindsight patients, especially with rapidly moving or suddenly appearing stimuli, have a kind of 'awareness'. Under other conditions, excellent discrimination is still possible even though the subject has no awareness whatever of moving stimuli. We have measured the stimulus parameters for moving stimuli for one blindsight subject, G.Y., in conditions where he acknowledges some awareness, and in other conditions where he has no awareness whatsoever. We did this using the 'commentary-key paradigm' to be described more fully in Chapters 3 and 6. The results suggest that there is a qualitative difference between the two functions, that the curve relating discrimination success to velocity and contrast of the moving stimulus when the subject is unaware is not just a pale shadow of the curve for when he is aware. The unaware function appears to be much more broadly tuned than the aware function. Such a result was also strongly suggested by studying the two conditions, unaware and aware, for another blindsight subject, D.B., again using a moving stimulus. A PET scan has already been obtained in G.Y. for the aware condition for moving bars. It remains to obtain a brain image of the aware and unaware conditions separately, which should indicate whether there are any brain structures uniquely involved in one or the other condition.

Can one plot the 'tuning curves' for the two conditions or modes, aware and unaware? Moving stimuli are not ideal for defining the entire curve, because above a certain velocity all movement remains aware for this subject (G.Y.). But this subject, like some other blindsight subjects, is also aware of stationary stimuli if they are made temporally transient, by sudden onset or by flickering. All monochromatic stimuli can be described and defined in terms of the spatial and temporal parameters for which they are effective. We have already measured those parameters for a blindsight patient, G.Y., who was presented with transient stimuli and was aware of them in his impaired visual hemifield. The tuning curve for his response is quite sharp, and shows a peak sensitivity at a low spatial frequency, about 1.3 cycles/degree. The results will be displayed in more detail in Fig. 6.8 and discussed in Chapter 6. It remains to measure his tuning curve for those stimulus conditions in which he can discriminate without awareness, and to determine whether it is, indeed, qualitatively different from the condition in which he is aware, and such an experiment should soon be conducted. And so the question of whether blindsight—discrimination without awareness—is just a weakened version of normal capacity for stimuli set well above the threshold for 'seeing' might be answered directly by experiment. Whatever answer emerges from such experiments is bound to have practical as well as theoretical interest.

It is premature to judge the outcome of such 'weakened normal function' explorations for all cognitive neuropsychological domains (and for all individual patients). But the appeal to a concept of 'normal function', weakened or otherwise, masks some complexities that are easily overlooked. There is a more subtle reason to question whether the idea of degraded normal function is itself a good model for anything, either in neuropsychology or in everyday life. There is no such creature in psychology as a *pure task*, nor will there ever be. All tasks consist of constellations of demands and capacities—perceptual demands, motor skills, motivation, etc., although tasks are designed such that some naturally come more to the fore than others. But these do not necessarily degrade equally with signal strength, or with a delay before testing memory, or what have you. A degraded normal task is not necessarily just a 'weaker' version of the strong normal task. Even within a single restricted domain, more than one process will be involved. In degrading from strong into weak versions of a task with normal subjects, it is possible that one is switching from one form of process to a qualitatively quite different one. In the case of vision this is obvious when one considers the sensitivity to stimuli under bright or dim illumination, because one switches from a predominant dependence on cone receptors to rod receptors in the eye, which have qualitatively quite different properties and sensitivities; for example one is colour blind and the other is not, and their peak sensitivities to a range of wavelengths are different—revealed in the well-known Purkinje shift, the name used to describe the fact that the eye is relatively insensitive to red wavelengths when dark-adapted, and so blue colours look brighter than red at dusk. And so it does not follow that even when a successful simulation of a deficit in a patient has been achieved by 'weakening' normal function, the residual function being simulated necessarily is *qualitatively* the same as normal 'unweakened' function. The question of relating clinical outcomes to normal function is much more complex than can be settled by such an easy comparison, which is why dissociations are so revealing. Pathological function is rarely just a pale shadow, just a weakened version of normality.

Double dissociations when found, as we have argued, can cut through this problem, for example, when it is discovered that blindsight fields are biased towards detection and are poor at identification, and intact fields are just the opposite. But the devil can also have an advocate here and return the argument, because it may be that weakened vision itself has such a bias as does blindsight, without there being any other qualitative difference. That is, even *within* a system there can be double dissociation. Elsewhere I (in agreement with others) have argued that the value of double dissociations in leading one to inferences of independent systems is pragmatic rather than logically decisive (Weiskrantz, 1968).

As amnesia research has taken one to the position, now widely accepted, of independent (but normally interacting and conjoint) memory systems, one can be confident that the claim of residual function equals weakened normal function will not be universal for all forms of residual function, and my prediction is that few of the double dissociations, if any, that are of the pure and absolute form (i.e., not partial or relative deficits) will end up having that status, although no doubt detailed theoretical analysis may argue for elevated thresholds for sub-components of a system (rather than a complete destruction or disconnexion, e.g. Andy Young, 1994). Or, if they do have such a status, it will be because, as has just been argued, the weakened *normal* homologue is actually different.

There is another aspect of the body of neuropsychological evidence that is clearly relevant to the search for mechanisms: it is that the deficits are *domain-specific* and can be, and often are, highly constrained (cf. Schacter *et al.*, 1988 for a good account of this and related issues). A blindsight patient can be, and usually is, perfectly normal in all other cognitive domains, and an agnosic patient can have normal episodic memory for events (for example, remembering that he had been shown a picture of a face, and that he could not recognize it on that occasion). This has led some to argue that there are domain-specific 'awareness' modules or capacities that are separately damaged in these various syndromes, or that there is a single awareness module but with different inputs from several separate cognitive systems, each of which can be independently disconnected from the awareness module. The latter position has one serious difficulty, namely that it should be possible, even if rarely, for a single *general awareness* module to be damaged—so that one would be left with just a bundle of implicit processors, a true zombie, if you will. In the tens of thousands of neuropsychological case reports, no such case has been reported, so far as I am aware. Admittedly, there are many cases of generally 'reduced' vigilance in association, for example, with damage to the midbrain or thalamic reticular formation even, at the extreme end of the spectrum, of coma, but these patients have severe problems in directing or maintaining attention. They are amnesic, for example, because they do not attend or take in material, not because they have a demonstrable and independent memory problem. However, one should not reject out-of-hand the possible *conjoint* role of the reticular system in conjunction with other particular domain-specific cognitive systems, a speculation to which we will return later.

An alternative to considering *either* domain-specific awareness modules, *or* a common module that can be selectively disconnected ('first-order' explanations according to Schacter, 1992), is to consider multiple systems within each of the domains, some of which allow implicit processing to occur, and others of which are invoked in the service of explicit processing ('second-order' explanations). The best-known and clearest example is from research on memory dysfunctions, where it is argued that the episodic memory system (which is, goes the argument, by its very nature explicit and which necessarily entails conscious awareness of past events) is selectively impaired in the amnesic syndrome. Similarly, in blindsight it has been argued that a system specialized for object identification is selectively damaged, such identification normally being accompanied by acknowledged awareness. Remaining visual systems, such as that controlling saccadic eye movements to sudden peripheral visual events, for example, can operate without recourse to awareness (and without recourse to the striate cortex). Or, to take another dichotomy, responses mediated by the autonomic nervous system can be, and usually are, 'unconscious', whereas cognitive cortical processing is inherently 'conscious'. Thus, a blindsight subject still shows a galvanic skin response to visual stimuli, and a prosopagnosic subject still shows such a response to familiar faces, these stimuli being processed over quite separate pathways from those involved in normal 'seeing' and recognition of familiar faces.

Thus far we have considered the various dissociations of residual function from awareness as having certain underlying formal similarities. But clearly in more than one sense they differ in important ways. In blindsight, or blind touch, the subject is unaware of the very material being processed. In the amnesic syndrome, the subject is very well aware of the material on which he or she is being tested, but is unaware that the positive response to a prime demonstrates good retention and, moreover, that it demonstrates the intactness of a capacity. It is a failure of awareness of the capacity itself, whereas in blindsight it is a failure of knowledge of the input and, unless there is knowledge of results, of the outcome as well. And so the examples differ in whether the knowledge is overt or covert with respect to the material and to the outcome. It is a distinction between awareness *of* and awareness *that*.

They also differ in the way in which the capacity is attacked experimentally. In some tests the method is direct: 'do you or do you not recall the words presented in the list?' Or, 'guess whether the unseen stimulus is moving or stationary.' In other tests the method is indirect and more cunning, as when it uses influences of visual stimuli in the blind hemifield on the truly 'seen' perception of stimuli in the intact visual field. The subject's direct response is to the seen stimulus, but the experimenter can infer the impact of the unseen stimulus of which the subject is not consciously aware. It is, in a completely innocent sense, an exercise in deception.

Just how one talks about the residual capacity in a theoretical sense is, of course, optional, although I think it is convenient to refer to it, as is commonly done, as an 'implicit' *process*, that is, an inference that something is going on even though at some level the subject is unable to acknowledge this explicitly. There are a number of other terms, such as 'automatic' or 'procedural' which intrude in the discussion of specific examples; these will be dispatched to the Appendix and need not intrude further here.

But apart these simple matters—the method of experimental attack, the status of the subjects' knowledge, and terminology—there is another sense in which the examples differ. It is in the logical structure of the inferences that can be drawn. In an anatomical arrangement such as underlies blindsight, where we have a number of parallel and independent pathways going from the retina to different targets in the cerebrum, it is reasonable to analyse the outcome in terms of *fractionation* of a capacity. Where one finds *double dissociations* of function, with convergent anatomical or physiological evidence of independent pathways, one has a necessary and a sound basis for inferring independent components or biases. As mentioned above, Warrington and I found just this type of double dissociation in a blindsight patient. The blindsight field was more biased towards detection, *qua* detection, than the intact 'seeing' field, whereas just the opposite was the case for form discrimination. And beyond striate cortex, there are multiple and parallel outputs, and so independent components of vision are emerging, for example, movement, colour, and form, each of which may well turn out to be associated with its variety of blindsight. That is, not only are there multiple dissociations between different types of attributes, dissociations among items arranged, as it were, in a horizontal array, but for each there may also be examples of 'vertical' dissociations between the particular attribute, such as colour, and its dissociation from conscious awareness of the residual capacity. Similarly, with memory disorders, there has been a host of instances of fractionation of 'memory' into different memory sub-systems, for example short-term vs. long-term, episodic vs. semantic, declarative vs. procedural. Some of these are accompanied by awareness, and others are not, as we have seen. It must be stressed, again, that double dissociations are necessary but not sufficient for demonstrating functionally separate components. They provide a good basis for making theoretical inferences, but the ultimate success of these inferences depends upon the mustering of converging evidence, and not on dissociations alone.

Fractionation is a division into potentially equally autonomous components. But there are other examples where the break-up is anything but equal, and one draws an inference that there is a hierarchical structure. In Lotty Tyler's evidence from aphasia, for example, where she finds that 'on-line' processing is intact, but 'off-line' is severely impaired, it is hard to conceive of a dissociation ever going in the opposite direction; that is, where a patient showed an insensitivity to grammatical and semantic structure when tested on-line by reaction time, but was nevertheless normal in comprehension and speech. It is not impossible, of course—neuropsychology is full of surprises. But the logical structure in this instance is probably is much closer to one of *hierarchical* levels of functioning in the brain, such as that advanced by Hughlings Jackson, the great nineteenth-century neurological pioneer. He argued that 'higher' functions were more fragile and vulnerable to assault, whereas the 'lower' more primitive functions were more robust. Thus, an aphasic patient may lose the capacity for fluent discourse in speech, but when provoked could still swear! I occasionally meet people whose speech is so replete with profanity that I wonder if they are thereby protected from ever becoming aphasic.

Disentangling deficits by dissociations, and the constructing of hypotheses about independence and hierarchical structure, is the very meat of day-to-day neuropsychological analysis and theorizing, and it is especially important in revealing aspects of mental structure that may not be easily seen in normal function. It is the case, as we have seen, that the examples of function without acknowledged awareness are domain-specific. The various examples are not only doubly dissociable but multiply dissociable: blindsight, agnosia, aphasia, and neglect can each occur as separate, isolated deficits. Each thus will invite, indeed demand, theoretical speculation within its own domain. Trying to speculate about the difference between the critical demands involved in seeing with or without awareness may not bear any close terminological or theoretical similarity to speculations about memory with or without experienced remembering, or with face identification without recognition, or any of the other residual phenomena. And certainly one can say that their respective neuropathologies have little, if anything, in common.

Speculating about features or properties that these implicit residual phenomena do *not* share, or how they have come about either theoretically or neuropathologically, may not be productive. But can we speculate about what they *do* share? That is the task we set ourselves in chapters to come. All the patients share the loss of awareness *of* or awareness *that*, all examples of which entail the loss of the capacity to make a commentary about something that remains intact. The relationship between commentaries and awareness will be a recurring theme. What does it require, in functional and neural terms, for capacities to be properly 'connected with' acknowledged awareness? What is it that allows some processes to be endowed with awareness? What is the change in the brain of the brain-damaged subject that dis-endows them? That is a tough one, but we will have a go in the chapter on 'How?' Finally, while dissociations of residual function from awareness are domain-specific, nevertheless the patients share a common handicap in their everyday lives, and this bears on the question of why awareness is important in an evolutionary sense. This will be the topic of Chapter 7, on 'Why?'

3

The 'What?' of consciousness

I often wonder what reaction a visitor from Mars might have if (he/she/it) happened to land in an airport waiting lounge. He might see, amongst the bustle, countless human creatures sitting silently and relatively motionless in front of sheets of paper, occasionally turning a paper over. More puzzlingly, others are to be seen sitting with a strange apparatus attached to their heads. Some would have their eyes closed, others not; the heads of some might seem to oscillate from side to side. If he manages to be able to talk to a native, he would be told that some are 'listening' to 'personal cassette players', others are asleep with the machine still working, and others have the apparatus on but their batteries have run down. However, he is told, you cannot tell the difference just by looking, or even by talking to them. What is going on inside them, asks the Martian? Why is the cassette player important? Well, the answer is, they find it an enjoyable experience to listen to music. Really?, says the Martian. And what is going on inside their heads (an advanced Martian theorist, this) when that happens? End of conversation.

The Martian then proceeds on a guided trip of so-called universities, where he encounters other equally silent creatures sitting directly in front of boxes, occasionally pushing keys with their fingers. He wonders if it is another way of enjoying music, or perhaps absorbing some strange sort of energy. His guide tells him that the countless creatures in room after room are 'computing' and 'thinking'. Again, he wonders what goes on inside their heads when they 'think'. His guide might offer some answer about 'something like how a computer works', but our Martian presses for an answer, not an analogy. End of conversation. The Martian concludes that on their planet the larger mass of earth creatures are more or less continuously immobilized in front of machines or with wires attached to their heads.

There used to be a lot of embarrassment and impatience amongst scientists when questions of experience or consciousness arose. They were said to involve 'subjective' matters that were beyond the scope of science—worse than that, everyday discourse involving the words was dreadfully messy and inconsistent. Science could only deal with the 'objective', the overt, visible, and the measurable. But, at the same time, we can point to persons who are 'unconscious', or sleep-walking, or persons who 'act without thinking', and presumably the brain activity in such cases must be different from those who are not or do not, and is this not a challenge for science to address? The layman has no doubt about the importance of his own consciousness and his own thoughts, and has an abiding curiosity about them which was not damped by scientists shunning the topic in the heyday of behaviourists' self-denial. On the contrary, it led to deep scepticism about behaviourism itself.

Nowadays, if anything, we are embarrassed by the plethora of scientists offering solutions to the 'problem of consciousness'. It has been described by John Searle (1995) as 'the most important problem in the biological sciences'. Searle puts that challenge quite directly: 'How exactly do neurobiological processes in the brain cause consciousness? The enormous variety of stimuli that affect us—for example, when we taste wine, look at the sky, smell a rose, listen to a concert—trigger sequences of neurobiological processes that eventually cause unified, well-ordered, coherent, inner, subjective states of awareness of sentience.' It is almost *de rigueur* for Nobel Laureates to enter the fray. Even the Royal Society has recently held a press conference on the topic of 'consciousness' and has sponsored a public lecture on it. I take this to be a happy state of tolerance, even of self-indulgence, and am optimistic about finding not *a single solution*, but a family of solutions. Instead of Occam's razor, we may well have a full-blown bushy beard. And, if we find that neuroscience is forced to retreat battered and bloody without any answers—which I cannot accept as at all likely—then we might be convinced that we need a wholly new approach that goes even beyond the mysteries of old-fashioned (but still impenetrable to me) quantum mechanics.

I believe that neuropsychology is partly responsible for this quantum leap in interest. The various syndromes all arise from known or knowable brain dysfunction, and they all have credible relevance precisely because they have been based on hard—often hard-earned—empirical evidence. The claims have been honed in the tough world of checking and counter-checking of experimental results, of replications and understanding of reasons for non-replications, when they occur—the stuff of science. And the results, by general agreement, certainly deal with the awareness. But, while philosophers of mind have also become interested in 'cognitive neuropsychology', it is still necessary to try to formulate one's position regarding the concept of awareness in the context of its disconnexion in the various syndromes which have come to light.

The first stand to take is to not retreat from the problem, not to redefine awareness out of existence as an important issue. The temptation for 'reduction' in science is powerful and easy to understand. Equally strong is the drive towards arriving at precise definitions, with frustration sometimes intense in their absence. The fact that definitions are difficult to reach, however, does not remove the importance of a domain. What is the definition of 'red'? Here is the definition in the *Oxford English Dictionary*: 'of or near the colour *seen* at the least-refracted end of the visible spectrum, of shades ranging from that of blood to pink or deep orange.' (italics added). The fact that it is associated with 'the least-refracted end of the visible spectrum' does not say what it is *like* to experience red. The directness of the experience of colour remains, even if it is 'reduced' to a part of the spectrum, to particular receptors in the eye that are sensitive to that part of the spectrum, and to particular brain regions to which they might project. Note that the best the Oxford Dictionary can do, beyond telling us of wavelengths of light, is to describe red in terms of other ineffable colours, like blood or pink or deep orange. More tellingly, try to tell a sufferer of a toothache that it is just a matter of the 'central grey' of his nervous system being a bit over-active. In seeking an explanation *of* a phenomenon it is important not to lose sight of the object of the *of*. Definitions come late in science, after one understands something, rather than as strait-jackets to be applied before one understands the lawfulness of phenomena. Faraday did not need Ohm's law.

And so, rather than seeking to 'reduce' varieties of awareness to a lower level, I believe it is more valuable to '*elevate*' explanations of the nervous system to a level that can do justice to the phenomena we seek to explain, and to study those aspects of the nervous system that might actually address them at that level. The spinal cord consists of perfectly robust nerve cells, and yet the spinal cortex isolated from the brain does not generate awareness (but does still show responsiveness). The brain also consists of robust nerve cells, and the paraplegic whose spinal cord is isolated is perfectly aware of his world (aside from stimuli impinging on the cord itself). The essential functional difference between the collection of nerve cells at the level of the cord and at the level of the brain inevitably implies (to me) that the awareness must be a matter of *organization* of systems, a matter we will pursue in Chapter 8 on 'How?' I am a materialist—I believe that awareness ultimately is a matter of brain activity and that its understanding is part and parcel of understanding brain activity, but I am an 'elevationist' rather than a 'reductionist'.

That much is a matter of a general outlook, a general stance. But while we should not be driven or constrained by definitions, or the lack of them, some preliminary distinctions, which can already be seen when we return to the possible ruminations of the Martian visitor, are pertinent. He will note different levels of sheer activity, and such levels of activation are themselves given descriptions in terms of 'levels of consciousness'. A comatose creature is said to be 'unconscious', and a very active and alert one said to be 'highly conscious'. This aspect of the subject is one which I shall *not* pursue, as important as it is. My concern is much closer to that of Nicholas Humphrey's in which he puts the position that 'to be conscious is essentially to have sensations: that is, to have affect-laden mental representations of something happening here and now to *me*.' (1992, p. 97, italics added). I stop, however, before the word 'me'. I am not concerned with whether awareness is 'self-awareness'; indeed, I think that particular concern has been over-stressed in discussions of consciousness. I also choose not to become distracted by the age-old problems of distinguishing sensation from perception, as when Humphrey states: 'All other mental activities (whether they occur in human beings, non-human animals or even in machines) are outside of consciousness.' (p. 180). Perceptions are 'affect-neutral representations of "what is happening out there".' (p. 179), which leads him to conclude that perception is more primitive than sensation. That does at least turn the historical distinction on its head. The quagmire into which that distinction between sensation and perception has become enmeshed can be left to others to pursue; I find the distinction to be unhelpful, perhaps because of my early Gestaltist imprinting. Conscious awareness in my discussion will be independent of its content, whether this be of the self, of a bodily twinge, an emotional reaction, an event in the world, or of knowledge. It is a question of experience, and not of its referents, which can be various.

The 'subjective' nature of experience, of course, is troublesome, and is at the root of traditional prohibitions in science as well as contributing to the vagaries and difficulties of definitions. There is also a traditional reluctance to engage in 'single person discourse', to converse with a single individual rather than characterize groups of subjects so as to arrive at general laws. But there are some paradigms that help both to refine and to open up the matter. It is curious that no one has either a *philosophical* or a *scientific* problem with '*single person discourse*' in classical psychophysics, that is with the measurement of the responses of a subject to stimuli varying along some physical dimension, for example intensity, so as to define his sensory threshold or his judgment of loudness, or what have you. One varies the stimuli, and the subject responds to each by 'yes' or 'no' or 'louder' or 'less loud', or may even assign a number on a scale to it. The methods are well-established, and the ordering of a subject's responses into 'psychophysical' determination is straightforward. There are, of course, as with any method, questions of how to deal with borderline phenomena, such as the precise definition of a threshold, and rather searching questions about how to vary or calculate the criterion that a subject adopts in making his responses, but the evidence from psychophysics is rich and invaluable in characterizing a person's sensory sensitivities. When the pattern of psychophysical results for the individual is orderly—is *lawful*—we accept it without qualms. We can and do fit mathematical functions to it.

A typical question that the subject is instructed to answer in psychophysical determinations might be 'was there a sound?', if so, then answer 'yes', if not, answer 'no' or press the appropriate key. Or, in the commonly used 'two-alternative forced-choice' situation, 'press key A if the sound was in the first of two temporal intervals, and key B if it was in the second interval'. All quite straightforward. But, note, implicit in this is that we are asking the subject to tell us when he or she is *aware* of a stimulus or not aware. Indeed, that is usually directly and implicitly embedded in the instructions we put to the subject: 'press key A if you *see* the light'. But by 'see' both subject and experimenter mean 'when you are *aware* of the light'. We are not troubled by the fact that this entire procedure is concerned with 'subjective' experience if the results are systematic, reliable, and lawful.

Typically, no distinction is made in this instruction with normal subjects between 'seeing' and being 'aware', unless we have a particular interest in subliminal perception or some such topic. Indeed, many would balk at the idea. But in blindsight we *do* distinguish, because of the discovery that a subject can press the discrimination keys appropriately even without seeing, without being aware. The psychophysical paradigm can still be used, because we change the instruction from seeing to guessing. If the results are systematic and lawful, they have precisely the same status as in normal psychophysics. There is no problem of dealing with the absence of subjective experience, any more than there is in dealing with its presence.

We can go beyond that, because some blindsight subject do have an experience of awareness for moving and transient stimuli under certain conditions, a matter that will be explored more fully in a later chapter. But under certain other conditions they do not have any awareness, yet they still demonstrate blindsight; that is, they can discriminate very well (in some examples, perfectly) by guessing. We can now expand our psychophysical procedure to four keys instead of two. With two of the keys the subject signals his discrimination, for example, 'present' or 'not present', *even when forced to guess*, and with the other two he signals whether he had *any* awareness of the event, or whether he did not. This paradigm, the 'commentary-key paradigm', as will be seen, also generates lawful results for *both* sets of keys. That is, one can determine the stimulus parameters that yield correct discrimination and, independently, that yield awareness. The status of the psychophysical procedure remains unchanged, we are simply expanding our single person discourse to include more than a single set of choices.

And so not only is the positivistic scepticism of a critical review unjustified in its declaration that 'from the theoretical point of view the unconscious aspect of blindsight is hence essentially trivial, and from the practical point of view it is impossible to treat scientifically' (Campion *et al.*, 1983, p. 427), but, on the contrary, the psychophysical procedure allows one to open up fresh investigations of the nervous system that bear directly on the issue of possible mechanisms of the 'unconscious' aspect.

Not all of the neuropsychological syndromes allow such a transparently direct psychophysical approach. It would be possible, in principle, but a bit awkward in practice, to set up a situation for an amnesic subject in which one interrogated both the 'associative' aspect of a stimulus and its 'recognition' aspect after each trial. In classical conditioning, for example, one could measure the conditioned response, and on each trial ask the subject whether he recognizes the C.S. (the light or sound) as having occurred before. Something like this actually has been done informally for blocks of trials, but not after each trial (Weiskrantz and Warrington, 1979). However, unlike the blindsight case, one cannot vary the nature and strength of the stimuli easily within a single psychophysical arrangement. Quite aside from this, there are no conditions for the densely amnesic subject in which he or she *does* acknowledge recognition after a suitable delay beyond the limits of short-time memory. And, of course, even if one could find such conditions, with the amnesic subject we are not dealing directly with whether or not the subject is aware of the event as such, but of lack of awareness of the covert mnemonic capacity—it is knowledge of which he is unaware, not stimuli as such.

This means that, for practical purposes, blindsight and related phenomena are much more convenient for pursuing the question and the limiting conditions of *awareness* experimentally. It is also the case that we know more about the physiology and anatomy of the visual system than the properties and anatomy of other systems in the brain, which makes it easier to form links in the discussion throughout the chapter. But, at this stage, the point to be stressed is that single person discourse and the psychophysics of awareness are not only admissible and permissible for scientific enquiry but are right in the thick of things.

That is all very well, but . . .

Appealing to single person discourse may be fine for considering the admissibility of evidence, but it does not address the deeper problem. The question remains: what is it that endows certain 'explicit' systems with the capacity for acknowledged awareness, and bars such access in other systems? Why should stimulus detection not necessarily entail awareness, whereas object identification apparently does (or does it always)? Why should the autonomic system be unconscious? Why should memory for an event typically lead to acknowledged awareness, whereas priming or memory for a conditioned association does not require it?

That is the nub of the problem of conscious awareness—the nettle to be grasped—for these neuropsychological syndromes. Many persons will duck this one, recognizing (nearly to mix the metaphor) the philosophical minefield in which such questions are fielded; indeed, it seems virtually impossible for explosions to be avoided! As usual, there are some ways of bypassing the problem. One is to deny the reality of the question by declaring it to be metaphysical, beyond scientific enquiry. Blindsight had such a brief characterization in its early days (viz. the comment already cited by Campion *et al.* that 'from the theoretical point of view the unconscious aspect of blindsight is hence essentially trivial, and from the practical point of view it is impossible to treat scientifically'). It is not only folk psychology that squirms at such a rejection, but also neuropsychology itself: it has been the patients, not the metaphysicians, who have driven us to try to understand the neurological underpinnings of these deficits. Fortunately, both scientists and philosophers are more tolerant about trying to understand consciousness these days, and there is a virtual plethora of nettle graspers, including those who take the neuropsychological evidence on board.

Another way of bypassing the problem is to declare that *normal* perception, memory, and other cognitive capacities are highly complex, and contain within them all the various strands that become unmasked or distorted by brain damage. This may be the view of some philosophers, such as Daniel Dennett, and his appeal to multiple drafts of cognitive functions whose apparent unity he judges to be illusory. Others may simply dismiss evidence from dysfunction altogether, declaring that it is fruitless to try to understand, let alone to reassemble, Humpty-Dumpty after he has been shattered. That used to be a common position, but fortunately even the experimental psychology of normal function now acknowledges that neuropsychological phenomena provide deep insights, and indeed the discipline has incorporated much of the evidence in analyses of normal implicit function. Within the neuropsychological field itself, another too easy solution is that by fiat, by definition: autonomic = without awareness; episodic = with conscious memory of a past event. And so forth. Not very satisfying. *Why* should episodic be conscious?

Yet another approach, potentially somewhat more satisfactory, is to try to determine what the members of the residual class have in common and, in contrast, what the members of the deficient explicit class have in common. This is an exercise in concept formation, and concepts might ease the way to more venturesome nettle grasping. In the early historical stages of research on each of the deficits, this seemed to be possible and promising, and for the amnesic syndrome—which has received the most concerted attention—there may still be some potential. But the class of stimuli which blindsight subjects, taken collectively, cannot discriminate by forced-choice guessing (the 'heroic' method) or by indirect methods, is gradually eroding (cf. reviews, Weiskrantz, 1986, 1990b). Not only normal spectral sensitivity, but also wavelength discrimination, is possible without acknowledged awareness. So is movement. So is simple form discrimination, according to some workers. (Further, its shape is reported to control the grasping by the hand of an object in the blind field, and there are claims by Tony Marcel, still unpublished, that words flashed in the blind field can generate semantic biasing of words subsequently shown in the seeing field.) So is completion of partial forms in the good 'seeing' hemifield helped by subparts presented in the blind field.

Again, in prosopagnosia the early findings emphasized autonomic responses, or forced-choice guessing of familiar vs. unfamiliar faces, that is, without any great demand on cognitive processing. But gradually the residual capacities have encompassed more demanding cognitive ones; for example, the abilities to attach correct, rather than incorrect, names more readily to unrecognized faces, and to classify the unrecognized faces into correct professional categories.

In aphasic research, the 'on-line' capabilities can be extraordinary: both syntactical and semantic skills can be intact when tested by indirect methods (but not, of course, in direct discourse). An aphasic patient, that is, need not have lost a sub-category of linguistic processing—except, that he cannot understand or use language!

The amnesic syndrome has received the most intensive examination, and in one way—but only in one way—is in better shape than the other deficits. The items in the 'explicit' category that are lost all involve recognition and/or recall. (Even here there is not always uniformity: recognition and recall can themselves be non-equally affected, and even dissociated.) But the items in the retained category defy simple conceptual specification, although they have sometimes been assigned a common label, 'procedural memory', implying an intact capacity to learn and retain skills. But in what sense is intact priming a procedural skill? What does classical conditioning have in common with priming or with motor learning? What does learning of anomalous sentences or anomalous pictures have in common with any of these other examples? In fact, virtually the whole arena of different types of long-term information has been reported to be capable of storage by amnesics, except for their recognition and recall.

What they all have in common in the amnesic syndrome, of course, is that they can occur without acknowledged awareness of being memories, but why should this be so? In the amnesic field, some speculation has been offered. For example, Daniel Schacter and colleagues have found (as discussed in Chapter 5) that priming for novel objects is still intact in amnesic subjects, a result that is important because it demonstrates that priming need not be facilitation just of old semantically-stored items. Schacter offers the explanation that 'since the structural description [of the previously presented object] does not contain information about the *time and place* that the object was encountered *or elaborations that tie the object to semantic or associative knowledge*, access to a structural description alone does not provide a basis for conscious recollection.' (Schacter 1992, p. 192, italics added).

This is an appeal to an implicit theory of explicit memory: that it requires contextual, spatial, and temporal information *or* semantic elaboration tying the item to-be-remembered to larger knowledge systems. Schacter acknowledges that such information might actually turn up in appropriate tests of implicit memory, which would be enough to destroy the theory, but no such evidence has been produced, nor actively sought (although there are claims that recency judgments can be intact in amnesic patients, and long ago Warrington and I (1971), demonstrated that such patients show normal benefit from clustering words to be recalled into similar semantic categories). But why should contextual information or semantic elaboration endow an item with the quality of being 'memorable'? Or, turning the question around, as I prefer to do, why should an item that is remembered allow one to ruminate about the time or place or other circumstances connected with the original event?

We are still at the stage of trying to understand the various domain-specific examples of function without acknowledged awareness in terms of theoretical speculation within each of the domains. Trying to speculate about the difference between the critical demands involved in seeing with or without awareness does not bear any close terminological or theoretical similarity to speculations about memory with or without 'experienced remembering', or to face identification without recognition, or to any of the other categories of residual phenomena we reviewed in Chapter 1. And certainly one can say that the respective neuropathologies have little, if anything, in common, at least as far as is presently known.

What all of the retained syndromes *do* share is that in none of them can the residual capacity be used by the patient in thinking or in imagery, and this is a severe handicap. This is a theme we will be addressing more fully when we discuss evolutionary aspects (Chapter 7). The amnesic patient cannot relate what is primed today to what was primed yesterday, or to any other item in memory, including time and place, and other (but not only) contextual information; he is functionally fixed in the semantic or procedural present. The blindsight subject cannot manipulate the stimulus, about which he has just guessed, in relation to other stimuli, or to their spatial setting; it cannot play a role in thought. He may be able to discriminate wavelengths by forced-choice guessing, but he cannot relate the colour of the current patch to the rainbow, the colour of his car, or the vase of daffodils, nor remember what the colour he guessed about yesterday was like. And obviously a stimulus that is omitted in the half-field of a patient with unilateral hemi-neglect will suffer the same fate. By definition, none of these patients can tell you that they have the contents of the residual capacities that they do have, and they cannot talk to themselves about them either. And, the actual items being imageless, nor can they imagine them in relation to other percepts (although in blindsight, of course, this does not preclude a subject from using the inputs to his intact hemifield for imagery in the normal way, nor his memory for familiar scenes, and attempting to imagine the unseen in those terms, but the patients' descriptions suggest it is very difficult and strange). The prosopagnosic is unaware of his ability to treat familiar faces as familiar in contrived test situations, and hence all faces, appearing unfamiliar, are merely isolated presentations unrelated to past associations or to each other.

Thus, the patients all share a lack of awareness of the positive powers that remain intact, and deal with the contents of the relevant events in their daily lives and experience as though they were powerless, as indeed they are in practical terms. In this sense, they are disconnected from a conscious acknowledged awareness of the true status of those events (using the term 'disconnected' descriptively and metaphorically, with no necessary implication as regards mechanism). They can *know* of their skill in an intellectual sense, but they remain unaware experientially.

Philosophers of course, have brought a diverse array of approaches and attitudes to bear on the question of awareness, helpfully reviewed by P. Churchland (1993). Some, of whom Daniel Dennett is one recent example, have a frank distrust of 'folk psychological' terminology; for them little in perception can be taken at face value; it is a mine-field and Dennett thinks that the answers will be found in appropriate forms of software, yet to be evolved. The grapes are as yet untrodden, and even if they turn out to mask other minefields, the explosion, nevertheless, might be more bearable if some fermentation has taken place. For others, no current form of computer software is going to solve the problem of how we comprehend both semantics and syntax of language. For those within a 'neurophilosophical' identity-theory outlook the question of consciousness will boil down to descriptions of the operation of the neural mechanisms themselves. Others embrace the folk psychological concept, at least of sensory awareness, but try to reduce it to particular brain activities. Others refine and dissect the way in which the term itself is used, and distinguish between the several different types of consciousness. Others speak of emergence of consciousness from the complexity of the brain, such that simple brains are not conscious and complex ones are. Others speak of the brain *causing* consciousness, leaving the question of cause to be solved by others. Another approach, such as by the mathematical physicist Roger Penrose (1994), appeals to Gödel's theorem, implying that it is necessary to go to a quite different level of explanation in terms of quantum mechanics, without spelling out the details of a solution, so in effect substituting one mystery for another. I realize that such a summary is a travesty, and each position would deserve and demand serious attention. Very good reviews exist of some of the main players in this arena, among them the recent series by John Searle (1995). A useful range of essays can be found in Davies and Humphreys (1993).

I prefer to approach the matter by considering the kinds of practical *operations* that are involved in deciding when a person is aware and when he or she is unaware. Beyond that, to see whether there might be a philosophical position onto which such operations might be mapped, but—as the lawyers say—without prejudice. And, finally, to see whether both the operations and the logical construction that flow from them might, in turn, map onto the nervous system.

Dan Dennett has helped me in this regard, perhaps unwittingly, in two ways. He has offered, firstly, a helpful review of some blindsight research together with a thoughtful and detailed speculation of some of its potential implications (Dennett, 1991). He has done this just wrongly enough to prompt my colleagues, John Barbur and Arash Sahraie, into doing further work. (More of that soon.) But he has also considered blindsight as a kind of degradation of normal vision. This is, as we have seen, a familiar argument, but he draws a comparison with normal peripheral vision. He comments, 'the vigorously moving object is not perceived by the blind-sight subject as having colour or shape, but so what? As we have proved to ourselves [earlier in his book] we can . . . identify a card held in peripheral vision without being able to identify either colours or its shapes. That's normal sight, not blindsight, so we should be reluctant on those grounds to deny visual experience.' (p. 338).

That passage yielded an eerie *déjà vu*, because we, too, long ago (Weiskrantz, 1972) had considered the same possibility that residual vision (in primates following striate cortex lesions) was like normal peripheral vision, which would have been in line, at the time, with certain contemporary versions of the 'two visual system' hypothesis (Ingle, 1967; Schneider, 1967; Trevarthen, 1968). It was necessary to shake ourselves free of this version of the view that blindsight was a form of degraded normal vision (cf. Weiskrantz, 1986, pp. 146–152). D.B. was deliberately put in the situation of comparing the far peripheral vision of his intact visual hemifield—with its characteristically severely degraded acuity and sensitivity—with his blind field. As we reported, 'on a number of occasions we presented a variety of stimuli to the far periphery of D.B.'s intact field and asked him whether they ever produced the quality of or had any other resemblance to any subjective experiences he had in his impaired field. The outcome was always quite firmly negative, and he remarked, "No, even way out there in that part of my field, I *see*." ' (p. 147).

There was also another study in which we compared his ability to detect and to discriminate, in a spared crescent-shaped sliver of intact but amblyopic vision at the edge of his hemianopic field, with his ability in the heart of his blind field. The amblyopic sliver permitted only very fuzzy perception. Nevertheless, he insisted that it was *vision*. As it happened, the measured visual acuity was actually poorer in the seeing crescent than in his unseeing blind field, where acuity had to be determined by forced-choice guessing of whether a variable-spacing grating did or did not have 'lines'. In the blind field, despite its higher acuity, he reported not being aware even of the bright back-projected display within which the acuity grating was generated, and of course did not see any lines (Weiskrantz, 1986, p. 30).

Finally, observations with detection of movement at first actually strongly tempted us to embrace the peripheral vision hypothesis, because D.B. was found to be much better in peripheral vision under one particular condition than in central vision, and he also had some kind of awareness in the periphery. But we had to abandon it when a simple variation showed that he was as good in his blind field as he was in his normal hemifield for central vision under conditions when he reported no visual experience whatever and was forced to guess (Weiskrantz, 1986, Chapter 13).

That experiment, like many others, came as a considerable surprise, in this case dashing hopes, soon after they were raised, that we had good evidence for the peripheral vision hypothesis. The sequence of events went as follows. Because D.B. reported awareness for some conditions of moving stimuli we were tempted to plot the sensitivity of one such stimulus—a moving dot oscillating rapidly up and down on an oscilloscope screen. The excursion of the dot could be varied, and the greater the excursion the easier it was to detect by normal observers, and by D.B. in his intact hemifield. D.B. adjusted the excursion traversed by the dot by repeatedly moving a knob on a potentiometer until he was at threshold—just barely aware of it. We found that he was very poor when the spot was placed near the fixation point, but improved markedly as the spot was moved farther away into peripheral vision, as shown in Fig. 3.1. And so it seemed that this aspect of residual vision—the sensitivity of the aware aspect—was biased towards peripheral vision. But then we decided to see how well D.B. did when he was forced to guess (moving or not moving) with the excursion of the spot set very far below threshold for awareness (on 50% of the trials the spot was moving, and on the other 50% the dot was stationary). To our surprise, his sensitivity was well within the range of normal sensitivity for detecting movement in his *good* hemifield, as also shown in Fig. 3.1. This was one of the first examples we had of a qualitative difference between the sensitivity of the aware and the unaware blindsight modes. In any event, it put to rest the idea of a direct equivalence of blindsight with peripheral sensitivity.

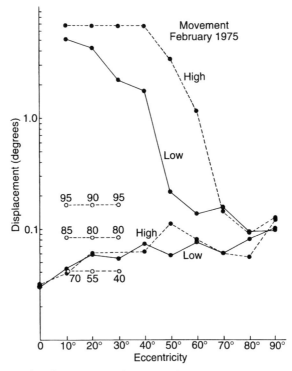

Figure 3.1. Results of a movement detection task with subject D.B. He was asked to adjust the excursion of a spot oscillating up and down until he was consciously aware of the movement. This was carried out at different locations in the affected and intact hemifields. The upper two graphs show that he was very poor when the spot was near the midline of the field, but improved when it was in more peripheral locations. (The two graphs are for different levels of background illumination.) But when he was required to guess whether the spot was moving or not when its excursion was well below his awareness threshold, his performance was approximately as good as that in his intact hemifield, shown on the bottom. The numbers indicate his per cent correct guesses, and the threshold would be calculated as the 75% correct value. (Reprinted with permission from Weiskrantz, 1986, Oxford University Press.).

But it was another report of Dan Dennett's that provoked us into actually doing some new research. He accurately recalled a video demonstration of a particular blindsight subject who can mimic, highly accurately, the path of motion of a visual stimulus (if it is moving at an appropriate speed) with a hand gesture.

> D.B. [in fact, it was G.Y., another subject], one of the subjects studied by Weiskrantz, has a right hemianopia and shows the classic blindsight capacity to guess above chance when cued. For instance, if a light is slowly moved

across his scotoma horizontally or vertically and he is prompted to guess 'vertical' or 'horizontal,' he does extremely well, while denying all consciousness of the motion. However, if the light is moved more swiftly, it becomes self-cueing: D.B. can volunteer without prompting a highly accurate report of the motion, and even mimic the motion with a hand gesture as soon as it occurs. And when asked, D.B. insists that *of course* he consciously experiences the motion—how else would he be able to report it? (Dennett, 1991, p. 332.)

Now, quite aside from mistaking the patient's identity (not serious in this case), Dennett reported an experiment that we simply never did. The reason is simple. The spot of light was a hand-held laser beam projected onto a screen. The account is correct that when it moved swiftly, G.Y. could accurately mimic the path. A plot of the various paths successfully mimicked in the video tape is shown in Fig. 3.2 (cf. Weiskrantz, 1995).

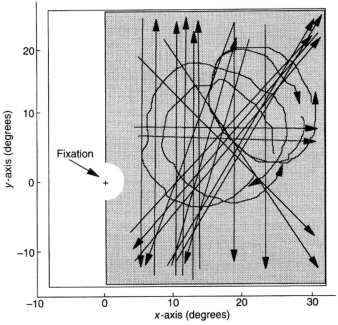

Figure 3.2. The paths of a small moving spot that subject G.Y. accurately mimicked with arm movements, as recorded on video tape. The arrows indicate the various direction of motion, both straight and curved. In the range of speeds used, performance was perfect. Fixation was well maintained throughout every trial. The hemifield in which G.Y. was tested is shown darkened in the figure to indicate his impairment (also shown is the small area of intact vision, 'macular sparing', intruding into his blind field, the white semicircle around the fixation point), but in fact both hemifields were uniformly and brightly illuminated. (From Weiskrantz, 1995, with permission.)

And it is also correct that when the light was moved slowly he did not even attempt to mimic—he did not detect it. But what was wrong in the account was that we did not make the 'classic blindsight' observation with the slow moving target—we did not even attempt it. The reason is that it is virtually impossible to control a hand-held laser projector so as to make it move slowly on the screen (less than about 5 degrees/sec) in a steady and smooth way. Too many jerky and tremorous movements occur, and we know very well that G.Y. responds sensitively to sudden transient changes in position of a target. Any results would confound slow velocity with jerky transients. I can only imagine that in chatting with Dan Dennett about this video, which was shown at a symposium in which we both participated, I might have hazarded a guess about what might happen *if* we had done the experiment, but I could not have reported the results of an undone experiment.

In any event, my colleagues and I thought it was actually worth doing the experiment, and not only to test Dennett's prescience. It was interesting in its own right, but even more important it also gave us the opportunity to try to determine in a formal way not only how well G.Y. could do while 'denying all consciousness of the motion' at slow speeds, but also how that related to those stimuli of which he had some conscious experience. For that it is necessary to try to find out whether the subject reports any awareness—at slow speeds, or other conditions of movement. We used the '*commentary-key*' paradigm, advocated some years earlier (Weiskrantz, 1986) but never actually used to map the boundary between 'conscious' and 'unconscious' in the same subject. It was necessary, of course, to use apparatus that accurately and smoothly controlled the speed, direction, length of excursion, and contrast of the laser beam, which took some little time for my colleagues John Barbur and Arash Sahraie to assemble.

G.Y. was given not two, but four keys to use *after every stimulus trial*. The first two were to be used to indicate, by guessing if necessary, which of two alternatives was presented in any trial, for example, whether the light had moved horizontally or not horizontally, or whether the horizontal movement occurred in the first or the second of two intervals; these are standard psychophysical procedures. The second two were commentary keys. He was repeatedly and insistently instructed that he was to press the 'yes' key if he had *any* experience whatsoever of the visual event, a feeling, a knowing, a tingle, or what have you. Only if he had no experience was he to press the 'no' key.

The result was that Dan Dennett was indeed prescient. G.Y. showed excellent discrimination even when he signalled having absolutely no awareness of the visual event. An example is shown in Fig. 3.3, but the matter and further examples will be discussed in more detail in Chapter 6. With slow velocities, G.Y. had no awareness, but performed very well. As velocity increased, awareness started to intrude, eventually dominating completely at higher speeds, with performance remaining high.

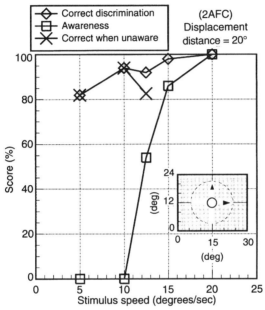

Figure 3.3. Performance with and without awareness by G.Y. He was required to indicate, by guessing if necessary, whether a spot moved horizontally or non-horizontally in his blind hemifield, and also to indicate on each trial whether he had any experience or awareness whatsoever of the visual event. (2AFC refers to the use of the 'two-alternative forced-choice' procedure, in which the subject has to indicate in which of two successive temporal intervals the horizontal movement occurred. The intervals were signalled by means of auditory beeps.) At velocities below 12.5° per second, he reported no experience but still performed at a high level of success. At higher speeds he reported awareness, and performance continued to be good. At higher speeds there were too few unaware discriminations for plotting. (Weiskrantz, *et al.*, 1995, with permission. © National Academy of Sciences, USA.)

Before leaving Dennett's account of the video demonstration of G.Y.'s mimicking the moving spot with his hand motion, we must just put a gloss on his comment that the subject 'insists that *of course* he consciously experiences the motion—how else would he be able to report it.'

G.Y. is far from insistent. His comment is recorded on the same video tape as his mimicry of the moving spot. He said, 'I *knew* that there was something moving, I was *aware*.' But the transcript then goes on: he was asked, 'Can you describe it?' Answer: 'No.' Question: 'What did you see?' Answer: 'I didn't see anything.' I did not present this phenomenon on video at the meeting as a pure case of blindsight, because there was actual awareness, a feeling. However, even here the subject insisted that it was not conscious *seeing*.

On another occasion, G.Y., in response to the same question in a closely similar stimulus situation, said it was difficult to know *how* to describe his experience. 'You do not actually really sense anything', he said. He then added that 'the difficulty is the same that one would have in trying to tell a blind man what it is like to see.' The nearest I have been able to come to a description of his awareness in this situation is that it is a kind of knowing that there is movement, as pure movement, and being aware of its direction, but in the complete absence of any identity of what it is that is moving—an awareness of contentless, directional movement. We will come back to this question in a later chapter, in relation to neural mechanisms.

We return to Dennett's comments on blindsight, in which he turns from the subject's responses to the experimenter's: 'the experiments couldn't be conducted if the experimenters couldn't give verbal instructions to the subjects, and the subjects' responses provide evidence of a startling phenomenon *only* when they are interpreted as speech acts. This is almost too obvious to notice, so I must pause to rub it in.' (p. 328). And later: 'Blindsight subjects have to be prompted or cued to give their better-than-chance "guesses".'

With forced-choice guessing, that is true. But the awkwardness of verbal exchange in such experiments, as we have just noted ('you do not actually really sense anything'), in blindsight and related syndromes is actually a nuisance, albeit a fascinating one. Many subjects, and no doubt experimenters alike, find it embarrassing to pretend that they can guess about something they cannot *see*. Indeed, some subjects refuse point blank. I have had a patient tell me, when encouraged to guess in the same way that one would back a horse, 'I do not gamble!' Another patient insisted, 'my brain is just not set up for *guessing*!' Another said, 'I *know* it's 50–50 of one or the other. But I can't guess.' In all the other neuropsychological syndromes we have discussed outside of blindsight, such convoluted verbal constraints do not apply. Instead, one uses *indirect methods* to infer the existence and operating characteristics of the residual capacity, for example priming in amnesia, reaction times to target words in aphasia, and so forth.

A range of such indirect procedures has evolved precisely to circumvent the dependence on verbal exchange (cf. review in Weiskrantz, 1990b). One general strategy is to see whether unseen stimuli in the blind field can influence the subject's response to stimuli in the *intact* field; the subject only reports what he sees in the intact field. For example, Carlo Marzi and colleagues have measured the reaction time to a light presented in the good field. If it is preceded just before by an unseen light in the blind field, the subject's reaction time is lengthened. The subject does not respond to the stimulus in the blind field when presented alone—he does not 'see' it, but we can infer from the increased reaction time to the light in the good field that the visual system is responding to it. A closely similar paradigm for saccadic eye movements has been published by Rafal et al., (1990); it has to be added that a colleague of mine (K. Cochrane, 1995) has had difficulty in replicating their findings for the type of hemianopes used in the Rafal et al., study, although it did work with G.Y. An older technique was introduced by Torjussen in 1976 and 1978. He showed that an incomplete circle in the *intact* hemifield was seen as complete when its other half was shown in the blind hemifield. If the incomplete circle was shown alone in the intact field, it was seen as just that—an incomplete circle. When shown in the blind hemifield, the subjects saw nothing (Fig. 3.4). The results for 3 hemianopic subjects are summarized in Fig. 3.5. A replication and extension of this result, using an after-image technique that controls absolutely for eye movements, has been produced by Tony Marcel (Fig. 3.6). Another visual effect and after-effect were exploited by Pizzamiglio et al. (1984) to demonstrate interactions between the impaired and intact hemifields. If a large disc, covered by random dots, is rotated in front of a subject, it produces a sensation of body rotation in the opposite direction; there is also a shift of the apparent vertical in the opposite direction, and torsion of the eyes in the same direction as the rotation. Pizzamiglio et al. showed that in normal subjects the effect is smaller when the rotating disc is presented to just one half-field rather than to the whole field. In patients, they found that exposing the disc to both the blind and intact hemifields produced a larger effect than when it was exposed only to the intact hemifield. (When presented to the blind field alone, the patients had no awareness of anything happening, although there was a small effect in the predicted direction.) Thus, there was a strengthening of the perceptual effect when the stimulus presented to the unseeing hemifield was added to that of the intact hemifield.

Another 'implicit' approach has been the use of pupillometry, attractive because it can be set directly beside results obtained along psychophysical

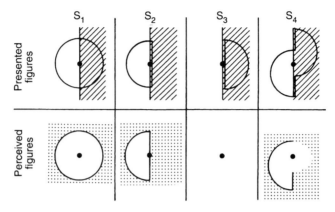

Figure 3.4. Stimuli presented to the cortically blind (hatched) and sighted fields, with the resulting perceptions seen by subjects, in experiments by Torjussen. The dot in the centre indicates fixation point. Radius of circle is $10°$. Note that a full circle is reported when it projects onto both the intact and the blind hemifields, but that the subject reports (correctly) only a half circle when projected onto the intact hemifield. A half circle entirely within the blind hemifield produces no response. (From Torjussen, 1976, with permission.)

		Subject 1		Subject 2		Subject 3	
S_1/S_2							
Response	◯	97.5	5.0	92.5	6.7	89.2	5.8
	◖	0.0	88.8	6.7	92.5	6.7	93.3

Figure 3.5. Results of Torjussen's experiments with three subjects, showing per cent of responses of full or half circles for stimulus conditions S_1 or S_2 of Fig. 3.4. (From Torjussen, 1976, with permission.)

dimensions. It turns out that the pupil of the eye contracts in response to a variety of visual stimuli, even when there is no change in light energy; the pupil is *not* just like the diaphragm of a camera. The amount of constriction varies with the spatial structure of a visual array, and indeed varies with the spatial frequency of a grating in a manner that allows one to measure visual acuity (Fig. 3.7). Such a measurement agrees closely with the acuity measured psychophysically (Fig. 3.8). Similarly, the pupil responds to the brief presentation of a coloured patch on a screen, even when the luminance is actually lower than the background. It also responds to

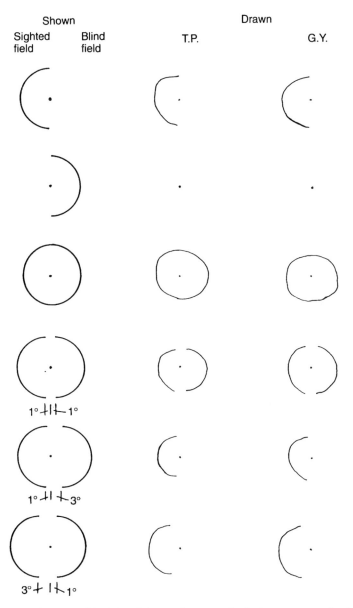

Figure 3.6. Figures used by Marcel (personal communication) to generate after-images (left column) by very brief and bright illumination with a photo-flash gun, and the drawings made by two blindsight subjects (T.P. and G.Y.) of their after-images. Such a procedure absolutely eliminates any artifact due to eye movements during the presentation of the stimuli or the after-effects, as the after-images move with the eyes. The stimuli were presented to the sighted and/or the blind fields. Note the similarity of results to those of Torjussen in Figs 3.4 and 3.5. (Reproduced with permission from Weiskrantz, 1990b, The Royal Society).

movement in the absence of a flux change. And so forth. The point is—
returning to Dennett's rubbing it in—that the pupil circumvents the need
for any awkward *verbal* instructions or exchanges. Provided the subject can
be persuaded to fixate a point on the screen, visual function can be
measured in the blind hemifield not only of a human adult, but also a
human infant (Cocker *et al.*, 1994), and an animal (Cowey and I,
unpublished, have recorded a pupil spatial frequency function in the
monkey which is closely similar to that of the human curve). Of
course, the method has to be validated against the measures obtained
by conventional psychophysics (including preference and habituation
techniques with infants (e.g. Spelke, 1988; Cohen, 1988)). So Dennett
was wrong in rubbing in a need for verbal instructions, at least when he
wrote about it, but I do not rub it in—the alternative methodology is
interesting in its own right. Further, as we shall see in Chapter 5, there is
reason to think that monkeys also have blindsight, and this was certainly
demonstrated without verbal instructions!

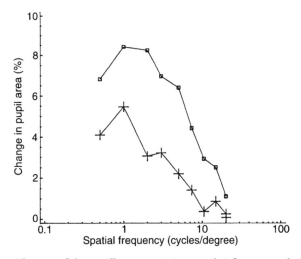

Figure 3.7. The size of the pupillary constriction to a briefly presented visual grating
(5° × 5°), centred either on the fixation point, (top line) or 8° peripherally, of a normal
subject. The total energy was kept constant over all values of spatial frequency. Note that
there is a peak at about 1 cycle per degree, with a decline to no constriction above 10 cycles
per degree, as the spacing in the grating becomes more and more crowded. The point on
the x-axis when zero constriction is first reached can be taken as a measure of visual acuity
for the pupillary response. (From Barbur and Thomson, 1987, with permission.)

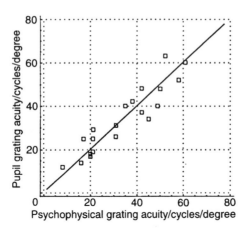

Figure 3.8. Plot of acuity measured behaviourally against acuity determined by pupillary response, showing excellent correspondence. Each point represents a different single subject. Solid line would represent a perfect correlation. (Modified from Barbur and Thomson, 1987, with permission.)

There is the second debt that I owe to Dan Dennett, which is for his lucid exposition of David Rosenthal's philosophical position (1986, 1990, 1993). The nub of Rosenthal's position is that 'conscious states must be accompanied by *higher-order thoughts*, and non-conscious states cannot be accompanied.' (1990, p. 16, italics added). 'A mental state is conscious . . . just in case one has a roughly contemporaneous thought to the effect that one is in that very mental state.' (1993, p. 199). A higher-order thought is a thought about a thought. A thought can be a perception, a detection, but it remains unconscious unless a higher-order thought accompanies. Rosenthal's account includes some strange terms, even within the context of folk-psychological language: for example unconscious thoughts, including unconscious higher-order thoughts that nevertheless render the first-order thoughts conscious. But so long as consistency is maintained, no matter. The main point is that unless you can have a thought *about* an input, it remains unconscious.

This is precisely what the patients cannot do: think about their inputs in relation to other inputs or contexts (I would extend thoughts, of course, to include images), to represent the content of their inputs to themselves. Rosenthal's approach has a similarity to my earlier attempt (1986, 1987c) to describe blindsight in terms of a failure of monitoring. Both approaches are subject to similar attacks: *who* is doing the monitoring?—is it another dreaded homunculus? But a new perceiver does not have to invent to perform in what Dennett calls the Cartesian Theatre. In talking to oneself rather than to someone else, one does not have to invent a new talker or new listener. Another worry: is there not a danger of an infinite regress— thoughts about thoughts about thoughts about thoughts, etc.? I, (like David Rosenthal, I think) have argued that logically an infinite regress is possible, but in practical terms is beyond normal capacity (Weiskrantz, 1987c). Rosenthal would argue, it seems, that even second-order thoughts are rarely conscious, that is, accompanied by third-order thoughts: 'They are the explicitly introspective thoughts that we would report (even to ourselves) only when in a state of hyper-self-consciousness' (Dennett, 1991, pp. 308–9). In any event, I distinguish logically between a monitoring system, which is sitting apart from what is actually going on, taking a peek at it from time to time, on the one hand, and a commentary system, on the other. The commentary system, which will enjoy a high citation index throughout this book, is the stage of the ongoing process of stimulus processing that is reached when it is capable of acknowledgment as such by the subject. It is what makes further elaborations and contextualization possible.

Dennett, while applauding Rosenthal's skilful manoeuvring and suc-cessful guidance through the folk psychology mine-field, nevertheless wishes to leave that mine-field, having more confidence that treading on software is mine-free (or mind-free). I wish to stay with it a bit longer, not only because I think we must tread there to reach our goal, but also because it does at least provide a unifying metaphor for describing the problem in all of the 'disconnected awareness' deficits. Beyond that, it also introduces the concept, or at least the possibility of hierarchical ordering, which provides one way of distinguishing among the various deficits.

Higher-order thoughts, indeed, suggest that thoughts are ordered in hierarchical ranks, from high to low. But this could be misleading in two ways: it suggests that the higher-order thought has greater generality or abstraction than the lower-order, like the trunk of a tree in relation to limbs, that is, that it is a superordinate. Second order, rather than higher-order, is sufficient to convey the notion that the second order is a thought about another thought, without implication as to its level of meaning, and is less likely to carry a misleading connotation. The second way in which a hierarchical connotation might mislead is if it is taken to imply that all of the individual deficits have the same underlying structure. Some of these are, indeed, break-downs within a hierarchical ordering, but others are not. For example, in aphasia it is hard to conceive that the implicit on–line processing of semantics and syntax, as studied by Lotty Tyler, could be damaged without the off-line explicit processing also being damaged. That is, there is a single rather than a double dissociation. On the other hand, in memory disorders and blindsight, it is reasonable to argue in terms of specific sub-systems being independently affected. In both cases, however, there is a lack of awareness of the content of the residual implicit capacity, the lack of a thought about a thought, in Rosenthal's terms. What is important about the second-order thought about a first-order thought is that it has to be a separable, even if contingent, thought.

Even as a metaphor, of course, it could be argued that second-order thoughts about first-order thoughts are just a redescription: it might be evident that if one cannot have a thought about a thought, in some sense the first thought must remain unconscious. There is also a possibility that the application of this approach would render us unconscious a good bit of the time—how often do we have thoughts about thoughts! In a very real sense we *are* often unconscious in these terms. But it does not mean that our automatic piloting of a car along the motor-way while thinking of tomorrow's committee meeting should be put in the same visual category as blindsight. In some respects it deserves to be, but the comparison forces us to remind ourselves that blindsight subjects' demonstrations of automatic skills are different from those of normal subjects in some important ways: they have a restricted visual pathway (restricted in the technical sense that their retinal cells themselves have changed), and, moreover, they cannot switch out of their state as the driver can. The driver can also call on visual memory, if typically fleetingly, of consciously seen events, like the sight of the police car lurking in the lay-by—an effective way of dismissing the automatic pilot! It is not incumbent on us to map the neurological deficits onto examples or lapses in our everyday lives, even if there are interesting and suggestive areas of overlap.

Rosenthal's position, that second-order thoughts about first-order thoughts are a necessary property for first-order thoughts to be conscious, tempts us to analyse the neurological disorders in terms of specific disconnexions or blockades between a first-order process and a second-order or higher-order stage that thereby lead to alterations in the states of awareness. It is a temptation to which I will succumb; that is, to link higher-order thoughts to the operation of the commentary system, specifically with reference to blindsight but also of wider application to other unconscious residual processes. Obviously the notion of higher-order thoughts is not to be taken literally as part of brain architecture. The point is that it is a logical structure onto which to map brain architecture, and vice versa.

The blindsight subject has no way of offering a contentful commentary on his discriminations. By this I do not mean that he is simply without words or language to communicate to others. I mean that he cannot offer a commentary to himself, let alone to anyone else. One realization that emerged from this approach was that (already reviewed) in order to diagnose whether a subject had blindsight one must not only offer the opportunity to make a visual discrimination (by forced-choice guessing or whatever), but also extract an accompanying commentary, typically verbal. But it *need* not be verbal, and if we ask whether an animal without striate cortex has blindsight, it cannot be verbal, and we will see that there is evidence that such an animal does, indeed, have blindsight (Chapter 4). Nor is it sufficient, tempting as it is, for the commentary response to be considered equivalent to the subjects' giving a rating as to how *confident* they were about their discriminative response, although that is of interest in its own right. In examining the verbal commentaries, together with confidence ratings and the performance of blindsight subjects (cf. Weiskrantz, 1986), there can be striking disjunctions. Confidence is not the same as content or commentary, nor does it always correlate with performance even when the subject is aware of the stimuli. Beyond that, confidence ratings normally are placed on a scale—say, of 1 to 10— which is a more complex analogue demand than requiring a binary choice between 'no awareness whatever' and 'some awareness'.

More broadly, it can be seen that *all* of the neuropsychological deficits we have considered—not only blindsight, but unilateral neglect, amnesia, aphasia, and so forth—are disjunctions in particular versions of the commentary-key paradigm. In amnesia, it is between the 'what is it' response for the prime, and the commentary keys, 'have you seen this before or not?' These disjunctions are not related to awareness *per se*, but to two different methods of testing for a capacity, or for two different forms of a capacity or, in multiple memory terms, for two different capacities. The dissociation of awareness in such a syndrome is a higher-order set of commentary-key responses that follow the response keys to the prime, of the variety, 'you were correct in your stem completion, but did you recognize that you had just seen that word a few minutes ago?' The answer, of course, would be 'no'. In neuropsychology, however, typically the order in which the commentary and the discrimination occur is in the reverse order. In blindsight, for example, it is first established by clinical examination that the subject says he or she is aware of nothing in one hemifield. Only later is it established whether or not the subject can discriminate by forced-choice guessing, or some other method. Indeed, historically speaking, *very* much later! Field defects were known to be blind for more than a century before the other two keys in the paradigm were introduced!

Indeed, in everyday life virtually all conversational interrogations take the form of a commentary-key paradigm but with verbal keys rather than mechanical ones, two verbal keys for 'did you see that car whiz by?' and 'was it a police car, yes or no?' Of course, the commentary keys expand often to a very much larger number than two, as when the optician asks (first set of keys): 'do you see the chart on the wall?' (two keys), and 'what are the letters on the bottom line?' (26 keys).

Commentary responses are necessary, in my view, as criteria in deciding issues about awareness of a discrimination, an identification, or of a capacity, but are they sufficient? Alas, probably not, because commentary responses, like any others, can become highly practised and automatic. A nice example, with literary license for exaggeration, is what I have termed the BWCS—the British Weather Conversation Syndrome. The British, as is well known, have the remarkable capacity to discuss the weather at length in something like a state of complete lack of unconsciousness, much like sleep-walking, except that even the sleep-walker can sometimes recollect what he or she has done. And so commentaries, in a literal sense, can become incorporated in a highly automatic routine—they are no longer commentaries but verbal extrusions. Indeed, one criterion for deciding whether a response is automatic in everyday life is precisely to determine whether there is a disjunction between a response and the subject's commentary—in much the same way as we determine that a paraplegic patient can emit a reflex response to a painful stimulus, but comments that he feels no pain. In more complex automatic skills, a practised car driver may be able to offer very little by way of commentary about what he has seen along the route, or even whether he has seen it. A BWCS emitter may be unable to tell you exactly what he said if queried immediately after their weather commentary!

Returning to neuropsychology, and blindsight in particular, the position we have come to, then, is that a commentary is a *sine qua non* for awareness. In the weak form of the hypothesis, awareness is *enabling* of the commentary, that is, allows it to occur. In this position, being able to offer the commentary that one has seen an event does not account for awareness *per se*. It is tempting to adopt a kind of identity theory for commentaries, but for some this will be too easy a solution for the qualia problem or the awareness problem. But at the very least one can say that the commentary provides a critical, even essential, criterion for deciding on the status of awareness. *This means that awareness always requires a parallel and separate response to the discrimination itself for it to be identified and acknowledged as such by the subject.* In the strong form of the hypothesis, the commentary itself is *endowing*. It is to say that it is the very achieving of the ability to make a commentary of any particular event that is what gives rise to awareness and it is what we mean by being conscious. To borrow a metaphor: the medium is the message—the achieving of the commentary is the awareness. It is what we mean by being aware, for an event to be experienced as such. The commentary need not be uttered; what matters is the state of 'comment-ability'. It is because of this approach to the issue that I find a distinction such as that between the 'phenomenal' and 'access' consciousness arguments (Ned Block, 1995), while instructive in its own right, orthogonal to the position taken here; phenomenal awareness itself, in our view, results from the delivery or potential delivery of a report.

There is a weaker form of the hypothesis, namely that awareness arises first, and that it leads to the possibility of a commentary being made. I know of no certain way, at this stage, of discriminating, of testing the difference between the weak and strong form of the status of the commentary, that is between the enablement and the endowment positions, although I prefer the strong form. The blindsight subject's autonomic nervous system might react vigorously to a visual stimulus, but without the subject being able to offer the commentary (although obviously, it need not necessarily actually be made) it is unfelt and unseen. Similarly, the paraplegic patient's limb withdraws from the noxious needle-prick, but he cannot acknowledge this to himself or to anyone else because the spinal cord lacks the organization by which to do it. Whichever form of the hypothesis one adopts, the advantage of this approach, while it admittedly, but tolerantly, suffers from the folk-psychological pitfalls, is that it is directly linked to the very methodology, and the operations themselves, which allow the limits of awareness to be defined; it is also linked to a philosophical position that attaches importance and meaning to thoughts about thoughts; and even more, it provides a skeleton on which to hang our consideration of the neural events that underlie awareness.

4

Animal consciousness—the problem of 'Whether?'

The question of animal consciousness is a relatively modern one, impelled by the Darwinian comparative perspective and more recently (and forcibly) by ethical issues. It was central to Descartes' position, of course, that all animals were machines without minds, and presumably that the human person minus a pineal gland would be a severely disabled creature because the mind could not affect the physical body. Even a modern dualist could not have such a simple get-out today! (Given the new-found importance for melatonin, a hormone secreted by the pineal gland and used by travellers for correcting jet-lag, perhaps there is a possibility of some helpful mind-bending after all from that part of the brain!) John Locke might have allowed animals some form of imagery, but he was grudging about their ability to think. He was able to pronounce with a flavour of certainty that it was 'positive . . . that the power of abstracting is not at all in them; [it is] an excellency which the faculties of brutes do by no means attain to.' (1690, p. 126). Contrast that with Darwin's quip that 'he who understands baboons would do more towards metaphysics than Locke.' (See Gruber, 1974, pp. 317–18.)

Philosophers do not hesitate to point out the manifold difficulties and ambiguities in the use of the term 'consciousness'. How much more uncertain is its application to animals, who may be entities of philosophical interest but who do not themselves philosophize. Of course, no one would have a problem in declaring a comatose animal to be unconscious, nor is there much quarrel in saying that a dog stalking its prey is conscious. In the absence of any verbal discourse with animals, and with the persistent lack of any objective criteria by which to make a judgment, we are thrown back on various deeply held intuitions and arguments derived from analogy with humans. The farther removed the creature is from the human, the more apt we are to deny it human attributes. Thus, we tend to assume that primates are 'more conscious' than, say, frogs, and certainly more than worms or paramecia, but such views are more intuitive than rational. The truth is that no one knows.

In fact, some naturalists have argued against any such phylogenetic tree of consciousness in animals. The American comparative naturalist, H.S. Jennings, took this very far. 'If *Amoeba* were a large animal, so as to come within the every-day experience of human beings, its behaviour would at once call forth the attribution to it of states of pleasure and pain, of hunger, desire, and the like, on precisely the same basis as we attribute these things to the dog.' And, he counsels, if *Amoeba* 'were as large as a whale, it is quite conceivable that occasions might arise when the attribution to it of the elemental states of consciousness might save the unsophisticated human being from destruction that would result from lack of such attribution.' That is, the attribution is adaptive *for us*. As Jennings remarked, 'We usually attribute consciousness . . . because this is useful; it enables us practically to appreciate, foresee, and control [an animal's] actions much more readily than we could otherwise do.' (1904, pp. 336–7).

Of course, this might be the case, but it is not a convincing argument for the attribution being *correctly* made. We attribute human-like qualities to objects in computer games, to servo-controlled missiles, to mechanical toys and robots; indeed, I suspect we are pre-wired to be animistic attributors to virtually every aspect of our environment, whether natural or man-made. But the fact that we can learn to predict and control does not require the attribution of anything at all *to the object* concerned. Indeed, the severe opponents of attributions argued that it actually impedes. Thus, Pavlov wrote, 'in our "psychical" experiments on the salivary glands at first we honestly endeavoured to explain our results by fancying the subjective condition of the animal. But nothing came of it except unsuccessful controversies, and individual, personal, uncoordinated opinions.' (1928, p. 50).

Pavlov no doubt would have made the same argument about the futility of the attribution of 'subjective conditions' to humans. But the thesis of 'other minds' in humans and chimps is a popular one, cast in just such positive utilitarian terms—that is, that making the assumption that a creature is conscious enables us to guess what it is thinking and hence to predict its course of action. With humans, it is argued, cheating is an example of deliberately misleading someone based on that presumption. And there are claims, some of them anecdotal (Byrne and Whiten, 1988) but not necessarily wrong on that account, of similar capacities for deception in the higher apes. Interestingly, however, when the *London Times* reported the account of the study by Woodruff and Premack to the effect that, among other things, their chimpanzee Sarah was 'the first non-human to be accused of lying', it provoked a speedy response two days later from no less a person than a past President of the British Academy. In his letter to *The Times* (22 October, 1981), he quoted the authority of Robert Louis Stevenson, who was convinced 'that all intelligent dogs are accomplished and incorrigible liars.' Indeed, 'pretence leg-cocking' by dogs taken out for their nightly toilet walk is seen by many dog owners. Many animals can change their colouring so as camouflage themselves. Others will remain motionless for long periods in a situation of danger. Do we have to attribute consciousness or intentionality to them, even though they succeed admirably in their deception? In other words, the difference between 'reflex' pretence and 'thoughtful' pretence, even if it could be drawn sharply, is a distinction between modes of *thinking* and its absence, and it might be considered that thought necessarily entails consciousness. Thought, in turn, is often linked to a capacity for language.

Language can be an important constituent of thinking, but Darwin concluded that 'that which distinguishes man from the lower animals is not the understanding of articulate sounds, for, as every one knows, dogs understand many words and sentences. In this respect they are at the same state of development as infants, between the ages of 10 and 12 months, who understand many words and short sentences, but cannot yet utter a single word.' (1871, p. 85). Lloyd Morgan's riposte is amusing: 'When I say "whisky" to my fox-terrier, he would at once sit up and beg: not because his tastes were as depraved as those of his master, but because the *isk* sound, common both to "whisky" and "biscuit", was what had for his ears the suggestive value.' (1900, p. 203). Whether or not dogs, or any other creature, can interpret language meaningfully while hearing it, curiously has received little systematic study. Much more has turned on the question of their capacity to generate meaningful language, in most cases, of course, either vocally, as in the warning signals of birds and monkeys, or by visual signs in the chimpanzee. The subject is deeply fraught. The criteria for accepting communicative utterances or visual signs as language are far from agreed upon, unless one rules out all shades of all sub-human varieties of communication.

But, leaving that issue aside, while language may be helpful for thought, it is certainly not the case that thought requires language. Thought without language can be seen in aphasic patients who have lost both receptive and expressive speech following brain damage. It is also seen in young pre-linguistic infants. And, most relevant in the present context, it is seen in animals (see treatments of all three areas in my book, *Thought without language*, 1988). Premack's juvenile chimpanzees, trained to learn the meaning of 'same/different' using tokens, for example, could solve the problem of adding ratios, even when the samples consisted of different types of items (Premack, 1988); for example:

1/4 apple plus 1/2 bottle = 3/4 disc or 1/4 disc?

The temptation to transfer thinking to possession of a language, even if one could agree on the minimal requirements for a language, will not work. And, returning to the start of this line of argument, even if we agreed that consciousness is a necessary condition for thought—which might readily be doubted by even 'soft AI'-ers—it is not a necessary condition for consciousness of sensory events as such. And so we are not much farther ahead.

This is not to say that language does not add a quantal leap. The adaptive advantages of being able to communicate are manifest, but the power to communicate in words requires both the capacity and the need, conjointly, to *abstract* and to *selectively represent*. Representation allows reference, but abstraction allows a world, a universe—even, said Romanes, a supernatural one—to be constructed that exists not only in the past but in the future.

Clearly, if animals are going to be declared to be conscious of this or that, of being conscious in the course of doing this or that, we will have to call on behavioural evidence. Behavioural evidence is often used to describe levels or stages of consciousness, meaning levels of activation ranging from coma to high arousal. But it is easy to demonstrate, or at least to argue convincingly, that a behavioural response to a stimulus may be necessary but it is certainly not sufficient for attributing conscious *awareness* of that stimulus to the responder. Consider the paraplegic human, in whom the spinal cord has been completely severed, leading to paralysis and anaesthesia of the lower limbs. As we have already noted, lower limb movements are still elicited by stimulation of the skin, and indeed it was those stimuli that normally are the most noxious that had the greatest effect. To repeat Sherrington's magisterial account, 'A needle-prick causes invariably the drawing up of the limb. . . . The nervous arcs of pain-nerves, broadly speaking, dominate the spinal centres . . . *where pain is, of course non-existent.*' (italics added, Sherrington 1957, pp. 227–8). And so the paraplegic's limb responds, but the person himself will tell you that he feels absolutely nothing (even if the 'feedback circuit 'is closed by his watching his limb move). It is no good arguing with the paraplegic that the *meaning* of consciousness is the butt of many arguments, that its semantic obscurities are such that some would even outlaw the term. The paraplegic—whether he is a scientist, a philosopher, or anyone else—will tell you he *knows* when he can feel—when the needle-prick is above the spinal cut—and when he cannot! No amount of argument about the philosophical basis of an experience can diminish the experience itself.

Obviously we must seek more complex behavioural criteria. William James (1890) considered *adaptive* behaviour to be the important test, 'the pursuance of future ends and the choice of means for their attainment', a definition that allowed him readily to endorse the view of some contemporary physiologists, such as Foster, that the spinal cord of the frog displays 'conscious intelligence'. That was because it was observed that if one limb's response of scratching at an irritating stimulus is blocked, the spinal frog will substitute another one directed at the same locus of irritation.

Well, does the spinal cord of the frog display conscious intelligence? I do not know if adaptive responses of a similar sort have been, or could be, demonstrated in the human paraplegic, but even if they could be, the paraplegic no doubt would still continue to tell you that he *feels* nothing, has no conscious awareness of the stimulation that led to the responses, and has no knowledge of having made the actual responses if he cannot see them or otherwise be indirectly informed. Very few would feel comfortable one way or the other about arbitrating on whether the isolated spine of the frog should be considered to be consciously aware.

Well, even more complex behaviour? Complexity is the domain in which most arbitrators have based their views: complexity of the nervous system and/or complexity of behaviour. Thus, Sperry (1969) and other theorists argue for consciousness being an 'emergent' property of the increasing *complexity* of the brain, absent in 'simple' brains but having gradually emerged in more complex ones. But why should neural complexity *per se* lead to such an outcome? And when, in the animal kingdom, is there enough complexity for consciousness to be above threshold for a given species? And *why* should it arise, anyway? Moreover, can we conclude that the loss of conscious awareness, as in the neuropsychological syndromes we have been considering, is caused merely by a loss of complexity? It seems unlikely that blindsight is caused by a reduction in the visual system's complexity *per se* in quantitative terms; if so, why is the precise locus of the lesion so important—why striate cortex rather than, for example, superior colliculus or the extensive inferotemporal cortex, which is also part of the visual cortical system? Even more remarkable would be the view that the Korsakoff amnesic patient does not recognize the items he has stored because of a quite small reduction in mass of the brain. Some Korsakoff patients who are severely amnesic have no other damage that can be seen microscopically other than a small but dense focus of degeneration in the mammillary bodies of the hypothalamus and a tiny strip of degeneration in the thalamus—the rest of the brain (including the hippocampal formation) appears quite normal (Mair et al., 1979). If a reduction in complexity will not account for the loss of awareness, why should adding complexity generate it? It is obvious that the answer must lie in the way the nervous system is organized, not its complexity as such. It may be that a complex nervous system is a prerequisite for certain organizational features to occur, but complexity per se does not reveal what they are.

As regards complexity of behaviour, if the reflex adaptiveness of the spinal frog seems a dubious criterion, what about even more complex capacities? Capacity to learn and to retain the products of learning seem unlikely to suffice, because they can be organized at quite a low level in the nervous system; for example classical eyelid conditioning is thought to be under the control of circuits in the cerebellum. Indeed, some have argued that changes in sensitization, which are posited to underlie learning, occur even in simple creatures such as sea slugs. Moreover, both classical and instrumental conditioning can occur in rats and rabbits with total decortication (Oakley, 1981; Oakley and Russell, 1977). That does not mean that such an animal is unaware of the stimuli about which it learns, but it also gives us little confidence that it is.

More elaborate learning? The ability to form environmental maps ('cognitive maps')? Perhaps, but not all primates possess this capacity to equal degrees, and there are patients who lose the ability (topographagnosia) who are most certainly not rendered unconscious of their environment. Again, as with other capacities, such as language and thinking, awareness may be necessary for cognitive maps, but cognitive maps are not necessary for awareness.

Complexity of behaviour, as a criterion, sometimes despairingly seems to depend on a blend of intuition and literary skill. 'The sort of consciousness . . . animals enjoy is dramatically truncated, compared to ours', Dennett tells us (p. 447). How do we know? Well, 'a bat, for instance, not only can't wonder whether it's Friday; it can't even wonder whether it's a bat.' One does not suppose that bats wonder about the days of the week (can we be *sure?*), but for some animals the time of the year matters much more than it does for us environmentally numb humans!

What about intelligence? It is not easy to design a measure of how smart an animal is, and anyway, we do not relate degrees of consciousness in humans to their intelligence. Another suggestion: 'fun seeking'? 'We certainly won't have a complete explanation of consciousness until we have accounted for its role in permitting us (and only us?) to have fun.' (Dennett, 1991, p. 62). But he rightly questions which animals can have fun. Simple observation of animals would suggest that young mammals are much more conscious, on that basis, because of their playfulness and frolicking. But playfulness will not do: academia is saturated with highly conscious adult creatures whose capacity for fun appears to have completely atrophied, and who may even resent others enjoying themselves.

The ability to reason? Anyone who has delved into the nineteenth-century literature will have derived great enjoyment from reading the observations of animal behaviour assiduously collected by the leisured classes. Darwin's friend and ardent admirer, George John Romanes (1882) gave accounts of the emotional and intellectual powers of molluscs, ants, bees, termites, spiders, fish, reptiles, birds, and mammals, with particular chapters on elephants, cats, foxes, dogs, monkeys, apes, and baboons. He enlisted the collaboration of his sister in making detailed observations on an allegedly tool-using monkey and a portrait-recognizing terrier. Hobhouse (1901) was direct: he went out and studied not only household pets, but also monkeys of several species, a chimpanzee, an elephant, and an otter. He did experiments with push-bolts on boxes, with stoppers, loops, weights, string-pulling, opening drawers, levers (anticipating the Skinner Box), door-pushing, and with pushing food out of long tubes with sticks, among other methods. This was a period of intense and intelligent fun, prompted by intrinsic curiosity but also spurred by Darwin's assumptions of emotional and intellectual continuity between animals and humans.

But all observers ran into the problem of not knowing just how to decide on the appropriate measurements, as well as the limits and the implications, of these tricks, leaving aside the question of species-specific constraints on 'intelligent' behaviour, such as whether the animal had colour vision, was territorial, diurnal, etc. All nineteenth-century observations of complex behaviour could be taken to be relevant to the question of consciousness if one accepted William James' criteria for consciousness, namely, the 'pursuance of future ends and the choice of means for their attainment'. This outlook was part of the animal folk psychology, not only of the nineteenth century, but frequently appealed to in the present day. The same argument applies, however, as it did to language and thinking: namely, that conscious awareness may be a necessary condition for the skills under examination to be exercised, but conscious awareness does not require them for its existence.

But there is a more fundamental weakness of all these approaches based on the *on-line* observations of animals, no matter how complex and engaging their skills and achievements. In the light of our criteria for demonstrating awareness in neurological patients, all of these approaches suffer from the same defect. In order to demonstrate awareness, we need to stand aside from the ongoing behaviour—we require an independent commentary or classification or judgment of the behaviour in question. This is because, as we have seen, quite remarkable residual capacities can remain intact in the absence of acknowledged awareness. We need an *off-line* commentary to know whether or not a behavioural capacity is accompanied by awareness.

Recall the commentary-key paradigm used in testing human blindsight, in which the patient was given four keys: two to signal his discrimination between two stimulus choices and two to signal whether he had any awareness of the visual event. Could not a similar approach be used with an animal? Does a monkey without striate cortex have blindsight? Does it discriminate without acknowledged awareness? We have good reason to assume that a monkey's visual system is organized like that of the human. That is, we know the neuroanatomy is closely similar and that striate cortex lesions produce field defects topographically like those in humans. We also know that a monkey without visual cortex can still detect and locate visual stimuli, can discriminate different orientations in the frontal plane, can discriminate moving from stationary stimuli, has a measurable visual acuity, and so forth. The same, or some of the same (depending on the patient and the pathological details) is true of human blindsight subjects, but they say they have no conscious awareness of the stimuli. Does the monkey, similarly, have no awareness of the stimuli it can nevertheless discriminate?

I have outlined a gedanken procedure in *Blindsight* (see also Weiskrantz, 1977, 1985). The animal would be provided with two sets of keys, one on which to make a discrimination between a pair of stimuli, and a second, independent, set of commentary keys. To teach an animal the meaning of the commentary keys, one could adopt an approach based on ostensive definitions, namely to give examples of 'see-able' visual events to a normal animal, and to give it other events that are below threshold, or masked, or simply not there. The commentary keys would be differentially rewarded, such that after a see-able discrimination it would learn to press the 'yes' key, and for the unsee-able, the 'no' key. The critical question is how it would respond to stimuli in the blind field following a striate cortex lesion.

A similar gedanken procedure has been proposed by Alan Cowey and Petra Stoerig (1992), which would also probably be practically much simpler. They suggest teaching a monkey to press one lever (A) when a light is presented, and another (B) when no light appears. The discrimination is then made more difficult by making the light progressively dimmer and dimmer, so that eventually it is only rewarded by chance on 50% of the trials. A third lever (C), however, is offered that will provide reward on 75% of the trials. If the monkey is a rational creature, when the target is so dim that it can only guess at the outcome with respect to pressing A vs. B, it should press lever C to improve its chances of reward. In other words, the monkey indicates, by pressing lever C, that it is reduced to just guessing on A vs. B. (There is an assumption here, of course, that the monkey would be rational about *switching* from 50% to 75% reward; in fact, animals are not always good judges of probability, but no doubt such sophistication could also be trained.) Again, the question is how it would respond to stimuli presented in a cortical field defect—will it press lever C, thereby indicating that it is just guessing? 'And', Cowey and Stoerig add importantly, 'would it then nevertheless perform excellently with levers A and B if the guessing mode lever is withdrawn, leaving the animal with a two-alternative forced-choice, as in blindsight?' (p. 27). (In my gedanken experiment, just reviewed, this would be determined independently on the discrimination keys.)

These methods are very close to the procedure that is adopted in some different contexts with human subjects, namely, to obtain a confidence rating by the subject as to how certain (on a scale, say, of 1 to 10), he or she was about the discriminative choice just made. But a confidence rating is not necessarily equivalent to a commentary about awareness. Subjects can be very confident even if they have no awareness, and can lack confidence even if they do. Some dissociations of that sort were seen in D.B.'s accounts, as reported in the *Blindsight* book (Weiskrantz, 1986). Instead of a confidence scale, with commentary keys we are dealing with the extremes of 'yes, I saw it' and 'no, I did not'. Also, it would no doubt be much simpler to teach an animal to indicate whether or not it saw something—which is just a two-alternative demand—rather than to teach it to make a confidence rating, which is typically a choice among several points on a confidence scale.

It can also be seen that the formal research question is closely similar to that involved in subception experiments, either with subthreshold stimuli or, more interestingly, with visual stimuli that are subjected to backward masking, a procedure in which a stimulus is followed soon afterwards by a brief presentation of a patterned stimulus which, if the interval is short enough, renders the first stimulus invisible. Nevertheless, under certain conditions visual discriminations are still possible even though the masked stimulus is unseen (Tony Marcel, 1983a, b). For example, even though subjects are at chance in reporting whether or not a sample word had been presented when it is masked, if asked to guess which of two visible words the masked sample word looked like or, in another condition, which of the two words had a similar meaning to the masked word, then they performed at well above chance (see Fig. 4.1). The question in the blindsight case with an animal is whether it would treat a normally see-able discrimination as unseeable, as indicated by the animal on the commentary keys, rather than whether a normally un-seeable subception stimulus nevertheless transmits information, but of course the commentary paradigm could in principle be extended to researching subception in animals.

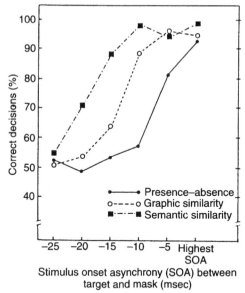

Figure 4.1. Results of Marcel (1983a). A visual target stimulus was presented just prior to a visual masking stimulus. The negative values on the abscissa indicate the time interval between the target and the mask. The effect of the mask is to sometimes make the preceding visual target stimulus invisible, depending on the temporal interval between the target and the mask. As can be seen, even when the subjects are at chance (50%) in detecting the target—cannot 'see' it—they can still make judgments of its similarity of appearance or of meaning with other unmasked visible words. See text. (From Marcel, 1983a, with permission.)

But we no longer have to speculate about gedanken experiments, because we now have a relevant experimental answer from Cowey and Stoerig about monkeys' residual vision and its similarity to human blindsight (1995). Their procedure consisted of two stages (see Fig. 4.2). It was first demonstrated, by way of confirmation of results already long known in the literature, that the animals with unilateral removal of striate cortex could respond accurately and reliably to a localized light flash in

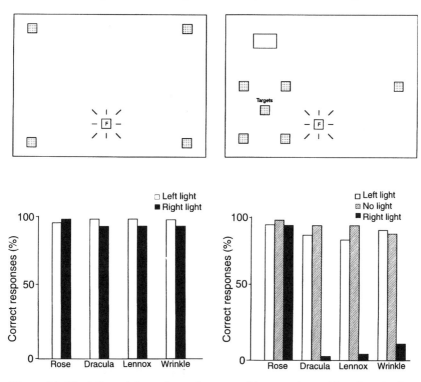

Figure 4.2. The left panel shows the performance of three monkeys with unilateral striate cortex removal, and one control monkey (Rose) in reaching for one of the four panels when briefly lit. The animals had been trained to maintain fixation on 'F'. Half of the lights appeared in the normal hemifield on the left (open bars) and half in the affected hemifield on the right. As can be seen, there is a slight reduction in performance on the affected side, but it is still excellent. The right panel shows the response of the animals when given the task of discriminating between lit panels or no light, presented in random order. If a panel was lit, they were to press it, but if no panel was lit they were to press the large panel. They learned the task very well. For lit stimuli on the left they performed very well. When lights appeared in the affected field on the right, they pressed the panel indicating 'no light'.

(Reprinted with permission from Cowey and Stoerig, 1995, *Nature*.)

their affected hemifield. The results of the first stage are shown in the left panel of the figure. In the second stage, the animals were taught to respond to the position of a lighted panel (after a warning signal) when it appeared in their *intact* hemifield, by reaching for and pressing any panel that had lit up. But on half of the trials, in a random sequence, no light appeared, and in that case the animal was rewarded for pressing a separate panel. Animals readily learned such a 'light–no-light' discrimination. After such training, from time to time 'probe' trials were inserted in which a light stimulus was presented on a panel in the *blind* hemifield. The critical question is how would the animals classify these probes? Would they press the 'light' panel, or treat the stimulus (which they had been demonstrated to be able to detect) as a non-light? The answer was very clear: as shown in the right panel of Fig. 4.2, the animals consistently treated the light in the blind hemifield as 'no light'; that is, they pressed the 'no light' panel. Thus, the very same stimulus that the animals could detect and localize with great success was classified by them as a non-light. We already know that a blindsight subject would behave in the same way.

Ideally the experiment should be run with a commentary response after every trial, as in the human demonstration with G.Y., instead of having to depend for the interpretation on how the animal has treated the discriminative stimuli in the blind field in a past testing session. It could be argued, for example, that in the final 'light–no-light session', the animal's *attention* is focused on the intact hemifield and so it ignores the stimuli in the blind field—even though when it has *only* the blind field to attend to, it can readily display its ability to detect and localize the stimuli. But it has proved difficult so far to train an animal with a commentary response after every trial, although no doubt this could be accomplished. Meanwhile, Cowey and Stoerig report (personal communication) that even increasing the frequency of blind hemifield presentations, and making them much more salient by flickering, etc., does not change the basic pattern of results: the animals continue to treat the stimuli in their blind hemifields as non-lights.

Their experiment could be extended, as Cowey and Stoerig suggest, to allow the animal to indicate whether a light in the blind hemifield was treated as *something*, but not necessarily visual. Nicholas Humphrey (unpublished) had shown earlier that a monkey with striate cortex removed bilaterally could be trained to respond to brief light flashes, and also to auditory clicks, but it had great difficulty in telling the difference between lights and clicks, a task that is kindergarten-simple for a normal monkey. It was as though the animal was responding to an 'amodal' stimulus, one that could not be readily classified as belonging to either the visual or auditory mode. This suggestion could be tested in an extension of the Cowey and Stoerig paradigm by actually providing the animal not only with keys for 'light' or 'no light', but also one for a real non-visual event, e.g. an auditory click. Its performance could indicate whether the animal treats a light stimulus in its blind hemifield as a real, but non-visual, event.

Another recent study also explicitly draws a direct parallel between human and monkey blindsight. Charles Gross and his colleagues (Moore *et al.*, 1995), demonstrated that a particular set of conditions were necessary for revealing the existence of residual visual function in the monkey after unilateral visual cortex ablation. The monkeys had to first fix their gaze on a fixation point, but they were also trained to make a rapid ('saccadic') eye movement from the point of fixation to a visual target in either hemifield. In that situation, which is analogous to clinical perimetry, in which subjects must respond whenever a light is detected, the monkeys failed to initiate saccades to targets presented in the affected hemifield, and hence—like patients—would have been deemed to be 'blind'. But when the fixation point was turned off simultaneously with the onset of the target—thus giving the animal a signal as to when to respond—the monkeys were able to make accurate saccades to stimuli in their blind field. They link this outcome with comparable procedures in human blindsight, where typically a warning signal is presented before requiring a forced-choice response. Typically, human blindsight subjects do not respond spontaneously to events in their blind fields, but this is a question that would benefit from much more exploration, and especially with patients with bilateral occipital damage.

The general underlying strategy in the commentary-key approach is similar to a much earlier one used by Beninger *et al.* (1974), who asked laboratory rats if they 'knew what they were doing'. On any trial, the experimenters waited until rats made one of four possible, and highly probable responses: face-washing, rearing, walking, or remaining immobile. There were no constraints on which of the four was allowed. But in order to get food, the rat had to press one of four different response levers to indicate which of the four responses they had just made. Rats can learn to do this. No doubt monkeys could as well. Could a frog (for appropriate high probability frog-acts)? Or a bird? There are, of course, horrendous technical training problems, plus the interesting and inevitable question of what would happen as discriminative skills became highly practised and 'automatic'. But the general strategy, in a formal sense, is clear: not merely to ask how well or how complex a discrimination an animal can make, but to step outside the discrimination situation itself and ask the animal to make a judgment *about* the discrimination or give some independent indication as to how it classifies it.

So far we have considered direct approaches to asking animals commentary questions, trying to design analogies with the questions we would ask of human blindsight subjects (or others who lack acknowledged conscious awareness of sensory events, such as paraplegics). But there are, as we have seen, also implicit approaches. These do not require any attention to be explicitly directed to stimuli in the unconscious domain. Instead, one determines whether responses to stimuli in the intact field are influenced by those in the blind field; there are a number of intact–blind field interactions available (cf. above, and Weiskrantz, 1990b; also Marzi *et al.*, 1986; Rafal *et al.*, 1990). For an animal this would be a two-stage procedure. Cowey and Stoerig (1992), here too, provide a clear outline of an appropriate gedanken experiment of this type). First, one would determine whether the reaction time of, say, a lever-press or a saccadic eye movement to a stimulus in the intact field is altered by a stimulus presented just before in the blind field, the strength and direction of the effect depending on the time interval between the two stimuli. Second, *if* such an effect were found, one would wish to know whether the animal 'saw' the stimulus in the blind field that was having the effect on the reaction in the intact field. This could be pursued by asking the animal to discriminate two vs. one stimuli, or one stimulus vs. no stimulus, with the constraint that the animal's intact field had to be involved in the initial training, so that the animal knows the difference between seeing and not seeing. That is, one wants to ensure that when it does not respond to the effective stimulus in the blind field it is because it does not see it, as we would expect if it had blindsight.

In the comparable human blindsight procedures used by Rafal *et al.* (1990) and by Marzi *et al.* (1986), subjects' attention was directed to the intact field, and no responses were found to single stimuli in the blind field. No doubt with explicit forced-choice procedures one could obtain evidence of detection of a stimulus in the blind field, or even of between-field matching—this is after all what blindsight research has revealed. But by training with a predominance of stimuli to the intact field before embarking on the critical tests with monkeys, it seems likely that one would obtain results parallel to those in humans.

The essence of this procedure, thus, is to compare an animal's *failure* to respond instrumentally to a stimulus in the blind field with positive evidence that the stimulus is nevertheless having an influence on the nervous system. That is important for analysing the capacity and sensitivity of extra-striate pathways, but it does not tell one if such a detection stimulus in the blind field would be potentially accessible to direct forced-choice methods. That is a separate question, but positive evidence from the implicit procedure could at least be taken as prima facie potentially confirmable, to be validated by independent observation.

An example of where there has been such confirmation is with a human subject, G.Y., with whom there was no indication that a visual grating in the blind field had any measurable effect on the pupil, whereas the pupil showed the characteristic constriction to the grating (without any change in total flux) when presented to the intact hemifield. But presenting a grating to *both* half-fields simultaneously appeared to generate a larger pupillary response than that to the good half-field alone; that is, there was a suggestion of facilitation by a stimulus in the impaired half-field even though it did not generate a response on its own. Until that point G.Y. had shown no indication of responding above chance to a grating stimulus by two-alternative forced-choice guessing. Subsequently, once the spatial and temporal parameters became refined (see Chapter 6 for an account), he could be shown to be capable of excellent performance in detecting a grating with forced-choice guessing in the blind hemifield alone (cf. Weiskrantz, *et al.*, 1991). Another positive result has emerged from measuring the pupillary response to *coloured* stimuli. The pupil shows a clear response to coloured stimuli in the intact field; it also responded in G.Y. to coloured stimuli, especially red, presented to the blind field. Blindsight subjects report that they do not *see* any colour in such an experiment. But, as already reviewed in Chapter 1, they can demonstrate good wavelength detection and discrimination psychophysically when tested with forced-choice guessing, and these have been compared with the pupillary response to the same stimuli (Barbur *et al.*, 1994b). Thus, the indirect, 'implicit' methods can be validated, and thereafter be used as good indicators of blindsight. But the final proof of the pudding must always be whether the subject *acknowledges or fails to acknowledge* the stimulus to which the pupil responds.

A pupillary constriction occurs without direct awareness of the response as such, and presumably is doomed to remain unconscious and impervious to direct voluntary control (indeed, it is good thing that it is; what a waste of neural capacity otherwise!). A question arises as to the unity and respective sensitivities of the set of all 'unconscious' measures, including of course not only the subject's own verbal commentaries in the psychophysical domain, but also autonomic measures, and all other possible non-verbal voluntary responses. Some have argued for their non-equivalence with regard to blindsight. Thus, Zihl and von Cramon (1980) studied three response modes separately in three subjects in whom lights were flashed into their blind fields: a voluntary eye-blink, key press, and a verbal 'yes' whenever they 'felt' that a light stimulus was present. They were able to perform well by blinking or key pressing after practice ('even though they never reported seeing a light target', p. 291), whereas in contrast their verbal responses to lights vs. 'blanks' remained at chance. Tony Marcel, in an unpublished study (cf. Dennett, 1991, p. 248), has also argued for a disjunction between a verbal response, a key press, and blinking in a blindsight subject.

It is not surprising that the range of different response modes, extending from pupillary constriction through to verbal commentaries, should yield different sensitivities to stimuli in the blind field—they may well involve different branches of the multiple, parallel visual pathways—although I do find it puzzling that *voluntary* verbal vs. non-verbal response do not co-vary (cf. Weiskrantz, 1986, p. 126) with other voluntary responses, such as key presses. But it does mean that when we study subjects in whom it is not possible to obtain the equivalent of a commentary response, or at the very least, an instrumental discriminative response—e.g. human infants, or animals without formal training—it remains impossible to draw any conclusions as to whether the creature is aware of the stimuli that can elicit involuntary responses in the putatively blind field, or whether it is not. And so, in the context of animal consciousness, one cannot learn anything about *awareness* from implicit responses *per se*, only that one of the visual pathways is open. Of course, that can be invaluable evidence not only for unravelling the neurological organization, but also in confronting sceptics who would wish to believe that blind means non-functioning. But that is another matter.

For each of the neuropsychological syndromes with disconnected awareness we have considered, it would be necessary to fashion a particular version of the commentary keys if we wanted to draw conclusions about their homologues in animals. For the amnesic syndrome something like this has already done in an elegant study by David Gaffan (1974). A monkey with a lesion in the part of the diencephalon (the fornix, the major output tract from the hippocampus, and which is putatively involved in the human amnesic syndrome) can successfully learn, and continue to perform correctly, a discrimination between two visual objects on the basis of one of them being consistently associated with food reward. But Gaffan showed, in an independent test in the same apparatus, that the animals fail to *recognize* the objects which they can learn to associate correctly with food. The way the experiment was designed was as follows: to test the association of objects and reward, several series of miscellaneous objects were presented, one at a time, over a central well in which a reward could be placed. The animal could displace the object to uncover the well and secure food if it was there. Half of the objects were rewarded, and half were not, in random sequence. To test retention, the objects were presented once again, one at a time, over a well on the right side of the test board. If the presented object had previously been rewarded, the monkey was again rewarded for picking it up. But if it had been an unrewarded object, the animal was not to select it but instead secured reward by displacing a brass disc placed over a well on the left-hand side of the board. To test recognition, in contrast, single objects were again presented one at a time, but all of them were rewarded. During the retention test, these were presented again as well as with objects that had never been seen. The animals were rewarded if they chose a familiar object that had already been presented, but for an unfamiliar object they were rewarded for choosing the brass disc over the left-hand well. As can be seen in the two panels of Fig. 4.3, the monkeys with fornix lesions were just as good as controls in learning and retaining the reward associations, but were poor in the recognition task. In other words, one might say there was evidence of learning and memory of an association in the absence of an acknowledged awareness of 'memory' itself.

The remaining neuropsychological syndromes are still unexplored with animals. There is no demonstration, to my knowledge, of prosopagnosia in animals (although there have been some unsuccessful attempts). Other varieties of putative agnosias are produced by amygdala lesions (a homo-logue of associative agnosia?) and posterior inferotemporal lesions (ap-perceptive agnosia?), but nothing like a commentary analysis has been attempted. Nor for unilateral neglect (which is produced, albeit tempora-rily, by unilateral parietal lobe lesions in the monkey). Even in this restricted domain of mammalian neuropsychology, there is enough to keep one busy for a long time.

Let's go back to the spinal cord. It is clear what the commentary-key responses would be for the paraplegic patient. His leg might respond differently to touch and non-touch, or to sharp needle vs. blunt needle, but he surely would respond with the 'no' or 'guessing' key for all trials. How would the spinal frog perform? For that matter, how would the *intact* frog perform? It is not sufficient, as we have argued, just to see whether it responds to noxious, painful stimuli—the paraplegic does, but without feeling them. If one is interested in knowing whether a frog suffers pain (at the heart of the animal experimentation debate), why not ask it? The gedanken experiment I suggested is in the grand tradition of academic philosophical detachment—with a capital G! I would not like my life to depend on being able to teach a frog to press four levers, or for it to generate commentary responses, or to estimate relative probabilities of reward.

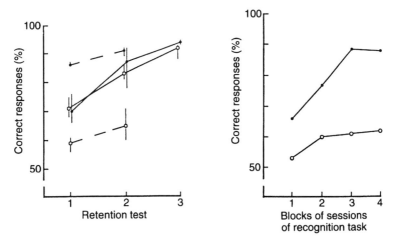

Figure 4.3. The effect of a fornix lesion on learning visual reward association vs. visual recognition problems. On the left panel is shown the animals' success in the association task (solid lines) and in the recognition task (dashed lines). The closed circles represent controls and the open circles the fornix-transected group. As can be seen the two groups of animals are equivalent on the association task, but the operated-on animals fall well below the controls on the recognition task. The right panel shows the performance on 5 successive days of testing on both tasks. The fornix group perform the recognition task much more poorly than the controls. (Reprinted with permission from Gaffan, 1974. © American Psychological Association.)

But, even assuming I could do so, there is of course a catch—in fact, a Catch 22. In order to train the frog to tell you, you must start with a situation that one assumes *is* painful to the frog. And so, alas, as a solution to the problem of animal awareness, commentary keys by themselves will not do. They will only do for *changes* in awareness induced by imposed treatments or environmental or some other independent variation. In other words we might find out something, perhaps something quite interesting, about the *spinal* frog *if* one could first train the normal frog to respond in a commentary fashion.

But animals are not unique in this respect. Humans are animals, *and precisely the same Catch 22 arises!* We must also assume that the human who is given a commentary key is also reporting on his or her *experience*. Humans, like other primates, have to learn the meaning of a commentary. In ourselves, this learning and this capacity are so ubiquitous, and so heavily reinforced by everyday language, that we often are unaware of the steps involved and the achievement reached when there is consistent agreement about the meaning and use of commentaries. Communication involves mutual pointing and exposure to events, and an agreement on how to use words such as 'I see' or 'I do not see'. But *direct* exposure of our experience to another person is not what is essential for the commentary system. We treat other people as being like ourselves, even when we cannot talk to them, through analogy, and we empathize with their pain or their sighting of a rainbow. Primates and humans are very similar as long as the importance of language for thought is not over-emphasized. Language without thought makes no sense, while thought without language does.

With animals such as monkeys, there is no difficulty in accepting a comparable analogy with humans that they can indicate whether or not they have an experience. That is why it is easy to accept—but not to prove—that the Cowey and Stoerig experiment does bear directly on whether the animal 'sees' or does not 'see' in its impaired hemifield. But with the spinal frog it is another matter. Or with the famous unknowable (but unknowing?) bat. The difficulty is not that we cannot share their experience—we cannot do that with people either. The difficulty is that we are not clear whether or not they have, or could be taught to have, a commentary system and if so how we are to read it.

I do not think language is necessary for a commentary system to develop, although it is immeasurably easier with it. But I suspect that much of animal interaction provides its own commentary training. Much of animal play I would take to have that character. One young squirrel teases another, and waits to see if that is effective not only in producing a fixed response, but in generating a whole cascade of responses that involve prediction, say, about which branch the teaser will jump to. Squirrels appear to make 'other minds' assumptions, and perhaps so do bats. Games are difficult to play unconsciously, although human games sometimes produce unconsciousness as an end result!

But, still we do not have a *direct* confirmation that an animal's response to an event, no matter how provocative the event and no matter how complex the response, is equivalent to a commentary. We must start with an assumption, helped whenever we can by ostensive definitions such as seeing vs. no seeing for light vs. no light. We can also teach an animal to guess by rewarding it on an unpredictable schedule without any visual stimuli. And as outlined above, if we could teach an animal to switch to a guessing lever when the stimulus becomes weak in the course of our determining its threshold on some sensory dimension, we might usefully infer that it, too, knows the difference between seeing and guessing. In other words, the guessing lever becomes our commentary response.

This may provide a theoretically interesting situation, and it may actually work in practical terms for highly evolved mammals. But in practice very few persons will take on the task of teaching a frog to guess about lights or flies, let alone noxious stimuli. And a failed attempt to teach an animal will leave us exactly where we started—not knowing.

There is another Catch 22 aspect to the study of animal awareness using commentary keys. If we train an animal to respond to light with one key, and to respond to the absence of light with another, what does requiring the pressing of a commentary key add to our knowledge? It is redundant in itself. Its value comes when we use the commentary key to mark *changes* in presumed awareness, or different states of awareness. The major way in which this has been accomplished has been, in fact, by changing the state of the nervous system, as with brain lesions, brain cooling, or some other intervention. In the course of doing so, and exploiting the commentary key to mark whether the animal has awareness analogous with human patients, we are likely to find that the animals, at least the higher mammals, show the same changes in awareness as the human patients have demonstrated. This was, after all, the implication of the Cowey and Stoerig experiment on blindsight in monkeys. This outcome has obvious theoretical and practical outcomes for understanding the organization of the brain as well as getting an entrée to the animal's awareness of its changed state. But it also bears directly ethical criteria, because it tells one something about the animal's conscious awareness, and whether the experiment has wrought the analogous loss of awareness as occurs in the human. The outcome of experiment on, say, awareness of pain by an animal, thus, acts to foreclose further research. This is, of course, the underlying conflict in all animal research. Even if one provides chickens with the opportunity to choose large cages over small ones, the group with the small cages may be suffering in order to tell us the answer! In the case of unilateral lesions of striate cortex, there is the saving knowledge that there is no major loss of power to negotiate the visual world—patently evident both in human and animal subjects—because only part of the visual field has contracted. The remaining field, with head and eye movements, can be used so efficiently that even skilled observers may fail to detect it in human subjects, and the subjects themselves become unaware of the field constriction. Unawareness of unawareness, so to speak.

Nevertheless, the major Catch 22 ethical issue remains, and becomes more pressing the more closely the experiments mirror a painful situation in humans. If one succeeds in finding out whether the spinal frog has lost its sense of pain, this will have been because one succeeded in inflicting pain in the normal frog, in exactly the same way that one makes that comparison in a paraplegic human patient. Broader ethical issues are then brought into play. As in all research, one uses the knowledge to establish one's criteria for further decisions, and to invoke the difficult calculus in which benefit, for animals as well as humans, is pitted against the procedures that wrought the benefit.

Is there any other approach to this problem that circumvents the practical need to have a commentary response? There is a simpler line of attack, along the lines advanced by Marian Dawkins (1980, 1987, 1990), which depends on allowing an animal to display a relative preference between two conditions or two situations, as in small vs. large cages for chickens. Of course, one cannot take a zero preference as indicating *no* difference in perceptual awareness. The much more difficult question is whether a positive preference between two situations indicates an awareness of the situations, in the absence of a parallel commentary (and sometimes even with it, as in sleep-walking!). I can well imagine that a frog would show a preference for an unshocked vs. a shocked compartment, without my being convinced that the frog experienced pain. Similarly the leg of a human paraplegic would demonstrate a preference for a position that eliminates the noxious, but unfelt stimulus.

The bottom line is that *ongoing behaviour, without an independent commentary or classification of that behaviour, falls short of answering questions about awareness.* There can be behaviour, quite complex behaviour, without awareness. Extending the behavioural responses to include the whole gamut of bodily reactions, as a solution discussed interestingly in Antonio Damasio's (1994) *Descartes' error*, does not work either; it simply increases the catalogue of responses with which one defines 'mind'. Moreover, if it implied that without bodily responses awareness is diminished, our paraplegic subject might well take exception. And there can be simple and undemanding behavioural tasks for which an animal *can* be assumed to be aware, with but the simplest constellation of bodily responses, as in the Cowey and Stoerig experiment with light vs. no–light discrimination applied to blindsight.

If thinking is not necessary for sensory awareness, some forms of thinking do obviously involve awareness of the events or the representations being thought about. This at least does provide one alternative to approaching the question of animal awareness. Can animals think? More precisely, do they demonstrate *intentionality*? Tony Dickinson has suggested a useful practical approach to the question of intentionality in animals. He makes the assumption that 'reasonable' behaviour requires continuing adjustment of the behaviour to conform to the animal's beliefs.

> I assume that an intentional account of behaviour is justified if that behaviour can be shown to be dependent on, in the sense of being a rational consequence of, a set of beliefs and desires about the world. In the present context this translates into the requirement that conditioned actions are reasonable with respect to the beliefs and desires whose content matches the conditioning schedule, reinforcer type and drive state. To be reasonable the behaviour must serve to bring about the occurrence of the reinforcer if it has positive value for the animal (and its non-occurrence when it has negative value) in a way that conforms with the content of the belief supported by the conditioning schedule. Moreover, if an intentional account is to be anything more than a redescription of behaviour, the animal must, when faced with a change in conditioning schedule, reinforcer type, or drive state, adjust its actions to maintain their goal-directedness in a way that conforms to content of the beliefs and desires supported by the new state of affairs. (1988, p. 307).

The situation in which Dickinson applied this approach was to ask whether rats could adjust their behaviour appropriately in an instrumental situation when the reward was weakened after training. He studied the conditions under which the rats could or could not adjust. If the reward is degraded after the animal has learned the task, will it proceed automatically in reeling off a fixed 'habit', or will it change its responding appropriately to indicate that it is less interested in working for the less desirable end product? Dickinson found, among other results, that rats would demonstrate their altered anticipations if they were not over-trained such that the response pattern became automatic.

Anticipation is a prerequisite for intentionality: we can be reasonably confident that the human paraplegic, and probably the spinal frog, could not learn to anticipate a noxious stimulus of which they never became aware. But the sufficient condition is not whether the animal or person anticipates, but whether it changes its anticipation in the light of the altered reward or punishment. The issue for animal consciousness is not the static preference, but how a preference changes as the contingencies change. You can see that we have returned, in the absence of commentary responses, to William James' criterion of 'the pursuance of future ends and the choice of means for their attainment'. It might even be argued that an animal which can rationally adjust its anticipatory behaviour could be said to be having a thought about a thought, in David Rosenthal's terms.

And so in terms of the more general comparative issue, one can still ask the simpler question of whether frogs could adapt to Dickinsonian reward degradation—this requires just a single lever! Similarly, if one is concerned with the question of an animal's capacity to suffer, one can apply the same strategy: does it alter its behaviour rationally when the value of the negative reinforcer is shifted? Significantly, *both* the 'switch to higher reward key instead of guessing' approach in the context of the gedanken blindsight experiments, and the 'intentional-stance' approach to conscious awareness require that the animal makes a rational change in its behaviour when a change in its situation would make it appropriate to do so, and providing explicit commentary keys implicitly assumes that the animal could elect to switch from 'guessing' to 'better than guessing', in parallel with its pattern of responding on the commentary keys. Linking conscious awareness to rationality should not mislead one into making the two equivalent: Rosenthal's thought about a thought need not be a rational thought. But it does help if we have a rational animal in order to find out if it has such a thought.

More simply, the position we have reached is this: that ongoing behaviour, no matter how rich in detail, does not necessarily involve awareness of the events controlling the behaviour. A person or an animal can show excellent capacities without awareness. A commentary-type response is required, and this is especially the case for sensory awareness. Neither humans nor animals come with a commentary system ready-made and transparent, although humans are immeasurably helped by language. But animals can also be trained to indicate whether they see or do not see, or whether they recognize or do not, which allows us to infer about their experience or lack of it by analogy with ourselves. When this is done it offers a direct attack on the question of such issues as blindsight in animals, with evidence suggesting that monkeys without striate cortex—like their comparable human counterparts—can detect and discriminate visual stimuli in the absence of any awareness of them as *visual* stimuli. In the absence of commentary responses, one can still use animal situations in which intentionality is exhibited, which entails the adjustment of anticipatory responses to *changes* in end-goals. Considerations of commentaries, intentionality, and changing preferences converge, even if they focus on different aspects of experience. We might, after all, be able to say something one day about the spinal frog.

5

The memory commentary is NOW

Historically, probably the first major example of preserved function in the absence of awareness with brain lesions was the amnesic syndrome, as reviewed in Chapter 1. It is a devastating condition, probably the most disabling of all the syndromes we have considered. To prime the reader (but who is not assumed to be amnesic): the patients apparently cannot recognize or recall the occurrence of any event after a delay of only a minute or so. They usually declare bluntly that they do not know the experimenter—with whom they may have had a lengthy interview ending just a short time before—or, in some cases, they say they recognize *everyone*, whether or not they have any right to do so. They may be able to remember events that occurred some years earlier, such as where they went to school or where they lived as a child, but in severe cases the retrograde amnesia may extend back for as long as 30 years or more, so that they may no longer remember how many children they have or whether their spouse is still alive. They also need have no intellectual impairment—their IQs can be unchanged; they can carry out complex mental operations, as in problem solving or arithmetic, provided there is not a critical memory gap to be bridged. Their short-term memory can be quite normal, as assessed by how many digits they can recite back, or in more formal tests of short-term memory as designed by experimental psychologists (such as the 'recency effect' in the serial position curve for free recall).

The condition is usually permanent, and almost always requires custodial care, although there are degrees of severity. It is as if their current experiences are written with rapidly fading ink, and as a result they are locked into the immediate present. They do not know whom they have seen, what or when they have eaten on that day, or even what day it is, or where they are or have been, or whether the attendant is someone they already know. The medical causes are various. One of the common ones is chronic alcoholism, which was recognized a century ago and given the name of Korsakoff's psychosis, after the Russian neurologist who described the condition. The name is something of a misnomer, because it is not really a psychosis as this term is normally used. Another cause—typically producing some of the most severe cases—is herpes simplex encephalitis. It can also be caused by head injury or stroke. Whatever the immediate cause, all of them involve damage to particular structures in the brain, notably in the medial temporal lobe, or in sub-cortical structures closely related to these anatomically, in the medial thalamus and the mammillary bodies of the hypothalamus. There is still some disagreement about the details of which structures are absolutely critical, as there is also about whether qualitatively different varieties of the amnesic syndrome exist, depending on which structures are damaged. Herpes simplex encephalitis is, in my view, one of the most frightening, because there is no way of protecting oneself against it. It can start as a common cold, and whether and how far it proceeds into the nervous system is just as unpredictable. When it leads to the amnesic syndrome, the virus starts its destructive incursion by travelling up the olfactory nerves, branches of which terminate at the front end of each temporal lobe (more specifically in the amygdala). Travelling further into the brain from that point, it carves a lesion along the medial portions of the temporal lobe, including the hippocampus and the surrounding neocortex and the inter-connecting white matter.

That lesion corresponds rather closely to that described in the most famous modern example of the syndrome, patient H.M., as discussed briefly in Chapter 1. This young engineer suffered from intractable temporal lobe epilepsy. Other treatments having failed, a neurosurgeon, William Scoville, removed the medial portions of both temporal lobes in 1956 (Scoville and Milner, 1957). The treatment was a success for controlling the epilepsy, but the devastating outcome was that H.M. was immediately transformed into an amnesic case, and has remained so ever since. The surgery in H.M.'s case was to *both* cerebral hemispheres, but other surgical cases have been produced by lesioning just one medial temporal lobe when, it has turned out retrospectively, the other temporal lobe happened to have had pre-existing pathology (Penfield and Milner, 1958; Warrington and Duchen, 1992). Nowadays there is no justification for surgery producing amnesia because one can determine in advance whether there is pre-existing damage or dysfunction in one or other temporal lobe by temporarily anaesthetizing it with sodium amytal (the 'Wada technique') or by imaging. Actually, it must also be said that recent brain images of H.M., who is still very much alive, reveal that the medial temporal lesion in either hemisphere does not extend as far back as Scoville originally estimated, and moreover that there is additional degeneration in a structure far removed from the surgical lesion, namely the cerebellum, where there is atrophy described as 'marked and diffuse' in the vermis and the hemispheres (Sue Corkin, personal communication). This is thought (Brenda Milner, personal communication) to have been the result of years of continuing chronic anti-convulsant treatment by phenytoin, which is now known to be associated with cerebellar toxicity.

The descriptions and tests of H.M. carried out by Brenda Milner and her colleagues (Scoville and Milner, 1957; Milner *et al.*, 1968; Corkin, 1968) provoked a virtual avalanche of interest and research, both with humans and animals. It seemed that at last, and after all, one might get a handle on one of the most intractable problems of the brain theory and function, namely how memory was stored. *At last*, because no one had witnessed the sudden conversion from normal to abnormal memory with the stroke of a knife. Previous accounts of the amnesic syndrome had been given in the nineteenth century, but these tended to be insidious in onset, variable in degree, confounded by confusional states, and the brain damage somewhat diffuse. Also, the memory dysfunctions themselves were not described in quantitative form.

And, *after all*, because the dominant influence at the time of H.M.'s surgery was Karl Lashley, one of the great pioneers of neuropsychology. Lashley had tried to localize the memory trace, the 'engram', in a long series of lesion experiments in rats that were taught tasks with a variety of demands and of graded difficulty (1950). He failed. Instead he concluded, with certain qualifications, that successful learning and memory correlated with the mass of cortical tissue left intact. Lashley was both a greatly influential figure and a launcher of a host of new techniques and approaches, some of which were brilliantly insightful and of crucial importance in testing particular hypotheses, especially in the fields of perception and learning theory. But he was deeply wrong about memory. His influence stemmed not only from his pioneering methodology and the centrality of the questions he posed, but also from his charisma. I experienced that personally, because he was one of my own teachers as a graduate student at Harvard, and no student survived the experience without being a bit dazzled by it. He was deeply wrong about memory because his experiments simply did not attack the more ventral and sub-cortical structures that subsequently were shown to be of critical and disproportionate importance. He tended to follow the great tradition from nineteenth-century neurology—that the human cerebral neocortex was not only the very pinnacle of evolutionary achievement but that it also took over many of the functions that were assigned to lower centres in lower creatures. Another great tradition from the nineteenth century, stemming from Hughlings Jackson, that suggested *levels* of hierarchical functioning in the brain, he tended to ignore. Even when he ventured into the sub-cortex in his writings, it tended to be in terms of a specific hypothesis (e.g., about emotion) rather than by incorporating it into his thinking more generally. He knew about amnesia—he knew just about everything that had been published!—but he was rather dismissive, not only of its sub-cortical components (which figure prominently in both the classical and his contemporary neuropathological literature), but of its importance: 'I believe the evidence strongly favours the view that amnesia from brain injury rarely, if ever, is due to the destruction of specific memory traces. Rather, the amnesias represent a lower level of vigilance, a greater difficulty in activating the organised pattern of traces, or a disturbance of some broader system of organised functions.' (1950, p. 475). I can recall his similar down-grading of the newly discovered strong evidence for a neocortical focus for visual pattern learning and memory in monkeys, situated in the inferotemporal region. When this is damaged, it really does seem to lead to 'the destruction of specific memory traces' in the monkey or, at the very least, is a critical structure for their establishment. When, in the early 1950s, he visited the Hartford laboratory in which Karl Pribram and Mort Mishkin were working, two workers whose research had played a key role in isolating this functional area (Mishkin and Pribram, 1954; Mishkin, 1954), he suggested the deficit was just a failure of 'visual attention'. (I can also recall the quite different, perhaps more imaginative, but equally misleading, interpretation of the inferotemporal deficit by another one of my teachers, the great Gestalt psychologist, Wolfgang Köhler, when *he* visited Hartford—it was, he suggested, that the inferotemporal cortex was oriented at $90°$ in relation to the striate cortex, and hence ideally placed to intercept the standing electrical waves that were generated there!) Of course, Lashley's statements about amnesia are so sufficiently general as to be non-disconfirmable (Lashley once remarked that he had the choice either of being vague, or of being wrong). Ironically, many modern proponents of connexionism and artificial intelligence still enthusiastically embrace Lashley's views on mass action in unadulterated form, because for some it is convenient to postulate that changes associated with learning in a theoretical network involve alterations widely distributed throughout the network.

It was against this background of Lashley's lengthy experimental pro-gramme and his sceptical conclusion that the report on H.M. burst upon the scene. There was another reason why the timing was propitious. Memory theorists had formulated the process of storage of new information as occurring in two stages, a short-term temporary stage which then fed serially into a more permanent long-term mode of storage that, in turn, was mediated by actual structural changes in the nerve cells and which could withstand changes in electrical activity (including, in an extreme example, its cessation caused by lowered brain temperature, Andjus *et al.*, 1955). That view is still widely held (although it can be severely challenged because, for example, there are cases of patients with selective and severe deficits in short-term memory whose long-term memory is nevertheless intact, Warrington and Shallice, 1969; Shallice and Warrington, 1970). Another hypothesis, related but distinct, was that there was a failure of 'consolidation' in long-term memory; that is, in the process whereby the long-term structural change finally is complete (although the consolidation view, as judged from evidence on retrograde amnesia, is also flawed because the retrograde amnesia can extend backwards in time for decades, and is not always permanent; cf. Weiskrantz, 1985). In any event, against the views held at the time, the evidence from H.M. almost irresistibly pointed to the hypothesis that there was a blockade at just the point at which short-term processes would normally transfer into long-term storage.

It was against that background, as reviewed in Chapter 1, that it only gradually became realized that, in fact, new learning *could* take place and that its results could be maintained over long periods of time by such patients. Sue Corkin, an associate of Brenda Milner's, reported in 1968 that H.M. could learn and retain perceptual–motor tasks quite well, even though he acknowledged no explicit recognition of the tasks, a result confirmed by others. For example (see Fig. 2.1), he can learn to follow a particular track on a pursuit rotor, or to do mirror drawing, and his improvement is sustained over days, probably weeks, findings replicated by others (e.g. Brooks and Baddeley, 1976). But when he returns to the apparatus he denies ever having done the experiment or having seen the apparatus before. Such perceptual–motor 'non–cognitive' tasks, however, could be conceived of as not depending critically on the hippocampus (which at the time was assumed to be the only critical structure for cognitive learning). Motor learning, it was suggested, could take place over other routes.

Many animal experiments were conducted attempting to replicate the lesions and the results in H.M. If one is going to work out the anatomical circuitry with any precision, it will require animal models. But for several years the results were very disappointing. Monkeys with medial temporal lobes lesions could learn and retain a variety of tasks apparently normally, and did not display the devastating kind of failure seen in H.M. Indeed, hippocampal lesions were used as an innocuous control procedure to compare with *neocortical* inferior temporal lobe lesions, which in contrast really *did* cause severe deficits in the learning of visual pattern discriminations! (Mishkin, 1954). Also, electrical stimulation of the hippocampus in the monkey had very little effect on learning and memeory, in contrast to frontal lobe stimulation (Weiskrantz et al., 1962). It took several years for the picture to become clear, and to dovetail with those emerging from the clinic with human amnesic patients (Weiskrantz et al., 1962). We will fill in the rest of that story a little later. But it was because of the largely negative results with medial temporal lesions at the time that I personally turned to the study of human patients, in collaboration with Elizabeth Warrington at the National Hospital, London, which was greatly enlightening and productive for me. The idea was to reexamine amnesic patients and to see whether they, when tested with procedures mirroring the monkey experiments, would show parallel findings. As it turned out, the experiments turned up some surprises.

We tried a number of conventional human learning and retention experiments that did not yield anything startling except to document the severity of the condition (Warrington and Weiskrantz, 1968b), but did show that the amnesic subjects were sensitive to the same cognitive organizational factors in learning (e.g. category cueing, clustering, isolation) as normal controls (1971). But about the same time a breakthrough occurred that is relevant to a seemingly paradoxical fact about amnesic patients, namely that they can remember that their memory capacity is shot—can remember, as it were, that they cannot remember. Amnesic patients are not always pleased by experimenters' insistently asking them to recall items from a list that they know they do not and cannot remember. (Knowing that they should be able to remember might be said to be part of 'semantic knowledge' in these patients, just as they know that they should be able to walk or climb stairs normally, that they can speak and hear normally, and so forth. Already existing semantic knowledge is generally acknowledged to be intact in amnesic patients, in distinction to 'event' memory.) Elizabeth Warrington had the idea, back in 1967–8, of testing the patients' verbal and visual memory without having to ask them about their memory as such. Her idea was to use the graded series of fragmented drawings (the 'Gollin Figures'), not as a perceptual task, but as a memory test with verbal and pictorial material (see Fig. 5.1). The advantage was that, as far as the subject was concerned, it was simply a guessing game, deliberately devoid of questions of the sort, 'do you remember the list of words?' or 'do you recognize having seen this picture?' and the like. Instead, the subject could simply be asked to try to guess the identity of a fragmented drawing.

Figure 5.1. Exemplars of fragmented material used to test learning and retention of amnesic patients. As used in the original experiment, subjects were first presented with the most incomplete drawing, and then succeeding versions until there was correct identification. The series were subsequently repeated and level of difficulty of drawing correctly identified was scored. It was found that amnesic patients and controls alike could identify the increasingly fragmented drawings more readily with repetition, and that this facilitation was retained over days, and even, in one amnesic patient, after 4 months. The facilitation was specific to material tested, that is, was not a general non-specific improvement. (Reprinted with permission from Warrington and Weiskrantz, 1968a, *Nature*.)

The surprising outcome was that our first patient, a woman who had become densely amnesic after temporal lobe surgery, showed good learning and retention between days, and this was also true of a larger group of 5 Korsakoff patients (Warrington and Weiskrantz, 1968a). That is, there was a clear demonstration of *priming*, the facilitation induced by prior exposure of items when the subjects were subsequently given the task of identifying the complex items from the fragmented bits, known as the 'primes'. This was in contrast to their hopeless failure to recognize those items or to recall them—the hallmark of the amnesic syndrome. We extended this pattern of findings to other amnesic patients in addition to the surgical and Korsakoff cases, especially including encephalitics.

This was more than a little surprising to us—the amnesic subjects were succeeding in showing excellent retention for the very items that they failed to recognize. But it was still possible to argue, and it was argued, that learning to identify drawings from fragments was an example of 'perceptual learning'. Perhaps perceptual learning, like the motor learning involved in mastering a pursuit rotor, did not require the hippocampus. But when it was demonstrated that amnesic patients were able to learn and retain *verbal* material using fragmented cues—the very same verbal items that were apparently inaccessible to recall or recognition—the results increasingly became deeply counter-intuitive (see Fig. 5.2). By arranging fragments of words in a priming paradigm (that is, studying the facilitation of the exposed words on one occasion when tested later by partial information primes, such as the initial three letters of the words), one could examine all aspects of acquisition, retention, and forgetting of verbal material. Indeed, by varying the relationship between the fragments and the complete stimulus items, we could measure the effects of both proactive and retroactive interference, or even use material designed to be interference-free (by using common words that are uniquely identified by their first three letters, such as GAO for GAOL, YAC for YACHT, ENI for ENIGMA, JUI for JUICE, and so forth). Meanwhile, Warrington and I extended the nature of the cues to semantic content, to interference phenomena, and also to classical eyelid conditioning (Warrington and Weiskrantz, 1971, 1973, 1978, 1982; Weiskrantz and Warrington, 1970, 1979). We carried out the conditioning experiment because of the anecdote told by Claparède (see Chapter 1) about the amnesic lady who continued to withdraw her hand whenever she saw him, but did not know why (the reason was that he had stuck a pin in it in a routine procedure to test her sense of touch!). Just as with Claparède, the subjects showed excellent conditioning and good retention over hours, but despite the hundreds of trials never recognized the unusual-looking apparatus, even when they continued to sit directly in front of it, nor could they recount the highly distinctive events—the pairing of a light and a sound with a puff of air to the eye—that took place. But despite this, after conditioning, whenever the light and sound came on, the conditioned response emerged without fail. In Chapter 1 there is an account of one of the subjects, a highly inventive Korsakoff patient (an ex-school teacher with knowledge of several languages), who suggested that we were trying to test his knowledge of Eastern languages. The only comment that bore any relationship to the experiment was the casual remark that 'he had a weak right eye because someone had once blown some air into it'.

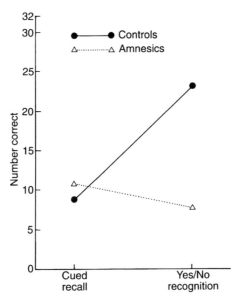

Figure 5.2. The contrast between retention by prompting with the first three letters of words, and with recognition of the words, in amnesic patients vs. normal control subjects. With priming by the first three letters ('cued recall') controls and amnesic subjects perform equally well. But when asked to recognize those words that had been presented before ('yes'), as distinct from test words that had not been presented ('no'), the control group is excellent and the amnesic group is markedly impaired. (Reprinted from Warrington and Weiskrantz, 1974, with kind permission from Elsevier Science, Ltd, The Boulevard, Langford Lane, Kidlington OX5 1GB, UK.)

My *meta*-memories about memory fragments from those early days are still vivid. Anyone working with densely amnesic patients, who appear not to retain new information beyond a minute or so, finds evidence of good retention over long intervals hard to swallow (in H.M. there was evidence of retention after 4 months (Milner *et al.*, 1968). I can still recall the frank and irrepressible disbelief after having testing the first amnesic patients—the good retention *must* have been a fluke, a chance result; it surely would not be confirmed on the next occasion or the next patient. But it was.

The counter-intuitive aspect also elicited sharp scepticism from a number of other persons in the field, and we went through what was probably a necessary period of sustained and intensive doubting and disbelief that lasted some years. It was claimed, for example, that the fragmented tasks were just easier ('even a child could learn them', was a comment made in one paper), that amnesic patients were not absolutely up to normal levels with fragmented cues, and so maybe amnesic patients were just like weak normal subjects. A certain measure of confusion also intruded because what we had called 'cued recall' from the very outset in 1968 became used, instead, as the example of a mode of retention in which subjects were explicitly asked to remember items from a list. We did not explicitly publish our instructions for testing retention in amnesic subjects although, as mentioned, the original use of fragmented material was certainly chosen to avoid having to ask explicit-type questions. We might ask a subject whether he could recall the fragmented item as having been part of an item from a previous list (but, of course, typically drawing a blank), and then go on to insist that the subject 'just guess' what it might be. The importance and the operational distinction between the instructions for the two modes of testing retention was later demonstrated and sharpened by Graf *et al.* (1984).

The fact that the very same items were accessible through indirect testing, but could not be accessed through direct methods of testing, led to the suggestion that there was a failure of retrieval in amnesic subjects. Interference—traditionally accepted as a strong factor in normal forgetting—seemed a reasonable hypothesis to underlie a retrieval difficulty. Work by Cermak *et al.* (1974) and others on the release-from-proactive-interference phenomenon suggested excessive interference in amnesic patients with verbal material. Indeed, as mentioned above, it was possible to arrange the fragmented cues so as to constrain interference by varying the number of alternative English words with which they might fit. Eventually we rejected the interference hypothesis (at least one version of it) because we could not find an excessive rate of false positive intrusions on the first occasion when they might be expected to have been exhibited (Warrington and Weiskrantz, 1978). A recent analysis by Baddeley and Wilson (1994) also concludes that the pattern of intrusion errors is the same for amnesic patients and controls, but that the loss of explicit recollection by amnesic patients does not allow them to eliminate intrusion errors when they occur. On the other hand, Tulving and his colleagues (1991; Hayman *et al.*, 1993) have shown that a densely impaired amnesic subject (K.C.) was helped in acquiring new factual knowledge by taking pains to constrain the degree of interference in the learning list. Retrieval impairments may still be of considerable importance, for example, in considering shrinkage of retrograde amnesia in some amnesic patients (cf. discussion in Weiskrantz, 1985). Retrieval is also a very tempting interpretation when one realizes that amnesic patients can actually acquire new knowledge of faces and facts about people they must have read about or seen on television, but with whom such knowledge remains covert to the patients themselves. Thus Marslen-Wilson and Teuber (1975) demonstrated that amnesic subjects (H.M. and Korsakoff patients) showed very impressive identification of the photographs of public figures (politicians, sports figures, etc.) who came into prominence only *after* the onset of the amnesic condition. The subjects showed no overt recognition of these photographs—they had 'never seen them before'—but could correctly guess their names when prompted by partial letters of the names or by circumstantial information about them. As these authors commented about that outcome, 'the findings of our present study may serve to underscore the extent to which, even in an amnesia as severe as H.M.'s, such an uncovering of seemingly lost memory traces is possible.' (p. 361).

The normality of priming, combined with the handicap of a severe disability of recognition, gives rise to some interesting perseverations in amnesic patients, presenting the appearance of their memories being *too* good. As we have indicated, using initial triplets of letters as the priming cues, amnesic patients show normal priming. But words in the English language have a very useful property, because it is possible to find examples where only two common words start with the same initial letters, for example, COT (COTTON, COTTAGE), ALC (ALCOHOL, AL-COVE). If the patients are first exposed to one list, COTTON . . . ALCOVE . . . etc., they are just as good as controls in showing the facilitated retention to the cues COT, ALC, etc. But when they are then asked to read the list with the alternate words (COTTAGE, ALCOVE, etc.), they persist in giving the words in the first list as their answers to the primes. They cannot benefit from recognizing that the list has changed, because they cannot remember the first list! And so they go on presenting the items for which they were first successfully primed (Warrington and Weiskrantz, 1978), as shown in Fig. 5.3. A very similar result was obtained when the rule was changed from one semantic category to another, but using the same priming words to elicit an associated word (Winocur and Weiskrantz, 1976). Anyone who knows amnesic patients will know that they persist in telling the same story, or the same joke—often with self-generated gales of laughter—after even short intervals. They cannot remember having done so, and hence do not remember not to persist.

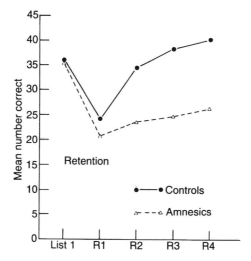

Figure 5.3. 'Reversal' learning. For each priming cue (the initial three letters) there were only 2 common English words available as possible responses. Subjects were first taught one set of words (List 1) and then given 4 trials with the alternative set (R1234). The same cues were used throughout. It can be seen that the amnesic patients were as good as controls on the initial list, but were impaired in switching to the alternative list. As there were only two words available for each prime, a mistake during the reversal stage is actually a perseverative response from the initial list. (Reprinted from Warrington and Weiskrantz, 1978, with kind permission from Elsevier Science, Ltd, The Boulevard, Langford Lane, Kidlington OX5 1GB, UK.)

Meanwhile, animal work continued apace. It gradually became realized that the very types of problems that animals with H.M.-type, or anatomically related, lesions could learn were somehow similar to those that human amnesic subjects could acquire, although it is difficult to make exact comparisons between verbal learning—or non-verbal learning but with verbal instructions—of human subjects and the types of tests available to animal workers. But simple associative learning could be compared with recognition memory in animals. A key experiment in the history of the subject was published by Gaffan, in 1974. As reviewed in Chapter 4, and summarized here briefly again, he trained monkeys with fornix lesions on two types of tasks (the fornix is one of the major direct targets of the output from the hippocampus, and can cause amnesia in human subjects, although this point is not entirely free from controversy). In one task the animals had to remember which objects were associated with food reward, a traditional 'reward-association' task. The experimental animals had absolutely no problem with that—they were as good as control animals. But in the other task the animal had to recognize whether an object had been presented in the previous set of objects. If a novel object was presented they were trained not to respond to it, but to a metal disc. The control animals had no great difficulty with that task, but the experimental animals were markedly impaired. That is, the fornix-sectioned animals could learn stable associations of objects with reward, but could not recognize having seen the objects. This is very close to the hallmark of the human amnesic syndrome, in which there is no recognition of knowledge that they can be shown to have acquired. A whole family of related and new tasks has been used with monkeys, and it is clear that what was originally taken to be a serious gap between brain function in sub-human primates and humans is being closed. More precisely, it seems that recognition is impaired with lesions that are similar to that imposed surgically on H.M. (or structures closely related anatomically) but that other forms of learning can proceed more or less normally. In contrast, monkeys with *neocortical* lesions in the inferior part of the temporal lobe, lying on the lateral surface of the brain, are deficient in learning visual associative problems. In rats with hippocampal lesions an interesting set of dissociations can be dissected in an apparatus known as the 'radial maze'. This has several arms arranged like spokes of a wheel, with one piece of food placed at the end each spoke which the animals can retrieve in any order they wish. Normal rats are able to remember remarkably well which spokes they have recently sampled, and do not bother to return to them. But rats with hippocampal damage have a great deal of trouble. On the other hand, they have no problem if only one or a few arms are consistently rewarded from day to day, and others are not. Nor do they have difficulty in learning which arm to enter, even if the arms are changed from trial to trial, or day to day, if the correct arms are identified by a visual cue. This distinction between 'working memory' and 'reference memory', first elucidated in the radial-maze context by its inventor, the late David Olton (1979), has spawned a great deal of important and illuminating research.

A hypothesis about the hippocampus that has received wide attention in animal studies is that it is especially concerned with 'cognitive maps', that is, with constructing and storing the spatial arrangements in an environment that contains sets of complex but stable cues and landmarks (O'Keefe and Nadel, 1978). This first emerged from research demonstrating that particular neurones in the rat's hippocampus have a preference for firing when the animal moved to a particular location (or, more recently, when monkeys simply *look* towards a particular location). An apparatus that has been used a lot in this connexion is the water maze designed by Richard Morris. This is a platform, placed just under the surface of the water, onto which the animals can climb—when they find it—after they are released into the large bath. The question is whether the animals can remember, from spatial cues about the environment, where the platform is even when they cannot see it. Rats with hippocampal damage have considerable difficulty in doing so relative to controls, but have none in learning to swim to a visible platform or in using a visual stimulus to mark the position of an invisible but patent platform. This has also been used to test the hypothesis that certain neuro-transmitters, which have a role in sustaining a form of electrical activity in the hippocampus and other structures, also play a role in spatial learning. It is claimed that when these transmitters are blocked biochemically (by so-called NMDA antagonists) spatial memory is seriously impaired in the water maze. More recent results, however, suggest that the results have been caused by indirect side-effects rather than by direct effects on spatial memory as such. And other results have shown that such agents can even facilitate memory in a non-spatial task (Mondadori and Weiskrantz, 1991).

Another line of hippocampal research is linked to the fairly old idea of consolidation of memory traces based on the evidence that amnesic patients and animals can retain information normally over quite short intervals, but are impaired with longer delays. And also, that hippocampal lesions in animals interfere with recently acquired information, but not with the same information after a longer delay. The consolidation view is by no means free from various complications (cf. Weiskrantz, 1985), and in any event we have just seen that information in *some* form can be stored over long periods in patients. Is consolidation selective only for some expressions of stored information but not others? Does 'implicit memory' consolidate at a widely different rate from 'explicit memory'?

Thus, the animal field demonstrates a rich tapestry of results and hypotheses, but it is too soon to know whether spatial memory has some special leading role in animal homologues of the amnesic syndrome, whether temporal factors are serial in a single type of process or involve different systems with different time constants, and exactly how the evidence is to be integrated with that from human amnesic subjects. A helpful review by Eichenbaum *et al.* (1994) suggests two main types of function for hippocampal and neighbouring structures, one temporal, the other dealing with modes of representation. It must be said, also, that the actual precise and detailed location of the critical circuits in animals (and, of course, in humans as well) is the focus of much work. This is because special methods must be used to separate the effects of damage to neural cells in a particular location from damage to fibres from more distant neurones that just happen to be passing through the region under study. Thus, a classical and well-known set of studies of recognition memory in the monkey was pursued by Mort Mishkin and coworkers. They showed that monkeys with lesions meant to simulate H.M.'s quite closely (that is, to the hippocampus and the amygdala), had great difficulty in recognizing whether an object was one they had just seen recently (Mishkin, 1978). More precisely, each animal was first presented with a single object, which was rewarded. After a delay, the animal was presented with two objects, and it was only rewarded for choosing the one that had *not* been shown just before. Monkeys with damage to the hippocampus *plus* the amygdala (both of which were damaged in H.M.) had great trouble with this task (Mishkin, 1978). But recently it has emerged from Mort Mishkin and colleagues' own work that this was almost certainly caused by inadvertent damage, and not to the hippocampus and amygdala as such. When special methods were used (Jarrard, 1993) that leave these fibres intact and only damage nerve cells (because some toxic agents can be exploited that only affect nerve cells and not fibres), carefully placed lesions in the hippocampus and amygdala produced no problem whatever for animals with the recognition task. Instead, a deficit appeared when the damage was directed to nerve cells critically placed in a neighbouring zone, the so-called entorhinal area (O'Boyle *et al.*, 1993; Murray, 1996). Thus, we are not even certain whether the hippocampus has a role in non-spatial recognition memory, although it may turn out to have one in spatial recognition memory. The work with primates has parallels with related earlier work on the rat by Len Jarrard (1986) and his group, who pioneered much of the research using agents designed to leave fibres of passage intact.

Animal research has been drawn into a number of interesting ancillary hypotheses about different types of recognition memory, and the search for critical anatomical mechanisms is continuously being refined, but there is a clear parallel between the recognition failure seen in animals with medial temporal lobe damage and that found in human amnesic patients. At the human level, there is still active work on further refinement of the character of the amnesic syndrome itself. Serious issues still revolve around such matters as how extensive the retrograde amnesia is, that is, the memory for events prior to the pathology, and whether these show a gradient as a function of the interval between the event and the pathology. Also, there are questions about variations in the density of amnesia, as well as possible distinctions between different aetiologies of the amnesic syndrome—whether they contain the same underlying deficit with different cocktails of optional deficits, or are genuinely different in a basic and qualitative way. The importance of frontal–lobe contributions to phenomena in the release–from–proactive–interference paradigm has been identified (Moscovitch, 1982). The finer fractionation or separation of deficits in recall vs. recognition outside of the densely amnesic population has obvious relevance.

What is not in doubt is the abundant evidence, accumulated by many workers, of good residual retention in amnesic subjects using fragmented material or partial cues to access stored representations of previously exposed material. Several reviews exist (Schacter, 1993; Shimamura, 1986; Squire, 1987). Testing of verbal items by priming with fragmented material, and with primes of partial letters of words, under the heading of 'stem completion' have become popular. Facilitation through prior exposure, identified by primes, has emerged as a virtually indestructible capacity in amnesic patients, and has become something of an industry. One has had to change one's concept of what is counter-intuitive. I find it interesting to observe how intuitions change over time without any clear signals or markers. Textbooks now describe it as perfectly natural that there is a form of learning called 'implicit' that *of course* can be intact after destruction of other forms of memory. In the not so distant past, instead of 'of course' one would have read 'surprisingly'.

Throughout all of this development, there has been an implicit contrast between two different explanatory approaches, not always made explicit. It is between *processing* accounts (e.g. faulty retrieval, excessive interference, a disconnexion syndrome of a cognitive mediational system, depth of processing, restriction to a pre-semantic representational system for novel object priming) and accounts in terms of independent but interacting *multiple memory systems* in the brain, the latter having been bolstered by distinctions from experimental psychology such as episodic vs. semantic (Tulving, 1983), and procedural vs. declarative (Squire, 1987). Some ten or so years ago the relationship between the various memory systems entered what might be called the taxonomic stage, and we are still right in it. Taxonomy is a difficult, even contentious pursuit, as for example in trying to decide when memory for an episode (impaired in amnesia) becomes an item of semantic knowledge through rehearsal, either private or public; for example, when we remember a childhood accident which we have rehearsed repeatedly (semantic knowledge being said to be intact in amnesia). Or in trying to map that distinction onto the proposal that 'semantic memory consists of an accumulation of many episodes.' (Baddeley, 1995, p. 17).

Where one finds double or multiple dissociations, as between deficits in retention of perceptual–motor skills and verbal recognition, or between short-term and long-term memory tasks, it is reasonable to pursue hypotheses of multiple memory systems, especially when different structures are involved in the pathology or are differentially activated in brain scans of normal subjects, although double dissociation does not logically prove independence (see Appendix for a further discussion of dissociations). And concentrating on what it is that amnesic subjects can acquire that other types of patients cannot acquire, and vice versa, fuels taxonomic and diagram-drawing proclivities to the full. It tempts one towards naming as the name of the game. Thus, as we have seen, amnesic patients can acquire and retain eyelid conditioning. There is evidence that patients with cerebellar lesions cannot. In my own taxonomic offerings I have called this evidence for a stable-associative system (Weiskrantz, 1987b, 1990a). Amnesic patients can acquire perceptual–motor skills, but patients with basal ganglia lesions are impaired, and this has been called evidence for procedural memory. Again, amnesic patients can show normal short-term or 'working memory', whereas there are other lesions that selectively severely impair short-term memory, leading to the suggestion of a specific system for that. And so forth. (As an aside, it is unfortunate that the term working memory has come to be used in somewhat different ways in animal and human research. In human research it refers to short-term functions, for example, digit span and recency effects, which are characteristically intact in amnesic subjects, whereas in animal research, as in the reference to the radial maze above, it refers to memory for unique, spatially dispersed events, which are severely impaired in the rat with hippocampal damage.)

Note that these various deficits are caused by damage that is not only centred in different structures, but which is also very different in its dispersal. Thus, a severe Korsakoff amnesic syndrome can be caused by relatively minute sub-cortical lesions in the mammillary bodies of the hypothalamus plus in a thin strip of one of the thalamic nuclei, near the midline of the brain (cf. Mair *et al.*, 1979). The locus of the damage that causes a specific problem with eyelid conditioning is also relatively focused, and far removed, in the cerebellum. Short-term memory problems, however, are probably affected by more widely dispersed lesions in the frontal lobes *or* in regions close to the primary sensory receiving areas. Again, deficits in skilled movements, procedural memories, are seen after damage to basal ganglia. Deficits of semantic knowledge of objects, 'object agnosia', have been seen especially in patients with widespread, diffuse damage, such as that caused by carbon monoxide poisoning. Finally, no one has succeeded in demonstrating a brain lesion that uniquely damages priming *qua priming*, although there is some pharmacological evidence showing a differential effect on priming (Brown *et al.*, 1989). Priming probably reflects facilitation of activity at a number of different loci throughout the brain, depending on the kind of information being processed.

But, of course, even if one accepts the existence of multiple independent memory systems in the brain, which seems irresistible, there is still the question of the processing modes used in each—whether they are qualitatively different or share some basic logical structure. One is helped in such an exploration by first asking whether there is anything that amnesic patients *cannot* do, regardless of the learning paradigm that one happens to use, but given operative retrieval methods? Cannot do, that is, except for the subjects' own explicit denials of the demonstrable evidence?

Is the demonstration of priming in the amnesic patient based on the facilitation of items already in the subject's repertoire of stored items, for example, the 'airplane' when shown a picture of it, or any of the words available in everyday language? But can the patient learning anything *new*? Whether this is so turns, as discussed in Chapter 1, on what is meant by new. In everyday life, what is new is not always spanking fresh and novel, but recombinations of the old, or constructions that are similar to them. Well, what is the evidence? Amnesic subjects can acquire and retain a conditioned response (Weiskrantz and Warrington, 1979), which involves novel associations. More interestingly, they can learn new words. I well remember our teaching Elizabeth Warrington's and my first amnesic subject, N.T., a temporal lobe surgical patient, to complete the word that starts 'ENI. . .'. The first time she failed, but was then told the word. Thereafter, even after a delay of 24 hours she would say, when presented with the letters, 'Enigma, enigma? Is there such a word?' We did not attempt to teach her the meaning of the word; it was presumably just a nonsense word for her (but she had no problem as such with word meanings within her established vocabulary), although we cannot be certain that she never knew the meaning of that word. And there is other evidence about the acquisition of new *meanings* as such. Long ago

Warrington and I asked whether amnesic patients could learn and retain the meanings of pictures in the McGill Picture Anomalies collection. Such pictures are anomalous precisely because of a novel reordering of objects being portrayed; for example, a picture of an ape in a cage with a picture on the wall (Fig. 5.4). With the more difficult pictures in the set subjects have

Figure 5.4. A representative item from the McGill Picture Anomalies set. The subjects were required to find the anomalous feature, and were told the answer if they could not do so. This produced a facilitation of finding the feature on subsequent trials, another example of priming. Amnesic subjects showed priming equivalent to controls (see text).

difficulty in finding the anomaly, but when this is pointed out to them they are apt to be successful on subsequent trials. We found that amnesic patients could show good learning and long-term retention of anomalies in the pictures (Warrington and Weiskrantz, 1973). With verbal material the point is well made by the anomalous sentences pioneered by McAndrews *et al.* (1987). The subject is asked to provide a single word that would help to make sense of strange, odd sentences. For example, 'The haystack was important because the cloth ripped.' Answer: 'Parachute.' Or, 'The notes were sour because the seams split.' Answer: 'Bagpipe.' Most people are flummoxed by the questions, but when provided with a word that lends meaning to the sentence, retain the answers over hours or days. The point is that amnesic patients also retain them, even though they do not remember having heard the answers on a previous occasion. This must be considered as the acquisition of new meanings, in terms of the new associative structure in which 'bagpipe' and 'parachute' are now contained. Novel visual objects and visual patterns, such as those shown in Figs 5.5

and 5.6, have also been shown to be primed in amnesic patients (Gabrieli *et al.*, 1990; Schacter *et al.*, 1991). Warrington and I also found (unpublished) that patients would retain their increased speed of putting randomly arranged words into sentences—specific, of course, to the particular words and sentences to which they were exposed. Whether these examples are or are not semantic in character I leave aside, although, as

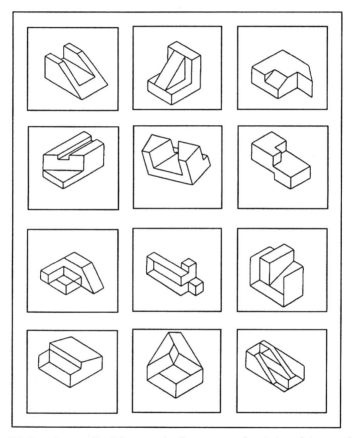

Figure 5.5. Drawings used by Schacter and colleagues to study priming of pictures of novel objects by amnesic patients and controls. The drawings in the top two rows are structurally possible as 3-D objects, and those in the bottom two rows would be impossible. Subjects were first exposed to some of the drawings in a control task, and then asked to judge whether each figure would be possible or impossible. Prior exposure to the possible drawings, but not the impossible ones, yielded increased accuracy in making the judgments, that is, priming. The amnesic subjects were equal to controls for priming, but were impaired on a test of explicit recognition of having seen the objects. (Reprinted with permission from Schacter *et al.*, 1991, M.I.T. Press.)

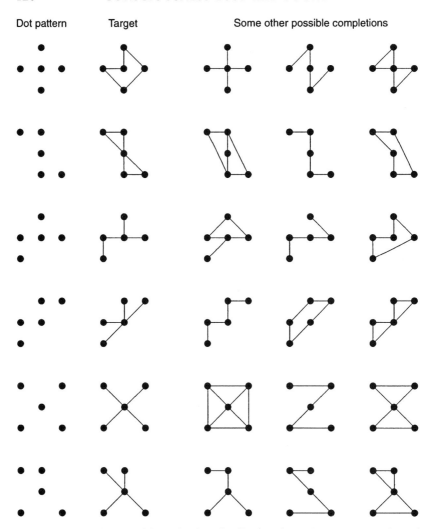

Figure 5.6. Drawings used by Gabrieli and colleagues for studying priming of novel drawings by amnesic patient H.M. and control subjects. Subjects were instructed to copy the target drawings (column 2) onto the dot patterns of column 1. Other possible completions are shown in the remaining columns. Subsequently the subjects were shown the dot patterns of column 1 and asked to connect the dots with 4 straight lines. Both amnesic and control subjects were influenced in the way they connected the dots by having carried out the prior task; that is, having drawn the target figure increased the probability of freely connecting the dots the same way later. But H.M. was impaired in explicit recognition of the connected dot patterns when required to select the target from a set of four possible completions. (Reprinted from Gabrieli *et al.*, 1990, with kind permission from Elsevier Science, Ltd, The Boulevard, Langford Lane, Kidlington OX5 1GB, UK.)

already noted, Endel Tulving and colleagues (Tulving *et al.*, 1991; Hayman *et al.*, 1993) have produced evidence of successful, if laboured, acquisition of new semantic information for one patient that bears directly on that issue. New rule learning has also been demonstrated, for example by Winocur and me (1976), for verbal paired associates, and Wood *et al.* (1982) for mathematical problems. Knowlton *et al.* (1992) have reported that amnesic patients can acquire a new artificial grammar. More recently, Squire and Knowlton (1995) have shown that a profoundly amnesic patient could classify novel drawings according to whether they belonged to the same category as a set of target drawings to which he had previously been exposed, despite his complete failure to recognize those target items as familiar, even when presented with them as many as 40 times in succession. Their findings, they comment, 'demonstrate that the ability to classify novel items, after experience with other items in the same category, is a separate and parallel memory function of the brain, independent of the . . . structures essential for remembering individual stimulus items.' (p. 12470).

And so positive evidence of retention encompasses a very broad range of cognitive content and demands, not only simple stable associations as in classical conditioning and priming for words, not only procedures involving new skills, both perceptual–motor and verbal, but also new meanings, new facts, and new systems of verbal rules. Amnesic patients can reason quite normally about information still preserved in their semantic store, for example, whether France is east or west of Poland. Indeed, looking at the inventory, it is a bit astonishing to tell someone that the origin of *all* of these studies is the fact that these patients cannot remember! It is even more difficult to persuade the amnesic patients themselves that they *can* remember, because remembering of new material (and much of old) as an *experience* is what they do not have.

Well, what is going on? Obviously one says that these patients cannot *recognize* current events in relation to stored items, or if they recall recent events (within the retrograde amnesia time window) they cannot recognize what it is they recall, or even that it is genuine recall. That, taxonomically, is the familiar loss of explicit memory or declarative memory, or of episodic memory, or, in Warrington's and my more cumbersome phrase, an impairment of 'cognitive mediational system'. But is there a more *general* formal characterization that one can advance? There may be one that goes along the following lines. In all the tasks we have been considering, it is of course essential, in displaying retention, that a currently presented item somehow gains access to material in which relationships had been previously established through prior experience. Different types of tasks involve different networks of relationships, from simple stimulus–reward associations, to categorical knowledge organized as superordinate and subordinate trees, to analogue dimensions of abstractions, to the more complex hierarchical networks of grammar and meanings that manipulators of models of parallel distributed processing are so actively pursuing. But for only a very limited set of these does retrieval depend on a specific interactive relationship between the current item and the stored items. For this limited set the current output is *critically* dependent upon the joint relationship *between* the current input and the stored network. This is precisely the situation with recognition. Output = f(current input × stored items). Similarly with recall, when it is acknowledged by the subject to be genuine recall, the items being produced must themselves be taken as the current items to be compared with the stored items. Of course, there are shades of differences in recognition vs. recall measures for different patients, although both are severely impaired in densely amnesic subjects, and I also recognize that there are several different meanings of recognition, for example, novelty vs. familiarity, that are not all relevant to this analysis, but the response to novelty need not involve recognition as such. There can be dishabituation without recognition. Stored events can also have different strengths, which can affect the strength of related responses, but without there being explicit recognition of these different strengths as such.

Of course, all memory involves both current inputs and relevant neural substrates altered by past events. But that observation in itself is necessary but trivial for demonstrations of retention. It equally applies to examples of metal fatigue or to our own muscular fatigue or to sensory adaptation, or to a compact disc. Without recognition, one cannot distinguish whether a stimulus is genuinely weak or is a strong stimulus acting upon an adapted substrate. When we speak of memory in a sense that also conveys the phenomenal property of '*having* a memory', the argument is that it requires a specific comparison between the current input and the substrate. The most common comparison, of course, is 'same' or 'different', but this is not the only possible comparison. It is the operation of such *a joint product* that is difficult for amnesic patients to operate. Of course, complex tasks, especially those that require repeated and recurrent rehearsal, and with high potential for interference, as in the learning of new complex semantic information, are compounds of several different processes and different demands, and to the extent that recognition is a critical feature in any of them, can be disturbed on that account in amnesia. And, for the normal subject, even though the task may nominally not *require* the operation of a joint product, of course recognition occurs willy-nilly, and will lead to rehearsal and cognitive manipulations during acquisition and retrieval.

A fortiori, it should be possible for amnesic subjects to demonstrate acquisition and retention for *any* task that does not critically depend on such a joint contingency between current input and stored network. No such contingency exists with any of the tasks for which amnesic subjects have been demonstrated to have retention. For example, in an associative conditioning task, the conditioned stimulus activates the C.S. representation, which in turn elicits the stored link with the U.S. that then can be outputted. In habituation and dishabituation, again, no joint contingency exists; the current stimulus activates a stored network in which activity diminishes in strength upon repetition. In a knowledge tree, similarly, the currently presented item activates its relevant part of the tree, which then can allow the rest of the tree to be retrieved. Similar arguments apply to motor, verbal, and perceptual skills (for the latter, see especially the evidence and thesis presented by David Milner and Mel Goodale, 1995). The argument is also clear in the case of priming, when the prime activates the originally stored representation (or node, or whatever theory one happens to have). In forms of learning of the non-episodic variety, no comparison need be made between the currently perceived event and its stored target. This is not, as just mentioned, that it cannot and will not occur—in normal subjects comparisons are made spontaneously, which in turn leads to active rehearsal and so forth. This is one of the reasons why direct quantitative measures of amnesic subjects vs. normal controls are often so difficult: the experimenter might consider that he/she is conducting a pure priming experiment, and indeed that might be true for the amnesic subject. But the normal subject indulges in all kinds of comparisons of the current stimulus with stored information as a result of recognizing or recalling the target of the prime.

This general approach is, of course, simplistic. Detailed analysis would be required for each of the various 'memory systems' in terms of how their outputs do or do not depend upon a joint multiplicative function. In particular, one would have to examine the form of the information that is actually retrieved in acquiring, say, a perceptual–motor tracking task or any other skill in which current performance is affected by previously acquired sequences; the argument would have to be that the entire learned sequence is activated and unrolled by the visual exposure. Beyond this, it is not necessary, when carrying out a perceptual–motor task, for the current scene to be explicitly recognized as being part of a larger stored sequence—

the task can be negotiated without that, but equally, without that attribute the task cannot be compared with similar tasks or identified within a temporal or spatial framework. The analysis of recall, and its relationship with recognition as a sub-process, is another classical issue, not to mention the analysis of recognition itself in terms of a dependence on contextual cues. The dynamic aspects of retrieval of episodic information (Warrington and Weiskrantz, 1982) are not considered here, but must be left to future treatment.

Given this general approach, in terms of whether an output is directly contingent on a joint interaction between current and stored events, it follows that Gollin pictorial fragments, or triplets of letters, or an incomplete array of letters in a stem completion task, have no special virtue as fragments *per se*. They are just darts that make an intrusion into a neural system that has been altered by past manipulations, darts, metaphorically speaking, that allow stored items to get a boost up or allow an activated network to generate its relevant output. The question is not whether the darts can hit their targets, but whether the subject's response must be based on a *comparison* of the dart and the intended target. Nor is it a hindrance to the acquisition of new relationships if they do not depend upon a continuous comparison of that sort. Clearly it is not necessary for the darts to be in fragmented form, nor do they have to act only by means of altered facilitation through repetition, as in priming. They can be whole words, as in a lexical decision task, or sounds or lights in a conditioning task, or a fun-and-games tracking apparatus, or the man named Claparède in the white coat with a pin in his hand. These different substrates may well be exemplars of different and potentially independent memory systems or of different processing activities, ordered in arbitrary taxonomic systems to suit whatever pleases the particular taxonomist. But they all share properties that allow accessing in the amnesic patient, in that such an access is not contingent on a current × past event interaction. Perhaps the time has come to go beyond taxonomy?

Without the capacity to compare current and stored items, thus, and to make one's responses dependent on that *acknowledged* comparison, one consequence is the loss of the ability to *think* with and about the stored items. The argument is that stored events do not lead to current events via recall, and hence different stored events cannot be manipulated and compared with each other in thought. Indeed, the hallmark of all the neuropsychological examples of residual implicit processing, in the absence of explicit forms, is precisely the loss of the patients' ability to think about, or to image (e.g. in blindsight) the content of material which they can be demonstrated to detect, discriminate, and/or retain.

This type of operation should be distinguished from those of a number of special purpose devices in the nervous system, which are essentially error-detecting, error-correcting, and parameter-setting mechanisms. The ability of the body to maintain homeostasis in vascular, metabolic, temperature, vestibular, and other systems, are obvious examples. These examples, too, depend on a specific relationship between a current input and a stored setting or standard. But these devices differ from the one postulated for explicit memory in a number of ways. First, an explicit memory mode differs from other special purpose 'error-correction' devices in that it is part of a much larger and richer set of cognitive relations. In saying that 'I recognize X', I am also acknowledging that X is not another person, 'Y', that I can compare X's situation now with what it was on an earlier occasion, that X is an example of a particular sort, such as an academic, or a technician, that X has a family, etc., that X must be some distance from his home base, etc. In other words, it engages a large number of contextual and associated networks of knowledge and other memories. It is this aspect of explicit memory that led Elizabeth Warrington and me to postulate a 'cognitive mediational system' that we suggested was disconnected in the amnesic syndrome.

The second way in which explicit memory—recognition and recall— differs from special purpose devices is central to our main theme: the special purpose bodily devices operate without any conscious experience. It might be that the rich cognitive set of complex inter-relationships entails just what it is when we speak of having a 'conscious experience' of remembering, and that no special device for 'awareness' is necessary. But without invoking a special device, how does this general picture of the amnesic syndrome meld with our general position regarding commentaries as an essential feature of awareness? It is precisely the achievement of a particular critical interaction between current and stored information that yields a commentary. Unless that relationship succeeds, the commentary fails. And, I would argue, without the commentary there is no awareness of the interaction between current and past items, and no way in which the subject can exploit that interactive outcome in his or her thinking. In other words, the joint interactive function between current and stored events is necessary but not sufficient for recognition. Just as in blindsight, where the subject can discriminate, but without the commentary cannot use the visual information in a see-able form, so the amnesic patient can access stored information remarkably well, but commentary-less it cannot be used in a remembered form. This is what I mean by saying that the 'memory commentary is NOW'. Memory involves a relationship between past and present events, but only when the commentary is achieved in the here-and-now does it provide for that relationship to possess the power that the amnesic patient so sorely lacks. Of course, having been made, the commentary can itself be incorporated in the stored record—one says 'I remembered seeing him at the football match', and 'I remembered remembering him . . . .' But that is storing the product rather than the commentary that endows a memory as such. An amnesic patient might acknowledge that he 'remembered going to such and such a school', but he will not be able to offer a commentary in the here-and-now that he recovered such a memory, nor will he remember it the next time he is asked the same question about his early schooling. The commentary is NOW.

As in blindsight, imaging holds out the hope of identifying where the commentary stage arises. The medial temporal structures and the ventral stream of pathways progressing from striate cortex downwards towards the temporal lobes are obvious candidates for such a function, given their rich two-way connexions with large domains of cerebral cortex, and given the wealth of information that demonstrates good storage *per se*, but no recognition, in the absence of medial temporal structures. It is interesting that one position that was long ago argued for the septal–hippocampal system is that it is a 'comparator' (Gray, 1982, p. 262ff., and 1995). But comparison *per se*, without commentary, is necessary but not sufficient for explicit memory. Increasingly, imaging information is pointing towards frontal lobe structures as being involved in explicit memory and, as in the case of striate cortex for vision, the medial temporal structures may be necessary but not sufficient for full awareness of the relationship between current and past events. We are at just the stage of technology where it is more prudent to await the outcome rather than to speculate about the details.

6

Attributes and possible pathways of residual visual capacity

As already noted in Chapter 1, there are at least nine pathways from the retina to targets in the brain that remain open after blockade or damage to the primary visual cortex. These are displayed in Fig. 6.1. (Note that this is an expansion on the 5 pathways listed in my 1986 monograph on blindsight, where nevertheless some of the evidence reviewed here can also be found in more detail. But the more recent review by Cowey and Stoerig (1991) brings one more up to date.) We still do not know whether these are parallel and *potentially independent* (but normally interacting) systems, each with a specialized function, and if so, what these functions might be. It is possible to speculate, for example, that the pathway terminating in the suprachiasmatic nucleus of the hypothalamus is specialized for the control of the diurnal sleep/wakefulness cycle by light, given that lesions in that structure interfere with that cycle. If we could study each pathway in the absence of the others it would be easier to arrive at conclusions about possible specialized functions of each. But this is far beyond any practical possibility, at least now. Instead of eliminating $n - 1$ pathways, we can only eliminate 1 or, at most, just a few of the pathways. We can also study their targets, but again not in isolation from all inputs except one. As the pathways can interact, even inferences from an $n - 1$ pathway isolation could well provide misleading results. However, some useful conclusions can be drawn from the study of the electro-physiological responses of the various targets, and we can also examine the effects of removal or blockade of any particular target.

The important point is that, in the absence of striate cortex, there are a number of routes over which information from the retina can reach, and be processed at, various stages in the brain. Even restricting ourselves to

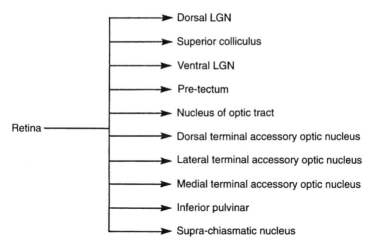

Figure 6.1. Diagram of connexions of the optic nerve with various brain targets (see text). The top route to the dorsal lateral geniculate nucleus (LGN), and thence to striate cortex (V1), is the major input from the eye to the cortex, and the most heavily studied. But the other pathways constitute about 10 to 15% of the optic nerve, which in total is greater than the number of fibres in the entire intact auditory nerve. (Reprinted with permission from Weiskrantz, 1990b, The Royal Society.)

just one extra-striate route from the retina to the brain, namely that to the superior colliculus, there is still a route open, for example, to visual cortical areas V2, V3, V4, even when striate cortex is completely removed or blocked, as is clear from Fig. 6.2. The point has been directly demonstrated by Rodman *et al.* (1989) for neurones in area MT, a region of cortex in the monkey in which cells respond especially to moving stimuli and their direction of movement. In the absence of striate cortex, cells in MT fire normally although the numbers doing so are reduced. It was demonstrated that the critical route sustaining the responses acts via the superior colliculus, and thence via the pulvinar to MT (see review by Gross, 1991). Retinal information can reach sub-cortical areas directly via the collicular and tectal routes, as well as via the accessory optic tract. And cortical areas can be reached via thalamic routes, the pulvinar and the LGN (Webster *et al.*, 1993; Hernandez-Gonzales and Reinoso-Suarez, 1994). Beyond that, information can reach large regions of the other, intact hemisphere, including its striate cortex, via brain commissures at both the sub-cortical and cortical levels.

And so the rest of the brain, in the absence of striate cortex, is in no sense completely deprived of visual information, although it may be reduced quantitatively. What is much less clear is how the residual information is processed qualitatively, and whether any particular pathways or their targets, or interactions with other targets or further projections, have a responsibility for any particular visual attribute. And, critically, whether the absence of striate cortex eliminates any particular attribute, and especially whether it eliminates visual *awareness*.

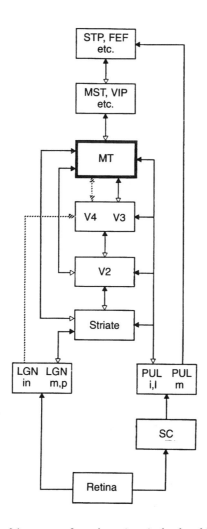

Figure 6.2. Schema of the outputs from the retina via the dorsal LGN and the superior colliculus (SC). It makes the point that even in the absence of striate cortex there are still routes open to other cortical areas. (From Rodman *et al.*, 1989, personal communication.)

In recent years a view has become popular that in the normal, intact primate brain various attributes of vision are organized in specialized areas of cortex (Zeki, 1993). It is said to reflect a general 'modular' organization. As examples, movement directionality is argued to be the speciality of MT (also known as V5) and colour opponency and constancy to be the speciality of V4. The argument is that V1 receives information coded appropriately for various attributes, and these are then projected differentially to specialized cortical areas. Evidence from brain imaging in normal human subjects has been taken to support such a view. But, in fact, *single* brain areas rarely light up (Gallows *et al.*, 1994)—as we shall note later in the case of movement—lesions of the cortical regions in the monkey that are highlighted by electrophysiology as being specialized for colour or movement do not entirely eliminate those capacities and, on the contrary, also produce different deficits, for example, for form (cf. Heywood *et al.*, 1992). The lesions in man that produce loss of colour vision ('achromatopsia') do not lie in the regions homologous to those in the monkey that have been suggested by electrophysiological evidence to be the special modules for colour processing. Nevertheless, there *are* patients with relatively selective perceptual loss of colour and other, rare, patients who have a loss of perceived movement, in both instances almost invariably combined with other 'agnosic' difficulties. To the extent that there is a degree of specialization in some cortical areas, it is to such targets that one naturally looks in considering where information may be processed in the absence of V1.

In one or another of patients with damage to striate cortex (see Chapter 1) there have been positive reports of the following visual attributes: detection, localization, orientation, movement, colour, and form. Not all of these are seen in every patient, for possible reasons which will be discussed a bit later. Nor, it should be stressed, do patients necessarily acknowledge 'seeing' those visual stimuli to which they can be shown to be sensitive. That question will also be addressed later. The question here is whether any of these attributes can be assigned to any particular visual pathways or targets. This is a difficult matter about which we are reduced to provisional speculation, although fortunately modern imaging methods hold out the promise of providing much more specific information, and already have started to make their impact.

The simplest index of *detection*, perhaps, is the response of the pupil itself to light, involving a relatively direct route from retina to pre-tectum and back, and a less direct loop via the cervical spinal cord (the sympathetic component of the pupillary response). A response of the pupil to an increase in luminance (the 'light reflex') is still found in patients with complete loss of V1 and adjoining cortex, although it is diminished in size (Barbur and Forsyth, 1986). It has even been found in a patient with a surgical hemispherectomy, in whom all cortex as well as parts of thalamus and the basal ganglia had been removed from one cerebral hemisphere (evidence by Mairie Keenleyside, shown in Weiskrantz, 1990b). But, as we have seen (Chapter 3), the pupil is exquisitely sensitive to more than mere changes in light intensity: it responds to colour, spatial structure—varying systematically with spatial frequency (see Figs 3.7 and 3.8)—and also to movement (Weiskrantz, 1990b). (Actually, one should say 'they', not 'it', because the two pupils are yoked together functionally and act in concert.) The sensitivity of the pupil in the normal subject responds to wavelength and to visual gratings, which reveal a visual spatial acuity that is equal to that obtained by psychophysical judgments (Barbur et al., 1987; Barbur and Thomson, 1987), as we have already seen in Fig. 3.7, in which acuity measured by pupillary constriction is compared with acuity as determined by the subjects' own perceptual judgments. That is, pupillary constriction is sensitive to just as fine a separation between lines on a grating as the subject him/herself is by looking at them. This strongly implies that the pupil receives a downstream control from cortex. It is also influenced by emotional events reflecting activity in the autonomic nervous system, which itself has a cortical component. And so even this primitive reflex does not operate in isolation. The potential attractiveness of the pupil as an indirect test of residual visual function has already been highlighted in Chapter 3. Another autonomic measure has also been used as an index of detection in blindsight, namely electrodermal responses to light, with positive and stable results reported by Zihl et al. (1980).

The pupil can serve as a useful index of detection, but it does not enter into a subject's instrumental behavioural response or judgments. Of course, all of the examples of discrimination in blindsight to be described below—position, orientation, wavelength, etc.—subsume detection as a prerequisite. But there are some clinical reports of detection, per se, without evidence of any further capacity. Thus, Brindley et al. (1969) reported that a subject with bilateral cortical blindness could detect a light being turned on, and a rather similar earlier report was made by Bender and Krieger (1951).

Spatial localization has been seen in 'cortically blind' patients, principally using two measures: saccadic or voluntary eye movements (e.g. Barbur et al., 1988; Zihl and Werth, 1984a, b), and manual reaching (Weiskrantz,

1986). A third measure was used in one study: teaching the subject to respond verbally to an estimated position on a memorized graticule, that is, a numerical spatial scale (Barbur *et al.*, 1980). It had been observed that monkeys without striate cortex will direct their eyes to a novel visual event (Humphrey and Weiskrantz, 1967; Humphrey, 1970, 1974; Denny-Brown and Chambers, 1955), and reach for briefly presented visual events (Humphrey, 1970, 1974; Weiskrantz *et al.*, 1977). The relationship between the activity of single neurones in the colliculus and saccadic eye movements provides a possible basis for residual capacity for localization: there is a topological map of the visual field in the colliculus. It was probably these considerations that led to the study by Pöppel, Held, and Frost (1973), who first demonstrated an ability of patients (war veterans) with cortical field defects to direct their eyes to the position of an 'unseen' visual flash in their blind fields. In the absence of V1, the evidence for the accurate control of the movement of the eye to the position of the target in a monkey's field defect has been shown to directly implicate a route via the superior colliculus. It has been known for some time, as mentioned, that a monkey without V1 can detect and localize visual stimuli, but its ability increases dramatically when trained to do so, that is, when it is *required* to respond to the stimuli in the affected part of the visual field to obtain its reward. Mohler and Wurtz (1977) trained monkeys to move their eyes to a target within a relatively small field defect produced by a restricted striate cortex removal. The animals improved with practice, as expected. They then located, by electrophysiological recording, precisely that region in the superior colliculus which received visual inputs from the retina corresponding to the recovered part of the visual field. When this was lesioned in turn, the field defect returned as permanent defect. But a superior colliculus lesion by itself, with striate cortex intact, had no effect. Hence, this is a direct demonstration of a 'take-over' of a capacity by a system when pressed into action. We have already seen a similar take-over in the evidence cited above by Rodman *et al.* (1989) for directional movement, with a relay via colliculus to area MT via the pulvinar. Whether the residual capacity for localization similarly requires a cortical target is not yet known.

Stimulus control of eye position is present in young infants, in whom it is assumed that cortical control has not yet matured (Braddick *et al.*, 1996). When it has done so, it is reasonable to speculate that the so-called 'dorsal cortical route' might be involved; this is the route coursing dorsally in the brain from its cells of origin in striate cortex (V1). Lesions along this route, especially in posterior parietal lobe, cause deficits in spatial localization in the monkey. On the other hand, the classical work of Sprague (1966) reveals a delicate sharing of control between cortex and superior colliculus, sufficient to transform a visual cortically induced scotoma into a seeing field. Similarly, the suggested role of inhibition between mirror-symmetric parts of the visual field, acting via putative midbrain pathways, was nicely demonstrated in interactions between points in 'blind' scotomata and mirror-symmetric points in the intact fields in human subjects by Singer *et al.* (1977), together with reports such as that by Pöppel and Richards (1974) of patients with enhanced sensitivity within scotomata that were mirror-symmetric to small scotomata in the other half-field. A balance of cortical and midbrain mechanisms is clearly demonstrated in such experiments. It is curious how short-lived are major fashions in science, and memories of them in the textbooks. There used to be, some 30 years ago, a very popular 'two-visual system' hypothesis—with cortex and midbrain as the players (Schneider, 1967; Trevarthen, 1968; Ingle, 1967). The cortical system processed 'what?' and the sub-cortical system 'where?' We now have a two-visual system hypothesis which is entirely cortical—the ventral stream leaving V1 for 'what?' and the dorsal system for 'where?', with the evidence for the earlier view neatly cast aside. It is not that the earlier hypothesis was wrong; it is just that we have a newer hypothesis, itself also not necessarily wrong. It is about time these two hypotheses were reunited.

The importance of practice—of forced use of parallel pathways—was demonstrated many years ago in monkeys with field defects caused by restricted V1 lesions (Cowey, 1967; Cowey and Weiskrantz, 1963; Weiskrantz and Cowey, 1970). It will be addressed more fully in a later section ('The evolutionary "Why?"', Chapter 7), but briefly, it was shown that the size of the field defect (itself characterized by a relative rather than an absolute loss of sensitivity for detection) remains quite stable over a two-year period, but shrinks as the animal is trained to use the information in the field defect. The sensitivity can improve by as much as a factor of 1000. The importance also emerges tellingly from Mohler and Wurtz's study; they carried out an ingenious control experiment bearing on the importance of practice. In one animal they 'trained' only one part of the field defect, and left the remainder naive and unpractised. The trained portion showed a clear differential improvement compared to its control within the same field defect. The Mohler and Wurtz study served as the impetus for studies by Sepp Zihl and colleagues using similar eye movement methods in human patients with V1 damage, reporting improvement that correlated with periods of practice (Zihl, 1980, 1981; Zihl and von Cramon, 1979, 1985).

Monkeys without striate cortex can discriminate the *orientation* of visual stimuli in the frontal plane, differing by as little as about 8°. Orientation was first studied systematically in a blindsight patient, D.B., who could discriminate a difference in gratings of 10° in his blind field (Weiskrantz, 1986). Various attempts have been made to find positive evidence in another well-studied patient, G.Y., with negative results using gratings. However, positive evidence has recently been obtained using single lines instead of gratings (Morland *et al.*, 1996). Sensitivity to orientation is strongly associated with the selective responses of cortical neurones. Indeed, it was this property found in neurones in V1 of monkey that led to the important breakthrough in the Nobel Prize work of Hubel and Wiesel (1962). Neurones sensitive to orientation are seen in a range of other visual cortical areas that receive inputs from V1 but also from extra-striate sub-cortical routes. On the other hand, sensitivity to orientation is not a feature of neurones in the superior colliculus. But this does not mean that the colliculus could not serve as an important *route* for a residual capacity for orientation. After all, the neurones of the LGN (which is the major relay point for neurones of the optic nerve from which fibres travel to V1) do not show any sensitivity to orientation, whereas neurones in V1 *are* sensitive. This sensitivity *must* arise from the way that neurones in the LGN distribute their targets to neurones in V1 along particular retinal orientations. In the same way, orientation sensitivity might arise at a later stage beyond the superior colliculus if its outputs were distributed in any of its targets along particular retinal orientations. It seems unlikely that a collicular mechanism alone, without a cortical target, could subserve orientation discrimination, but there are several cortical targets that receive inputs from the colliculus relayed via the pulvinar in the thalamus. We do not know the orientational properties of such extra-striate cortical areas in the absence of striate cortex, but in the intact primate brain orientation tuning of single neurones becomes less and less prominent a characteristic the farther away from V1 is the extra-striate visual area; that is, V5 shows less orientation sensitivity than V2. It seems likely that a residual capacity to discriminate orientation will be rather fragile in the absence of V1, and lesions to V1 in clinical patients almost invariably extend into surrounding areas. Patient D.B., who demonstrated good orientation discrimination, perhaps was unusual in having a relatively restricted surgical removal of a tumour lodged in V1.

Movement has to be considered in terms of detection of a moving event *per se*, as well as discrimination of the *direction* of such movement. Blindsight patients can discriminate direction of movement, and to the extent that cortical area MT plays an important or even critical role, we have seen that a relay via the colliculus allows MT to continue to function after striate cortex removal in the monkey (Rodman *et al.*, 1989). And in the human patient G.Y., we know from recent imaging evidence that area MT (V5), together with a number of other brain areas, lights up when he is making discriminations of direction of movement (Barbur *et al.*, 1993). We will be considering this imaging study in more detail when we discuss the 'blindness of blindsight' in the next section.

But it seems likely that movement *per se* does not require a cortical component. Marie-Therese Perenin's (1991) research with hemispherectomized patients found just that—an ability to detect moving spots, but not to discriminate their direction. The work with such patients has been subjected to renewed scrutiny recently, however, and it may be that this result will require confirmation before it can be established with certainty (King *et al.*, 1996). We know that neurones in the superior colliculus respond to visually moving stimuli in the monkey. The pupil constricts to a moving stimulus in the blind hemifield of patient G.Y. (with V1 damage); it remains to be seen whether it does so in the blind hemifield of a hemispherectomized patient. But, evidence from hemispherectomy aside (hemispherectomy, after all, is a massive insult on an already severely pathological nervous system, and extends well into subcortical regions; it is hard to know how intact, if at all, are the tectal pathways), it has also been reported that optokinetic reflexes were found in a patient with long-standing bilateral cortical blindness (ter Braak *et al.*, 1971).

Colour—or more strictly, wavelength sensitivity and discrimination in the absence of colour perception, *per se*—is one of the most intriguing features of blindsight: all of the examples of discrimination in blindsight are examples of 'missing qualia', but somehow the example of processing 'colour' in the absence of the quality of colour is more evocative. The constraints imposed by known mechanisms and pathways help to reduce the alternatives for wavelength processing in the absence of V1. The reason for this is that only one class of ganglion cells in the primate retina, the p-beta retinal ganglion cells, appear to be involved in initiating and transmitting the signals that give rise ultimately to colour contrast and constancy (ganglion cells are the cells of origin of the optic nerve). The p-beta cells project *only* to the dorsal LGN of the thalamus (and only to the parvo-cellular layers of that structure). Under daylight conditions, normal subjects show a characteristic profile of unequal sensitivities to different wavelengths of light—from red at one end of the wavelength continuum to blue at the other—with small peaks and troughs of sensitivity at particular wavelengths, thought to reflect the operation of colour contrast mechanisms. If these characteristic peaks and troughs were to be found in blindsight subjects, indicating the integrity of colour opponency, then no other candidate pathway would exist except that of the p-beta projection to LGN of the thalamus. The answer is that they *are* found, at least in some subjects: the *shape* of the spectral sensitivity curve of such selected blindsight subjects is normal (although its over-all sensitivity is reduced), and it contains the characteristic peaks and troughs (Stoerig and Cowey, 1989, 1991, 1992). In passing, it must be noted that it is much simpler to summarize this statement than actually to obtain the evidence. Stoerig and Cowey had to require their subjects to guess whether a stimulus was or was not present by forced-choice responding in order to obtain the thresholds for each of the individual wavelengths, even though the blindsight subjects could not 'see' any of the stimuli. This was an arduous and heroic achievement, on the part of subjects and experimenters alike, requiring days and days of testing.

It is not only that the shape of the sensitivity curve is normal, but also that subjects can discriminate *between* wavelengths, for example by being forced to guess whether a particular stimulus is 'red' or 'blue' (Stoerig and Cowey, 1992; Brent *et al.*, 1994; Barbur *et al.*, 1994b; and Stoerig, Barbur, Sahraie, and Weizkrantz, in press). G.Y., in fact, appears to have a relatively heightened sensitivity for green (Stoering *et al.*, in press).

From the last century until relatively recently, it was assumed that the LGN projected *only* to the striate cortex *and* that the neurones in that nucleus degenerated completely after striate cortex damage. If true, colour discrimination in blindsight would be impossible. But it has been discovered in recent years that both of these statements are false: there are still a small number of cells in the LGN that remain undegenerated— they are intra-laminar, that is, situated between the layers of the LGN (Fries, 1981; Yukie and Iwai, 1981; Benevento and Yoshida, 1981). Importantly, these cells project to extra-striate visual areas, as mentioned already in Chapter 1. The evidence for this projection, and existence of the retinal input to the intra-laminar layers, has been clearly demonstrated and reviewed by Cowey and Stoerig (1989, 1991).

But it is not only the LGN that undergoes a marked change following striate cortex damage, showing the characteristic degeneration back to the cell bodies of origin which lie within it. The damage is further reflected in changes in the retina itself; there is trans-neuronal retrograde degeneration

(Van Buren, 1963). As a result, there is a marked shift from a predominance of p-beta cells to a much stronger predominance of p-gamma cells and p-alpha cells in the retinal ganglionic distribution (Cowey *et al.*, 1989). Some p-beta cells remain, however, and hence there is a clear candidate for a unique pathway to mediate intact wavelength sensitivity and discrimination—as and when it is found.

Given the positive results with human patients for wavelength discrimination after V1 damage, it would be expected that monkeys with striate cortex lesions would also show some capacity for wavelength discrimination at photopic levels of illumination, and a Purkinje shift in spectral sensitivity with dark adaptation. Therefore the report of Malmo (1966), with a follow-up by Lepore *et al.* (1975), that destriated monkeys show only a sensitivity function characteristic of dark-adapted sensitivity, remains a puzzle. Perhaps their lesion included not only striate cortex (V1) but also extensive damage to extra-striate areas. In any event, with restricted lesions, but including the whole of V1, Cowey (personal communication) has found clear evidence of a Purkinje shift in the monkey. But, curiously, there is still little positive evidence, and some negative evidence, for wavelength discrimination in monkeys with striate cortical removal (Cowey, personal communication). The reason is unknown, but it could be because typically the lesions in monkeys rarely stop just at the border of V1, indeed it is virtually impossible for such a lesion to be made experimentally.

If light-adapted sensitivity and wavelength discrimination depend on an intact pathway via p-beta retinal ganglion cells to LGN intra-laminar layers, and thence to other extra-striate cortical regions, it obviously follows that such capacities should not be found in patients in whom critical extra-striate cortical areas are destroyed, and indeed only a proportion of the patients studied by Petra Stoerig (1987) had these capacities intact—presumably because of the disposition of the cortical damage in the other cases. The lesions in clinical cases obviously vary considerably, and are rarely placed to suit the neuroscientist; even modern high resolution imaging techniques are not adequate for assessing the precise limits of damage, especially given the convoluted layout of the brain within which visual cortical areas lie.

The evidence regarding *shape*, or *form*, is still incomplete. Indeed, just what is involved in shape discrimination itself is still a contentious issue, and a discrimination between shapes can involve subsidiary capacities or can be derived from other attributes. Monkeys without striate cortex are reported to be able to discriminate between 'simple' shapes, but also require a large amount of training to be able to do so (Schilder *et al.*, 1972). In the earlier literature, based on the classical experiments of Klüver (1942), such a capacity was thought to be impossible. Klüver concluded that such animals could only discriminate stimuli differing in total luminous flux, regardless of their spatial or configural distribution. But the lesions made by Klüver were quite extensive, reaching well outside V1. The Pasiks made more restricted lesions, largely confined to V1, and reported positive evidence for both spatial and shape discriminations (Pasik and Pasik, 1971, 1982; Miller *et al.*, 1980). The human patient D.B. was able to discriminate stimuli such as 'X' vs. 'O' (Weiskrantz *et al.*, 1974; Weiskrantz, 1986), but it was argued that this was likely to be based on his discriminating the orientation of the sub-components rather than the global shape as such (Weiskrantz, 1987a). That was because he had much difficulty in discriminating squares from rectangles, where the orientations of the sub-components were the same.

On the other hand, there have been reports of subjects being able to reach out to grasp a solid object, and while reaching, to adjust their hands to match the shape of the object being grasped. Tony Marcel (in press) was the first to report this. Another study has recently been reported by Perenin and Rossetti (1996; cf. Milner and Goodale, 1995, p. 76). Their hemi-anopic patient could not make perceptual judgments of the orientation of a slot verbally or by manual matching when the slot was projected to his blind hemifield—he performed at chance in this mode. However, when asked to place a card into an open slot, like a mail-box with its aperture skewed to different test orientations, the subject could perform reliably above chance. This type of capacity calls to mind the role of the so-called 'dorsal stream'—the pathway emanating from striate cortex and going to parietal lobes. It has been associated with the processing of spatial localization, whereas the 'ventral stream' is considered to process object identification. As reviewed earlier (Chapter 1), Milner and Goodale (1995) have made an alternative suggestion for its role, and have invoked it in patients who have perceptual difficulties in *perceiving* the shape and even the orientation of simple lines and objects, but who can nevertheless demonstrate that the information is available when they reach and *act* with respect to them. They argue, indeed, that the dorsal route subserves *visual action*, and that this function is characteristically carried out without acknowledged perceptual awareness. This is, in a sense, blindsight without blindness.

Another meaning of intact shape discrimination can be gleaned from the pathways involved in movement discrimination. G.Y. can mimic the path of a moving spot with his arm movement with quite remarkable skill—this evidence will also be discussed in another context in the next section. But the point is that he can do this even for circular and elliptical paths of movement, and probably for much more complex ones. From such an approach one might be able to determine just how readily patients could differentiate various 'shapes from movement'. Recently, Kentridge, Heywood, and I have established that G.Y. can, indeed, discriminate the shape emerging from motion–paths. He was able to discriminate a circular path from a triangular or rectangular one, and in fact to name some of the 'shapes' without prompting. He could also discriminate an erect from an inverted triangle, and also a 'figure 8' from a curvilinear 'squiggle' that was, in effect, an open '8'.

Another indirect indication of shape emerges from reports of 'completion' of shapes presented to both the intact and the blind hemifields of patients, as reviewed in Chapter 3. Patients report seeing the *complete* shape, for example, a circle, bridging both half-fields, but see nothing when a half circle is shown to the blind hemifield, and see only a half circle when only it is shown to the intact hemifield. Just how large a range and complexity of shapes the intact hemifield can persuade its blind partner to process is an interesting question.

Finally, a striking claim has been made by Tony Marcel which if confirmed would force a considerable expansion of the known capacity for residual perception of stationary shapes. In our own work, as just noted, we found that even simple shapes might be discriminated merely on the orientations of the principal components, rather than their global characteristics. But reading of words obviously demands a discrimination of shapes of letters, although it is possible that only partial shape information is required to activate already existing visual lexical groupings. Marcel has reported that words flashed into the blind hemifield can influence the interpretation of meanings of words subsequently shown in the intact hemifield. For example, 'money' in the blind field will bias the reported meaning of the ambiguous word 'bank' in the intact field—that is, bank can either relate to 'money' or to 'river'. It is now more than 10 years since this intriguing report was first made, but I understand from Tony Marcel that the material is now in press.

We are left with the questions, still unanswered, of just what is the striate cortex good for and, more importantly, what is it *essential* for? In a quantitatively reduced fashion, it would appear that virtually all visual attributes can somehow be processed in one or other of the group of patients lacking V1, although not all of them in all subjects. Given the plethora of parallel pathways perhaps this is not surprising, providing of course that the essential processing targets themselves are not damaged at the same time as V1. It would seem that so long as a possible route is open, and is pressed into use, any one of a wide spectrum of visual capacities can be processed.

It is worth reflecting on how much undue importance may become attached to the primate striate cortex in a comparative context, due to its accessibility and ready identification anatomically, the elegance of the electrophysiological studies, and of course to the striking nature of the cortical blindness. But throughout the vertebrate kingdom, there are homologues of both the geniculo–striate system and the tecto–pulvinar system (or more familiarly named the collicular–pulvinar system in primates), as shown schematically in Fig. 6.3. The balance of these two systems varies from species to species, and the geniculo–striate system is often subsidiary to the homologue of the tecto–pulvinar system. Many species of birds, for example, are accomplished visual creatures with excellent, even super-human acuity and good colour vision, and yet lesions of the pathway (the thalamo–wulst) homologous to the mammalian geniculo–striate pathway are virtually without effect on such visual capacities (Karten and Shimizu, 1991). The homologue of the mammalian tecto–pulvinar system (tectum—n. rotundus) pathway is more important in those creatures. It also develops earlier in the lives of birds and many mammals. Lesions in it produce severe deterioration of visual behaviour in birds. Even in some mammals, for example the tree shrew, the effects of collicular lesions far outweigh those of the geniculo–striate system (Casagrande and Diamond, 1974). The tree shrew, which is by some considered to be a primitive primate, still retains the capacity to discriminate colour, pattern, objects, and spatial localization vision in the absence of striate cortex (Killackey et al., 1971; Snyder et al., 1969; Ware et al., 1974). It would seem that much depends on the relative sizes of the midbrain and LGN pathways as to which would be dominant. This is not surprising in itself, but it does indicate that there is nothing sacrosanct about V1, per se, which endows it intrinsically with higher importance, although certainly in primates it is in a powerful position. An interesting speculation about its development derives from the fact that primates have forward-looking eyes and a large binocular field of vision, with the advantage that this allows for depth perception. In birds with forward-looking eyes, such as the owl, the thalamo–wulst pathway is apparently more important and larger than in birds with small binocular fields, such as the pigeon, where the effects of damage are slight (personal communication, Harvey Karten). The popularity of the primate visual cortex with visual scientists may have led to an understatement and underestimate of the capacity of the older pathway, and to its place in comparative evolution. Neurones, after all, are neurones, whether they happen to be upstairs or downstairs. What matters is their organization.

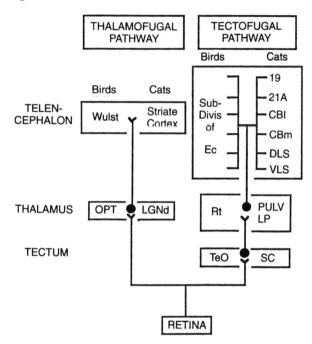

Figure 6.3. Schema of organization of two major visual pathways, seen widely throughout the vertebrate kingdom. The pathway on the left is via the LGN or its homologue, and the pathway on the right is via the SC or its homologue. The balance between these two routes varies from species to species. (From Karten and Shimizu, 1991, with permission.)

Missing from this review, because the evidence is too scanty, is a potentially important qualification that must be placed on all of the categories of residual function after V1 damage: it may well depend critically upon the age at which the damage occurred. It is found (Gross, personal communication) that infant monkeys with V1 lesions have a much greater ability to localize stimuli in their affected fields than do adults, despite the fact that changes in the retina itself caused by retrograde trans-neuronal degeneration of p-beta ganglion cells (see above) are probably more severe the earlier in life they occur. Some of the hemispherectomy patients whose brain damage initially occurred prenatally develop cognitive and linguistic capacities that are superior to patients in whom the damage occurs later, but the evidence for visual function is very thin. There are, however, some fascinating but scattered observations. For example, Damasio *et al.* (1975) reported a case of a 34-year-old woman who suffered brain damage at the age of five, and received a left hemispherectomy at the age of 20. Immediately after surgery the fields were markedly constricted (and the left eye virtually blind because of optic atrophy), but with the right eye 14 years later 'she had almost normal vision ... and showed no hemianopia.' A classical case is that of Jelsma (reported in Marquis, 1935), concerning a boy with a porencephalic cyst, presumably of prenatal origin, in the posterior left hemisphere, which was removed surgically at the age of 11. The boy's vision was remarkable. There was only slight constriction on the right side of his field, and he had normal colour vision. It was confirmed by an independent observer that 'the entire occipital lobe, with the complete calcarine fissure [in which V1 is located] was lacking.' This patient was said to have almost full fields in one eye some years after the hemispherectomy. The young damaged brain might have potentials not seen in adults, and so it is possible that other cases of more restricted early striate cortex damage would yield similar phenomena. Clear evidence of plasticity has been seen in the human somatosensory system, which gives hope for a similar potential in vision.

But, leaving these exceptional cases aside, no doubt the typical patient who lacks striate cortex will tell you in no uncertain terms that striate cortex is *essential* for normal perception, and, indeed, perhaps for any 'seen' perception whatever. And that brings us to the next question:

The blindness of blindsight

So far we have been strolling through the visual system, including the retina, in an effort to relate various subtypes of residual capacity (e.g. colour, orientation, movement,) to the known or putative properties of specific subparts of the extra-striate visual pathways and cortical areas. But nowhere in this tour has anything been revealed about the question of the *'blind'* aspect of blindsight. This breaks down into two questions; one is largely empirical, namely what brain structure or structures are necessary and/or sufficient for visual awareness to occur? The second is more theoretical and speculative: what is it that removes the experience from the discrimination in blindsight, and what might allow it to occur in normal perception?

It has to be confessed, of course, that no one knows the answer to either question; we are just at the beginning of the quest, but at least it is a quest that can be pursued. As regards a structure that is *critical*, it is obvious that the first candidate must be the striate cortex itself. It is, after all, the structure that when damaged gives rise to the phenomenon of blindsight—the intact discriminative performance in the absence of acknowledged awareness. No other structure is really a candidate.

But this candidate—striate cortex—runs into a spot of trouble regarding the experiential aspect. The first patient described in detail, D.B., *did* have some forms of visual *experience* in his blind field under certain stimulus conditions. Examples of this are described in detail throughout the book summarizing research on him (Weiskrantz, 1986). They were sometimes 'feelings' or an 'awareness', 'I got a movement' and with vigorously moving stimuli, actual 'seeing' of waves. These experiences were apt to mislead him by giving rise to complex experiences and wrong inferences. For example, in forced-choice discriminating between a curved and straight-sided triangle, he said, 'There is a movement. I said "straight" when the waves were thinner, and "curved" when they were thicker and quicker.' On another occasion, with the same discrimination, he said, 'it's a circle inside a square—that's the feeling I get.' But he typically insisted, when asked, that he was not actually *seeing*. Other researchers have described 'pin pricks' (Richards, 1973; Blythe et al., 1987). With D.B. these feelings, and especially the waves, were non-veridical but obviously attention-capturing for him.

Another well-studied subject, G.Y., who has a right hemianopia caused by head injury at the age of 8, also has experiences of transient stimuli but they *are* veridical (Blythe et al., 1986). In discriminating direction of movement of a target, such as a spot or a bar, provided it moves rapidly enough, he says he 'knows' that there is movement and 'knows' whether it is in this or that direction, even if he finds it difficult to describe the experience itself. D.B. had the ability to detect presence/absence with very slow onset times—taking as long as 10 seconds to reach full strength, for which he typically had no awareness. But, like G.Y., when stimuli moved rapidly or had rapid onset times, D.B. also reported experience, for example, he could describe and discriminate 'away' versus 'towards' for circular stimuli that were made to rapidly shrink or grow in diameter (Weiskrantz, 1986, p. 86). Because these 'waves' were so intrusive and attention-capturing, Warrington and I went to some trouble to try to arrange stimulus conditions to eliminate them, for example, by increasing ambient illumination and thus decreasing contrast (see Chapter 13,

Weiskrantz, 1986). Under those conditions, D.B.'s strikingly impressive performance could emerge for which he insisted that he had no experience whatever. In G.Y.'s case, however, because his perception of rapidly moving or transient stimuli *is* veridical, it has been much more tempting for experimenters and G.Y. alike to concentrate experimentally on stimuli that yield conscious awareness. That has resulted, with few exceptions until recently, in G.Y. not being tested under those conditions that yield *no* acknowledged experience, that is, what can be defined as genuine 'blindsight', as had been found in a range of tests with D.B. In a sense, it was fortunate that D.B.'s experiences were non-veridical because we could arrange to eliminate them and thus to explore genuine blindsight in a thorough-going way over the ten-year period in which he was studied.

A PET scan has been made of G.Y. discriminating the direction of movement of a bar, with the parameters deliberately set such that he had a kind of 'awareness'. But the report (Barbur *et al.*, 1993), especially, but not only, the title—'Conscious visual perception without V1'—might suggest to the casual reader that G.Y.'s experience was perceptually normal. The text reads, '. . . in spite of his "blindness", he was able to discriminate correctly and faultlessly and to have conscious awareness of *having seen* the particular visual stimulus' (p. 1295, italics added), although it later is conceded that 'his awareness is not the same as that of normal individuals' (p. 1301).

In fact, as was also the case in the video tape recording of D.B. transcribed in Chapter 3, G.Y.'s awareness is very far from normal *perception* and he denies that he is seeing. Here is an interview in full that was recorded a few months after the PET study was done:

L.W.: G., you remember the experiment that you did in the PET scan— with the moving bar? Can you tell me what sort of experience you had in that situation? What did you sense? What was it like?

G.Y.: You don't actually ever sense anything or see anything. That's where we get the mix-up, because the sensation I get I try to put into words. It's more an awareness but you don't *see* it [his emphasis].

L.W.: Did you know what it was?

G.Y.: The shape or the motion?

L.W.: The shape.

G.Y.: No. Roughly, but not sure about that.

L.W.: The direction?

G.Y.: Yes.

L.W.: What kind of words do you think you have to use? Is it like anything in your normal visual field?

G.Y.: The nearest I ever get, and it is not a fair comparison, is waving your hand in front of your eyes when they are closed. You are kind of aware that something has happened but you don't quite see it. You know something has moved. But that isn't a fair comparison to make.

L.W.: The nearest you can get is the sense of something happening, but you don't know what it is?

G.Y.: Yes.

L.W.: Anything else you can think of to describe it?

G.Y.: No, because it is a sense that I haven't got, if that makes sense. If you said something to try to describe sight to a blind man, we don't have the words to do it because he does not have the receptors or the reception, and that is the same with me. I mean I can't describe something I don't understand myself.

But even if the experience itself defies easy description, obviously experimenters—and subjects alike—feel more comfortable with having some sort of guidance and feedback from awareness of this kind, rather than being forced onto a pure 'guesswork' mode. For this reason, only rarely has G.Y. (and most other hemianopic subjects) been tested under conditions deliberately designed to eliminate the experiences. And so we recently tested him in the commentary-key paradigm, to determine conditions under which discrimination was accompanied by experience, of 'knowing', and to determine whether he, like D.B., could perform at high levels without any experience. This has already been discussed briefly in Chapter 3. G.Y. was asked to indicate on one of two response keys, by guessing if necessary, whether a small spot was moving in one or another specified direction. With two other keys he was to indicate, on every trial, whether he had any experience whatever of the event (press 'yes'), or absolutely none at all (press 'no'). The results showed that acknowledged experience of movement did not emerge until the spot reached a velocity of about $10°/sec$ or more and occupied an excursion of about $20°$. One result has already been shown earlier in the book in Fig. 3.3. Other examples can be seen in Figs 6.4 and 6.5. At slower speeds, he could still perform excellently. An even more telling example emerged when we increased the background luminance, holding the luminance of the target constant, thereby decreasing contrast. His awareness responses plunged down to practically zero, but with no change in his very high level of performance (Fig. 6.6), which remained at better than 90% correct. Actually, the result with high background luminance was anticipated: this

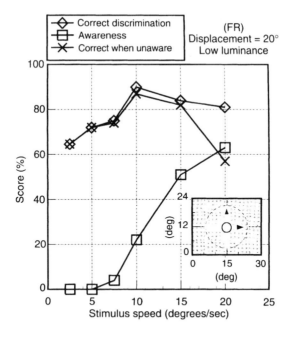

Figure 6.4. Performance by G.Y. in discriminating, by guessing if necessary, whether a spot moved horizontally or non-horizontally in his blind hemifield, and also in indicating whether he had any experience whatever of the event. (FR refers to use of 'forced-response' method, in which the subject must indicate, with a key press, which of the two alternatives occurred on each trial.) As speed increases, awareness increases, but performance is still very good on trials with low velocities in which he reports no awareness. See also Fig. 3.3. (From Weiskrantz *et al.*, 1995, with permission. © National Academy of Sciences, USA.)

was precisely the manoeuvre—flooding the background field with strong light—that we had used in earlier research with D.B. to abolish his awareness of moving stimuli. This was done to eliminate D.B.'s non-veridical and confusion experiences—he actually performed better without them (Weiskrantz, 1986, pp. 95–7 and *passim*).

When G.Y. did acknowledge awareness of visual events, as we have just seen, these experiences may have been odd and difficult to describe, but they were nevertheless genuine *experiences*. Therefore the PET scan taken under those conditions is of some interest: it showed activity increases in the 'conscious' movement discrimination task in 'human' V5, V3, area 7, other more anterior cortical areas, and vermis of cerebellum. The control subtraction task was discrimination of the position of a stationary bar. The authors stress the result with V5, but the activity increases were not confined to just that region.

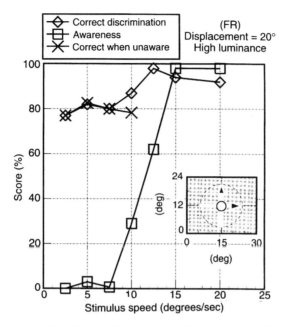

Figure 6.5. See legend for Fig. 6.4. The background luminance conditions differed from results shown in Fig. 6.4, but otherwise the experiment was the same. See also Fig. 3.3. (From Weiskrantz *et al.*, 1995, with permission. © National Academy of Sciences, USA.)

These results were obtained before the commentary-key paradigm was used with this subject, when it was not appreciated that he could discriminate so well without *any* acknowledged experience. Obviously, the next step is to scan him, and other subjects, separately while 'aware' and while 'unaware'. His performance levels in the aware mode and the unaware mode can be matched using the same kind of discrimination in both conditions (see, for example, Fig. 6.7). A comparison of the two scans should give us an indication of whether there are structures uniquely associated with visual awareness of *transient stimuli*. An exciting prospect. As this study is likely to be carried out in the near future, if it has not yet been finished before this book was printed, it is perhaps idle to speculate on what the result will be regarding the comparison between the aware and the unaware modes. The options seem three-fold: (a) the same structures will be involved, but with quantitatively different levels of activity; (b) there will be a non-identical set of structures, or (c) there will be no difference. The first result would suggest that the difference between the two modes is simply a matter of threshold; the second, which is the most interesting, would suggest that an additional step or a wider network is required to proceed from unaware to aware. The third alternative would suggest that conscious awareness is not a matter of which particular structures show activity, but would be compatible with views that particular temporal firing patterns are critical (e.g. the 40 hertz synchronization advanced as a mechanism for binding, Crick and Koch, 1990; Gray and Singer, 1989; Singer, 1993), which of course would be very unlikely to appear in functional imaging. In that case the appropriate methodology could be electrophysiological rather than locus of structure as such.

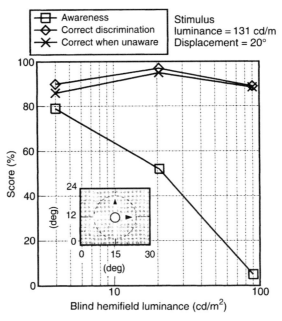

Figure 6.6. Effect of increasing background luminance (holding stimulus luminance constant), thereby decreasing contrast, on awareness and performance. G.Y. had to indicate, by guessing if necessary, whether a spot moved horizontally or non-horizontally in his blind hemifield, and also to indicate on every trial whether he had any experience whatever of the event. It can be seen that the percentage of trials on which he reports awareness plunges sharply as background luminance increases, while performance remains unaffected and at a high level. (From Weiskrantz et al., 1995, with permission. © National Academy of Sciences, USA.)

The emphasis that it is *transient* stimuli that are essential to generate an experience of awareness in the absence of striate cortex is important. These appear to be the only kinds of visual stimuli that generate experience in any of the blindsight subjects studied so far. Transient means either spatially *or* temporally transient. The sudden onset or offset of a stationary stimulus will also generate it. Thus, D.B. said he had a 'feeling of movement

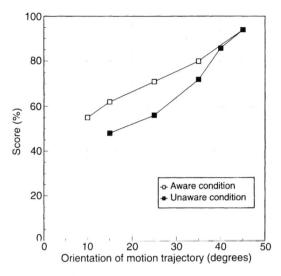

Figure 6.7. Comparison of G.Y.'s performance in his blind hemifield in a task with a moving spot at different directions of movement for conditions under which he reported no experience whatever vs. those for which he always reported experience. On any trial he had to indicate, by guessing if necessary, whether the spot moved horizontally or non-horizontally, and also to indicate whether he had any experience whatever of the event. As the orientation of the non-horizontal movement increasingly deviates from horizontal, his performance improves. But note that even when completely unaware he reaches the same high value, better than 90% correct, as when he reports awareness. The data for this graph can be found in Weiskrantz *et al.*, 1995.

sometimes' when a light was turned on abruptly, but when it came on slowly, taking more than about 2 seconds to reach its steady level, he commented, 'just guesswork, 50:50', that is, chance level; on half of the occasions, randomly, no light was actually presented. (He nevertheless performed at 90% correct; Weiskrantz, 1986, Chapter 9.)

What one would like to have is a precise measure of the conditions with transient stimuli that generate awareness and those that do not, while still allowing good discrimination to occur by 'guessing'. That is, one would like to have the 'tuning curves' for the two separate conditions. It will be seen from the results with moving stimuli, above, that the window of parameters that generates awareness is much more sharply tuned than the window for unawareness. In fact, stationary stimuli with sharp onsets and offsets probably are more suited to obtaining tuning curves. The reason is that the movement curve is one-sided—above a certain velocity, awareness is always found because the transient character remains sharp until, perhaps, one reaches very high velocities. But with stationary stimuli one can vary the spatial and temporal characteristics of stimuli that generate awareness. Such a study was carried out with subject G.Y. (Barbur *et al.*, 1994a) in an experiment in which he had to detect the occurrence of a grating. It was, indeed, found that the tuning was relatively sharp, with a peak of about 1.3 cycles/degree when the grating was also oscillated at about 10 times a second (Fig. 6.8). It now remains to determine the tuning curve for the unaware mode. It is certainly going to be much broader. Whether it will be similar in shape remains to be seen. Another exciting prospect.

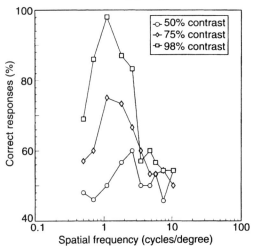

Figure 6.8. Spatiotemporal 'tuning' function for G.Y. He had to indicate in which of two successive time intervals a stimulus occurred. (The intervals were signalled by means of auditory beeps.) The stimuli always were presented to his blind hemifield. The contrast of the stimuli was modulated up and down sinusoidally at a rate of 6 times per second. The stimulus was a sine wave grating of different values. The contrast level was also varied, and results are plotted separately for three different levels. It can be seen that performance was sharply tuned to a spatial frequency of the grating of approximately 1.2 cycles per degree. (Reprinted with permission from Barbur *et al.*, 1994a, The Royal Society.)

And so, it may be possible to discover whether there are particular or unique neural structures associated with visual awareness, in contrast to those when there is no awareness but when the subject is performing equally well. And, quite independently, the psychophysical tuning curves for the two modes, aware and unaware are potentially measurable and can be compared with each other. For both approaches, we are half of the way there.

Returning to the question of whether striate cortex is necessary for visual awareness, the answer must be no for *transient* stimuli, with the qualification that the range of transient stimuli that evoke awareness is probably relatively narrow, and also that the experience of awareness is indeed far from normal.

But the answer appears to be yes for other visual attributes—the striate cortex *is* essential for experience. Thus, none of the subjects whose spectral sensitivity curves were measured, or those who could discriminate one wavelength from another, reported any experience of *colour*, as such. Stoerig and Cowey comment in their spectral sensitivity paper, 'The patients were often asked whether they could perceive anything when the blind field was tested. Throughout the experiments, which involved from 2 to 4 three-hour sessions per month for approximately 6 months, they consistently claimed that this was not the case and that they never saw or felt anything that was related to stimulus presentation.' (1991, p. 1496). Stoerig and I, and Stoerig, Barbur, and I (both studies unpublished) found good evidence of wavelength discrimination in G.Y., but he did not experience colour as such. In the study by Brent *et al.* (1994), G.Y. did report the transient experience of the onset of the stimulus, but not its *colour*. With D.B. similar findings were obtained for orientation discrimination. When he was required to guess whether the lines on a grating were horizontal or non-horizontal, under appropriate conditions D.B. reported 'an impression of something coming in' when the grating was flashed onto the screen in his blind field, but insisted that he was 'guessing about the orientation', although he in fact had performed at 95% correct! (Under other conditions, he performed in the complete blindsight mode for orientation discriminations; that is, he had no experience even of the flash itself but performed at a high level for orientation, indeed at 95% for discriminating by guessing the difference between a horizontal grating and another oriented at 45° from horizontal, Weiskrantz, 1986, p. 71.)

But hold on! A more radical view has recently been championed, namely that the striate cortex is not only essential for visual experience, but for blindsight itself! It has been suggested that perhaps there are tags, *islands* of striate cortex that escape damage, and it is these that are responsible for the residual capacity. Without striate cortex, no visual function, whether experienced or not. This view really harks back to an older view of the matter, already consolidated in the nineteenth century. William James summarized the contemporary wisdom: 'The literature is tedious *ad libitum* . . .'. The occipital lobes are indispensable for vision in man. Hemiopic disturbance comes from lesion of either one of them, and total blindness, sensorial as well as psychic, from destruction of both.' (1890, p. 47). From this knowledge, known even in James' time, that monkeys without visual cortex could still make visual discriminations, a thesis emerged that visual function in people becomes 'encephalized', that visual cortex may not be essential in monkeys but because of an upward evolutionary migration of function it becomes essential in humans (see Marquis, 1935, and critique by Weiskrantz, 1961).

It must be stressed once again that in humans damage to the brain is erratic—head injuries, surgery, and so forth do not reproduce exactly the same lesions from case to case—and no blindsight patient (fortunately) has yet come to post-mortem, so we do not know whether there are any tags. But the idea that such tags might be involved was advanced recently by Michael Gazzaniga and colleagues (Fendrich et al., 1992; Gazzaniga et al., 1994) because they found a tiny island of intact function in an otherwise dead visual hemifield of a patient with occipital damage. They found this using an 'eye tracker' which allowed the visual image to be absolutely immobile; if the eye moved, the image moved with it. Their patient was instructed, of course, to maintain fixation, but perhaps could not do so reliably. The result was that the patient could detect a dark spot on a light background at a level better than chance (about 65% correct, chance being 50%); it was blindsight because the patient did not acknowledge seeing it. They also found a bit of intact striate cortex at the occipital pole. It cannot be said, however, that this tissue corresponded to the island of function. That patient was entitled to have some intact striate cortex at the pole because he had macular sparing (i.e., some spared visual field near the fixation point; this is not uncommonly found in hemianopic patients, for reasons we need not go into here). Michael Gazzaniga and colleagues argue that the reason that not all hemianopic patients demonstrate blindsight is because they do not all have such tags of tissue. And so we should deal with the question of tags of tissue and patchy vision, and also the question of why not all patients demonstrate blindsight—if they do not.

It may well be that other cases like Fendrich et al.'s exist, but it is difficult to accept their interpretation as general for residual function (cf. Stoerig and Weiskrantz, 1993). First, it cannot apply to the animal evidence, where the completeness of the lesion and the absence of islands of striate cortex can be confirmed with certainty. We have seen, in fact, that the monkey without striate cortex in one hemisphere behaves like the human blindsight subject for visual events projected to the affected blind hemifield (see Chapters 1 and 4). But Gazzaniga et al. (1994) are unwilling to accept the animal evidence, even for this early stage of visual processing and despite the close similarity of the monkey's and human's visual pathways.

Another reason for doubting the generality of the 'island of cortex' explanation is provided by the remarkable ability of the blindsight subject G.Y. to mimic with hand movements the paths of motion of a small spot moved through a variety of trajectories spread out over a large area of his affected hemifield, as shown earlier in Fig. 3.2. For this capacity to be explained on the basis of tags of intact tissue would require a virtual archipelago, not just the odd single island (Weiskrantz, 1995)! But his high resolution scan does not show any striate cortex whatsoever, aside from the tissue at the occipital pole most reasonably related to his macular sparing. (Needless to say, the movement experiment was tested well outside that macular spared region.) Nor does his PET scan show any V1 activity during a movement discrimination task (and this is also confirmed in a recent fMRI study of G.Y.—no activity in V1 is detected, Steve Williams, personal communication). Finally, G.Y.'s ability to maintain visual fixation is incredibly good, and this has been measured as a matter of routine in many experiments. But to be certain that no islands were being missed, an eye tracker device was also used to carry out exactly the same experiment with G.Y. that Fendrich et al. (1992) had performed with their patient; we used the same model instrument and the same visual parameters. The result was that no isolated islands were discovered in G.Y. (Kentridge et al., in press); the functional area was more like a continent, although—pursuing this metaphor—the northern hemisphere was more sensitive than the southern. (In fact, it turned out that the original parameters chosen by Fendrich et al. were not optimal: better results were obtained with G.Y. with higher contrast and longer intervals, and it is possible that the residual island of Fendrich et al.'s patient might have expanded using those conditions.)

The question of the *incidence of blindsight*—indeed, of *all* the categories of residual capacity without acknowledged awareness reviewed in Chapter 1— remains to be explored more intensively. Certainly not all patients with damage to the visual cortex have yielded evidence of blindsight when tested; on evidence thus far, only a minority do. This contrasts with the amnesic syndrome, where it seems that the very large majority of patients do demonstrate implicit memory. But the true incidence of blindsight really is not yet known. There are several possible reasons for negative results in blindsight. The first reason, and almost certainly the most important, is that the location and extent of lesions are not uniform across patients. It is virtually impossible to have a pure V1 lesion in humans because V1 is buried deep in the brain. In monkeys if the lesion extends beyond V1, residual visual capacity becomes severely degraded (Pasik and Pasik, 1971).

A second reason is that the age at which the damage occurs may be important, as suggested by animal research on the visual system (Payne, 1994). Thus, patients whose injuries occurred early in life may be more likely to exhibit blindsight than patients whose injuries occurred later. D.B.'s brain damage, in fact, may have originated prenatally. G.Y.'s head injury occurred when he was 8 years old.

A third reason is that the stimulus parameters used when testing for blindsight can be critical, such that a person showing no evidence of residual function might yield different results when tested under different conditions. One cannot demonstrate the universal negative, but one can sometimes demonstrate that it does not hold. This was the case, for example, with G.Y. himself. When he was tested thoroughly under particular conditions that work well for normal vision, he was reported to show no evidence whatever of residual vision (Hess and Pointer, 1989), and the existence of residual function was dismissed, somewhat disparagingly it must be said. But when the speed of onset of the stimuli was increased just slightly, his performance jumped from chance to virtually perfect levels (Weiskrantz *et al.*, 1991), as shown in Fig. 6.9. The parameters that might work well for normal vision may not be optimal for blindsight.

A fourth reason for the variable incidence of blindsight is the very strangeness of the question the researcher asks a subject in such a study. 'Tell me whether the stimulus you could not see at all fell within the first or second of two successive time intervals', for example. Such questions do not favour easy cooperation or credibility. Indeed, some subjects refuse to play such a strange game, and some experimenters no doubt find it awkward to ask these strange questions and may well indicate shared, even bemused, scepticism when doing so. This last difficulty is compounded by the fact that systematic studies require thousands of trials over days or even months, so only long-suffering subjects are willing or able to be available. It is for such a reason, as already discussed in Chapter 3, that investigators interested in blindsight are currently developing implicit and indirect methods, such as pupillometry and 'visual completion', homologous to the indirect tests used to study aspects of cognitive processing in other syndromes after brain damage, such as amnesia.

There is another approach to the subject which, in a sense, is even more indirect: it is to seek blindsight in normal subjects. This quest is quite different, let it be said, from simply looking for above-chance performance in the vicinity of near-threshold performance. We argued in Chapter 2 that blindsight is not simply degraded normal perception, not just a pale shadow of the real thing. One reason for this, among others, is the high level of performance that can be achieved in blindsight, far above the need to appeal to squeezing statistical significance out of borderline, shadowy data.

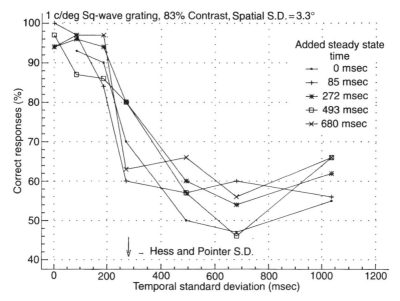

Figure 6.9. G.Y.'s performance in detecting the occurrence of a stimulus in his blind hemifield as a function of the steepness of its temporal onset and offset, in a two-alternative forced-choice paradigm. The size and structure of the stimulus were held constant, but randomly from trial to trial the temporal envelope was changed. (The steepness of the onset is measured in terms of the standard deviation of a Gaussian envelope, as shown on the x-axis—the smaller the standard deviation, the sharper the rise and fall of the stimulus.) It was also possible to vary the length of time the stimulus remained at its peak contrast level, resulting in the family of 5 curves shown. The results of Hess and Pointer (1989) could be confirmed using their temporal value. But a slight increase in the steepness of the onset and offset yielded sharply improved performance approaching perfection. (Reprinted with permission from Weiskrantz et al., 1991, Oxford University Press.)

But, without rehearsing that argument further, another approach has recently been suggested in a recent paper in *Nature* by Christof Kolb and Jochen Braun (1995), based directly on neurophysiological properties of visual cortex. They have reasoned that neurones in V1 are sensitive to some kinds or levels of visual information that cannot be processed by neurones in projection areas to which V1 sends information, especially V5. And so they designed their perceptual tests under two different condition, using stimuli which can be projected forwards by V1, and those which cannot. They report that normal subjects are aware of the former, but not the latter (the subjects had to report, by guessing if necessary, in which quadrant of a computer screen a critical target occurred). After each trial the subject also indicated whether he or she was confident about the correctness of the judgment. In the conditions in which the subjects were aware, they were also confident that they were discriminating correctly. However, the important finding is that when subjects were forced to guess about the critical non-projectable displays of which they were unaware, their discrimination was at well above chance levels, and showed no correlation whatever with their confidence estimates made after each trial. They argue that this blindsight information still reaches other relevant visual cortices over the more circuitous sub-cortical routes, rather than by a direct projection from V1. It is not clear, in that case, why the subjects are not aware of this information, which is good enough to sustain discrimination, a point that is not discussed in the paper by Kolb and Braun. Nor of course is their demonstration exactly like blindsight in a precise literal sense, because their subjects were very well aware of the highly visible stimulus screen as a whole. It is just the information on a projected-onto part of the screen that they missed. Nevertheless, the approach is a novel and interesting one, and shows promise of mapping onto the same mechanisms as are disturbed in patients. As it can be carried out on the voluminous supply of normal subjects, one would not have to depend on the smallish sample of brain damaged subjects and also, of course, PET and fMRI imaging could be used to investigate critical neural structures.

To return to the question of critical pathways for blindsight in patients. In those patients in whom it is found, we have seen that the striate cortex appears to be an essential player in the cortical cast for awareness of all types of visual stimuli, with the exception of transient visual events. But is it *sufficient*? We have seen, for example, that parietal lesions can lead to a hemifield of visual neglect even with striate cortex intact. More critically and importantly, what about experiments that remove *non-visual* cortex but leave visual cortex intact? The first study to attempt this was by Roger Sperry and colleagues (1960), at the California Institute of Technology, who removed 'most' of the non-visual neocortex in cats, but left visual cortices intact. This was done only in one hemisphere so that the animals were not paralysed. Visual inputs to the remaining hemisphere were blocked either by severing the inter-hemisphere commissure (the corpus callosum) and masking one eye, or by sectioning the optic fibres entering it. The animals had severe visual deficits on a variety of visual discriminations (most severe, interestingly, for an inverted vs. an erect 'V', in which the orientation of the components are identical—cf. above for 'form' discrimination in D.B.), but were able to recover some discriminative capacity, although the deficits remained severe. It is not possible to draw any firm inferences about which non-visual structures were important— 'removal of temporal cortex produced no greater, and perhaps somewhat less impairment of vision than did removal of the frontal region', and in no case was the non-visual neo-cortical removal complete.

Sperry, in the same paper, also mentioned a related experiment in progress with similar isolation of the occipital cortex in a split-brain monkey with removal of all or most of non-visual cortex but with sparing of the geniculo-striate tract. This was 'observed (Sperry, unpublished) to produce even a greater blinding effect than in the cat.' This must be the study subsequently published by Michael Gazzaniga (1966), one of Sperry's coworkers at the time, describing two monkeys with forebrain commissur-otomy and midline section of the optic chiasm such that the visual input to one hemisphere was removed without damaging visual cortex. Unilateral lesions were made in the other hemisphere of frontal parietal, and temporal cortex (Fig. 6.10), and the animals tested with a patch covering the eye projecting to the intact hemisphere. These monkeys 'appeared to be functionally blind. . . . Neither could track and neither would react to a threatening gesture.' They bumped into obstacles, and could not relearn a previously acquired pattern discrimination (only one animal tested). Both had a pupillary response to light. The animals were kept alive for only 26 and 30 days, and so the long-term effects could not be assessed.

This was not a problem in the studies carried out in monkeys by Richard Nakamura and Mortimer Mishkin, 1980 (1982, 1986) at the U.S. National Institutes of Health, who were able to study permanent effects. The lesion was only made in one hemisphere, with the forebrain commissures and the optic tract in the other hemisphere cut so as to remove any visual input to that hemisphere. The spared cortex included striate and prestriate cortex, inferotemporal cortex, cingulate gyrus, ventral frontal cortex and medial temporal cortex (Fig. 6.11). In the 1980 study, one monkey showed recovery of pattern discrimination after 40 days. But the other three remained blind for as long as they were tested, including one that was still blind after 2 years, when the paper was published. 'There was no detectable reaction to visually presented stimuli, whether these were food, fearful objects, threats, or sudden movements.' In a strange room they bumped into obstacles, and only found scattered peanuts by touching them accidentally. These three animals could not be retrained on a visual pattern discrimination.

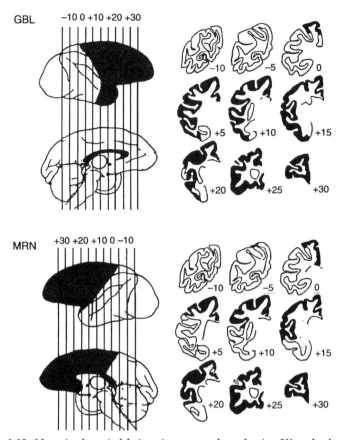

Figure 6.10. Non-visual cortical lesions in two monkeys, leaving V1 and other visual cortical areas intact. GBL and MRN are the codes for identifying the monkeys. The numbers on the lines traversing the brain diagrams refer to cross-sectional views. (Reprinted with permission from Gazzaniga, 1966.)

There is some ambiguity about the definitions of visual and non-visual cortical areas. Many regions that lie outside the more conventional definition of visual cortex will respond to visual stimulation. We use the term to refer to those cortical areas that are exclusively visual, or at least predominantly visual, and in which connexions with V1 have been mapped out—that is, the definition is distinctly V1-centric. Some of the maps of extra-striate areas have been refined, of course, since Gazzaniga's, and Nakamura and Mishkin's experiments. The lesions in those studies may be compared with a more recent summary of visual areas (Felleman and Van Essen, 1991; cf. also Crick, 1994) defined in this V1-centric manner. The relation between visual cortex and other more remote areas will be taken up more fully in Chapter 8.

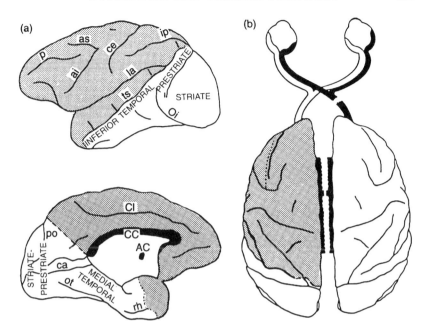

Figure 6.11. Non-visual cortical lesions in two monkeys, leaving V1 and other visual cortical areas intact. (Reprinted with permission from Nakamura and Mishkin, 1980.)

We do not know, as Nakamura and Mishkin acknowledge, whether the three animals that remained blind in the study just cited could have been shown to have residual vision if they were tested more extensively and sensitively, along the lines pursued by Humphrey (1974); Pasik and Pasik (1980); Keating (1980), although it seems unlikely that nothing would have been noted over a two-year period. However, perhaps some degree of spared vision might have emerged with more focused and more persistent testing. It is worth stressing that this result of the procedures used by Nakamura and Mishkin is far more extreme than that caused by bilateral V1 ablation itself, where after some time animals respond to moving stimuli with pursuit eye movements. Also, it is important to note that the non-visual cortex included the posterior parietal cortex, the target of the so-called visual dorsal stream leaving striate cortex which is essential for control of spatial functions such as visually guided reaching. David Milner and Mel Goodale argue that this visual 'action' may be mediated via the dorsal stream, and that such action may not require visual perceptual awareness. The matter is discussed in Chapter 8.

It would be of great interest to know whether there is any particular lesion of non-visual cortex that is absolutely crucial for producing this striking outcome. Nakamura and Mishkin followed this up, but unfortunately no clear conclusion can be reached. For example, were the forebrain commissures (the corpus callosum and the anterior commissure) an essential link in isolating the visual cortex when non-visual cortex in one hemisphere was removed; that is, would blindness result if the visual cortex remaining in one hemisphere could communicate with motor and other functional areas left intact in the other hemisphere if the commissures connecting the two were left intact? We already know that the commissures, by themselves, are not necessary for monkeys (or people) to use visual information from one hemisphere to guide the accurate reaching of the arm and hand controlled by the opposite hemisphere. Apparently sub-cortical pathways can mediate visuomotor control. Nevertheless, Nakamura and Mishkin did report in their 1986 paper that one animal with a contralateral non-visual lesion and a unilateral optic tract cut in the opposite hemisphere 'recovered vision within an average of 10 days of surgery. . . . Subsequent forebrain commissurotomy, however, rendered them permanently blind.' In contrast, however, in a study mentioned in their 1980 paper, total blindness was obtained in other monkeys even when the forebrain commissures were left intact, which means that the blindness in those animals cannot have been due simply to a disconnexion of visual from motor pathways. They conclude in those cases that 'the visual signal is not processed beyond striate cortex, for otherwise the signal should have been transmitted across the preserved commissural channels, which start at the striate–prestriate border.' Apparently the commissures are important in some animals but not in others as an essential constituent of recovery of visual function, depending presumably on the precise, but as yet undetermined, disposition of the non-cortical lesions. There might also be endogenous individual differences. In addition, there are some species differences, as it appeared that the same lesions in cynomologus monkeys produced a more severe effect than in the rhesus monkey (for which the authors give a reasonable account in terms of histology).

Nakamura and Mishkin also found that, in general, 'enlargement of the nonvisual ablation in rhesus monkeys so as to include all of the limbic cortex except the hippocampus and parahippocampal gyrus drastically exacerbates the loss of visual performance, transforming what had been a short-term and largely recoverable effect into an apparently permanent one'. However, it also appears from their diagrams that this enlargement included not only limbic cortex but also basal ganglia, which are important sub-cortical motor nuclei. Even so, there was a very instructive exception to the conclusion that enlargement to include limbic cortex played a crucial role: the exception was a cynomologus monkey

> in which the entire prefrontal cortex was purposely spared and in which there was also nearly complete sparing of cingulate gyrus [part of limbic cortex]. Yet, despite preservation of all limbic cortex [and all of prefrontal cortex], this animal remained blind until it was sacrificed about seven months postoperatively. . . . Apparently, far less than total ablation of nonvisual cortex may on occasion be sufficient to yield total and permanent loss of visual responsivity. (1986, p. 182).

This is obviously relevant to hypotheses that prefrontal cortex plays a critical role in visual awareness (Crick and Koch, 1995).

In an intriguing Society for Neuroscience Abstract, Nakamura and Mishkin (1982) state that 'the large nonvisual cortical lesion can be viewed as being composed of three major components: sensorimotor, limbic, and polysensory regions. Effects on vision of removing individual components as well as all two-component combinations indicate that the three regions are graded in importance, with polysensory cortex most and sensorimotor cortex least important; all components, however, make some contribution since some visual recovery is possible if any is preserved.' The evidence for this conclusion, unfortunately, has not been published. And so we still do not know if there is a critical focus or foci, or whether mass within a large subclass of cortex is important. These are difficult experiments leading to an extreme result, and we may never know from them alone. Fortunately, we now can see functional imaging methods providing some clues without the need for procedures as extreme as removing all non-visual cortex. But at least we do know that far less than total ablation may on occasion be sufficient, and also that in some cases the isolation of the visual cortex can be breached by a route via the commissures. Why this breach occurs in some animals, but not others, may turn on finer details of the non-visual lesions and incidental damage, or equally on individual differences between animals.

We *do* know, however, even in the face of ignorance of where such a route might lead, that the primary visual cortex itself is not 'turned off' by the lesion that renders the animals apparently blind (Nakamura and Mishkin, 1980, 1982, 1986; Nakamura *et al.*, 1986; Mishkin, personal communication). The striate cortex itself is still functional, because an evoked potential to a visual signal could be recorded in it, and single neurones also showed normal processing of information in V1 (Nakamura *et al.*, 1986).

The implications of this set of results are important. On the assumption that these animals had no visual *awareness*, it means that for awareness to occur there must be an interaction between visual cortex and structures lying entirely outside of them. Not only is striate cortex not sufficient for visual functioning, but neither is *any other area of extra-striate visual cortex*, working in tandem or hierarchically connected with it. The fact that striate cortex removal still leaves a visual function intact does not mean that one can simply transfer the burden from striate cortex to one of its neighbours; you have to go outside the whole set of visual cortices closely married to V1 before discovering what is important for allowing these visual areas to achieve awareness—if they do. To take one concrete example: G.Y., who has a V1 lesion, is aware of movement, and 'human V5' lights up in the PET scan when he is discriminating movement direction. From this it cannot be concluded that V5 is sufficient for awareness of movement. Indeed, it cannot be concluded that any of the other visual areas that light up (e.g. V3, area 7) are sufficient. The reason is that all of these areas were perfectly intact in the Nakamura and Mishkin preparation, and yet the animal failed to respond to motion or to threats. (There is a slight qualification to make to this conclusion in the Nakamura and Mishkin study, because it appears from the histological reconstructions (Nakamura and Mishkin, 1986) that V5, which lies at the depths of the superior temporal sulcus, might have been partly damaged, but it would seem that this was equally so in those monkeys that recovered as those that did not. No such qualification is necessary for the Gazzaniga study, in which the lesion ended well forward of the superior temporal gyrus; areas V1, V2, V3, V4 and probably V5 were left intact.) For the same reason, 're-entry'— the feeding of visual information back into itself to achieve a visual synthesis, as advanced by Edelman (1989) and Zeki (1993)—cannot work if the source of the re-entry is wholly confined to the visual cortices themselves, as we know them. There is nothing to stop re-entry within this domain in these monkey preparations.

Given that the striate cortex remains active, and yet the animal is rendered functionally blind by removal of non-visual cortex, what accounts for its inability to control visual behaviour? There are various possibilities. One is that there is a disconnexion between visual cortex and the motor system, that is, an interruption of the *output* from visual cortex to relevant motor systems, such that the animals can see, but not control, movements based on vision. The fact that they bump into objects, for example, means that they can locomote; and eye movement mechanisms should be available to them via the midbrain. Given that visual control can be affected over sub-cortical pathways to the contralateral hemisphere when the commissures are severed, it is difficult to see why this cannot also take place in these animals. It might also be that non-visual cortex exercises some kind of tonic control over visual cortex, related to arousal or some non-specific influence. That is, perhaps the non-visual cortical lesion removes an *input* into visual cortices. But, again, sub-cortical pathways might allow such an input via the sub-cortical routes, which typically involve anterograde as well as retrograde connexions and, in any event, we have seen that the visual cortices appear to retain normal electrophysiological properties. There is a third possibility, which is more bold than a disconnexion *to* the motor system, or *from* arousal influences. It is that the non-visual cortex is carrying out important processing itself, which may require an input from the striate cortex and its neighbours, but that also the visual cortices are modulated by an input *back* to it.

The hypothesis I would like to pursue is that what the Nakamura and Mishkin animals lack is visual *awareness*, and in the absence of the pathway essential for visual action, which does not require perceptual awareness, no visual behaviour can be initiated or provoked—at least, not without extensive training, which was not given to these animals. What the non-visual cortex lesion removes is the commentary stage, and the isolated visual cortex is unable to achieve a level at which vision becomes phenomenally *visual*. The interruption is both *to* that stage, and back *from* it, that is, the commentary stage leads to further processing and filtering with the visual cortices themselves. Wherever the assumed commentary stage exists, whether it is in one place or distributed, it must be in a form that normally is associated with integrated processing in coordinates in which objects are represented rather than retinal coordinates in which the earlier stages of visual processing are conducted (Marr, 1982). Also, in humans, it must be in a form that allows ready access to verbal and other communicative systems and similarly, in monkeys, that allows them to convey visual information to their fellows, and I would like to assume—as in humans—to themselves. In Chapter 8 we pursue the hypothesis further.

Before that, however, we will turn to a consideration of some aspects of the evolutionary issues of possession and loss of conscious awareness.

7

The evolutionary 'Why?'

If an attribute or capacity is worth having, why? In an evolutionary sense, what advantage accrues to consciousness? What has been, or is being selected? There have been countless suggestions, including one that declares consciousness to be nothing more than an epiphenomenon and hence rendering the question pointless. In this spirit, T.H. Huxley likened consciousness to a locomotive's steam-whistle; it has no effect on the engine but is there just as an ancillary and powerless gadget. To which came the counter from Lloyd Morgan (of canonical repute): if it is useless, why did it ever evolve? To which an evolutionist must provide an answer. For many, the evolutionary question has been put on hold until there is some philosophical or scientific resolution regarding its status. There are those who despair of coming to grips with such a vague concept, difficult to define, variable in its application to everyday usage, and dependent on private experience. It can be acknowledged that the term is used in a large variety of different ways and with all kinds of nuances, but here we restrict it to those dissociations that have emerged from the neuropsychological syndromes under review, as discussed in earlier chapters. Even within the neuropsychological arena, we distinguish between 'aware of' (such as blindsight, in which subjects discriminate stimuli *of* which they are unaware), and 'aware that' (such as amnesia, in which subjects are capable of demonstrating good learning and retention, but are not aware *that* they have such a capacity). It can be further acknowledged that the latter set of dissociations of awareness from residual function are the more varied and more difficult to come to grips with. But, in the end, we were driven to consider the question of such dissociations not because of any philosophical yearnings or obsessions with the mind–body problem. Indeed, thirty years ago, very few scientists would venture without trepidation into such a supposedly metaphysical realm if they wished to command the respect of colleagues or the support of a research council. But it was the patients themselves whom we encountered so long ago who forced us to recognize that they had lost their sense of awareness of capacities, and not their capacities as such, or at least not the whole of these capacities.

If a physical device, even one consisting of neurones, cannot instantiate conscious events without a radical change in our concepts of physics or their quantal applications (Penrose, 1989), mundane questions of evolutionary selection will also have to be recast. I do not know how selection might occur for events at a quantum mechanical level! On the other hand, if potentially a Turing post-doctoral computer with the right software is entitled, in principle, to have whatever attributes humans possess, including consciousness (Dennett, 1991), selection becomes more straightforward in principle, although of course one must decide just what aspect of capacity offers the selective advantage.

On this front, there have been two prominent suggestions, one based on social factors, the other on communication. The argument from social value turns on the advantages of understanding and predicting what goes on in the minds of other creatures. Such an interpretation is greatly aided by analogy with one's introspective understanding and knowledge of one's own motivations, anxieties, and past strategies. This I take to be important, but much too narrow and even misleading as an evolutionary advantage. Creatures are socially complicated throughout the vertebrate kingdom, and indeed throughout much of the invertebrate kingdom, but most have evolved perfectly good ways of dealing with their social demands without being burdened with a theory of the mind, or any other theory. Perversely, humans are the only creatures that have social problems of any serious kind. One reason for this is precisely because they are conscious and can fret and fantasize about all of the social complications that may be confronted; moreover, humans' introspective understandings and insights are often creative mnemonic embellishments and circumlocutions rather than direct records of historical truths about motives and causes. Paranoia is a species-specific penalty humans pay for this gift of consciousness. Perhaps chimpanzees can be paranoid, but I very much doubt that the bat or the frog or the tortoise can be.

On the other hand, it may well be that complex social exchanges, especially between parents and children, are crucial as a framework for the development of awareness. Horace Barlow (1988) put this eloquently:

> To enlarge [its] experience and bring it partly under his control the infant
> brain must build a model of what it is interacting with, that is a model of the

mother and her brain which will tell the infant when smiles will be returned, and when other responses and interactions will occur. . . . Thus the content and validity of introspection can be enlarged, but only by social experience leading to the incorporation of models of other people's minds. On this view the crucial feature of consciousness is that it *requires* a remembered partner for its introspection: consciousness is taught, awakened and maintained by interactions with other modelled minds. . . . Thus consciousness becomes the forum, not of a single mind, but of the social group with whom the individual interacts.

This definition of consciousness is much broader than the concept of sensory awareness *per se*—linked, as it is, to the introspective stream within and about a mental model—but its development may go hand in hand with sensory awareness. Ingenious studies of pre-linguistic human infants demonstrate a good capacity for a variety of visual discriminations. The human infant may not be able to locomote or to speak, but its eyes are very active. It will look preferentially at some visual stimuli over others (e.g. an arrangement of lines to make a sketch of a face as opposed to the same lines randomly arranged). It will also gradually lose interest if the same pattern is repeatedly presented, and direct its gaze to another stimulus, which demonstrates the discrimination. But Spelke, who carried out many of these experiments, suggests that 'infants do not perceive the unity, boundaries, and persistence of objects under all the conditions that are effective for adults.' She suggests that 'it may be misleading to say that objects are *perceived*. Objects may be known, instead, by virtue of an early developing *theory* of the physical world.' (1988, p. 168, italics in original). In other words, the mental models to which Barlow appeals may precede integrated perception itself. This is a difficult hypothesis to test; indeed, the whole question of how awareness develops—sensory, or otherwise—is virtually untouched by evidence. But because different pathways in the brain mature at different rates, it may eventually become possible to derive clues from the study of systems in the adult brain that are uniquely involved in awareness, if and when these emerge from imaging and neuropsychological studies.

Mental models not only have a framework and an extrapolation to other minds, they also have persistence. They also are readily invoked when the commentary stage is activated. And as children grow, knowledge of such persistence is projected into the future capabilities. All parents must have been struck by the behaviour of the young child who has suffered a fall: in seemingly intense (and noisy) agony one moment, smiling and romping happily the next. No adult sheds pain so rapidly! No adult, that is, unless the capacity has been shattered for remembering that pains persist. I have witnessed an Alzheimer patient shriek with pain because of movement by a nursing attendant of an arthritic limb, only for the blithely peaceful demeanour to return almost instantaneously when the movement stopped. Social complexity may enter into the genesis of consciousness, and may constitute an important part of the 'What?' of awareness, but is not in my view the main factor in the evolution of consciousness. As just argued, social arrangements have proved entirely satisfactory and stable for millions of years for practically the whole of the insect world and most of the vertebrate world. Man has an advantage over other creatures, but not primarily because of social arrangements or capacities as such.

Communication, especially in the form of human language, is another popular candidate for the evolutionary value of consciousness. Indeed, for some it is not only a prerequisite, it is synonymous with it. For Wittgenstein (1922, p. 5.62), 'the limits of language . . . mean the limits of my world.' If it were language that especially endowed one with consciousness, however, it would imply that only *Homo sapiens* were conscious, which few—and certainly not I—would wish to accept. That particular argument has been rehearsed in Chapter 4. But an argument could be developed along the line that consciousness, or awareness, for all individuals, of whatever species, is coextensive with their communicative behaviours. (I am indebted for this to my former teacher, Bill Verplanck, portions of whose recent e-mail correspondence I quote with permission.) 'In plain language, if I can tell you about "it" I am aware of "it", "it" is in consciousness. If I respond appropriately to what you say and do, then I am "conscious" of what you say and do.' The evolution of consciousness on such a view would go something like this: 'I tell you aloud what I see, what I am doing, and what you should do. I hear myself and say aloud, tell you (etc.), and as I tell you, I also tell myself aloud what I am telling you.' Finally, this overt communication becomes covert and unobservable by others, just as reading can be done silently. (Verplanck, incidentally, was one of the first to document evidence for learning without awareness, cf. his papers of 1955, 1956, and 1992.)

This position bears some relationship to the one that we have advanced throughout this book, namely that being aware means being able to make a commentary and, in the strong form of the hypothesis, that such a capacity may be endowing and not merely enabling, which in turn bears a formal, if not literal, relation to David Rosenthal's view that consciousness entails a thought about a thought. I distinguish the position we have advanced from one that simply defines awareness operationally in terms of the response by which it is measured. Obviously, one consequence of being aware is that one will able to communicate the commentary (not necessarily verbally, of course). But while a commentary entails communicative power, communicative power does not require awareness. Indeed, the sensitivity to 'body language' in 'giving the game away' means that communication has taken place without the communicator knowing that it has. The wagging of a dog's tail has high communicative value, but I have my doubts about whether the dog knows that it is communicating. (In fact, I have often wondered whether one could reward a dog for wagging its tail!) Many other animal signals are important for communication, but may be elicited automatically. The two positions, communicative behaviour and commentaries, come close together if one requires that the communicator *knows* that he or she is actually communicating, because I take it that a commentary has that epistemological status. But it clearly does not mean that a commentary necessarily leads to communication as such—it can remain private—nor that communication always entails awareness.

Bodily responses themselves, of course, can result in awareness—a sinking feeling in the gut or the pounding of one's heart. They stitch an important embroidered pattern on the fabric of emotional experience, and they play an important role in Antonio Damasio's intriguing discussion of 'somatic markers' (1994). The same question arises, however, for them, as for externally caused sensory events: how and when do felt bodily states themselves become conscious or, instead, remain unconscious, which may be their more typical state. That is, I contrast the present position with one that might endow felt bodily states, or their emotional concomitants, as being or providing the essential ingredients of awareness.

The clinical 'Why?'

The advocates for particular types of survival values leading to the evolution of consciousness have, thus far, argued from a priori positions, and in the nature of the situation have very little a posteriori evidence to bolster their positions. I take my own starting point from the clinic, based on the classical stance of drawing inferences about normal function from pathology. One way to find out what something is good for is to examine what it is like not to have it. We have seen that there is a broad spectrum of syndromes in which there is a loss of acknowledged awareness of capacities or their contents, ranging from detection, through selective attention, semantic and associative meaning, episodic memory, to language. These can occur, and typically do occur, as isolated deficits, but our quest is to see what difficulties they might share.

The message that emerges from the clinic is unmistakable: all of the syndromes can possess implicit processing, but none of the patients can live by implicit processing alone. It cannot be used by the patient in thinking or in imagery, and this is a severe penalty. The spectrum of impairments includes both those of knowledge (in prosopagnosia, amnesia, and aphasia, for example) and those of direct awareness of events as such (as in blindsight and unilateral neglect), and in that sense require quite different levels of analysis. But the patients all share a lack of awareness of the positive powers that remain intact, and deal with the contents of the relevant events in their daily lives and experience as though they were powerless, as indeed they are in practical terms. In this sense, they are disconnected from a conscious acknowledged awareness of the true status of those events (using the term disconnected descriptively and metaphorically, with no necessary implication as regards mechanism).

The amnesic patient is severely impaired, and requires continuous custodial care. Priming is intact, but of no evident use to the amnesic victim. He cannot relate what is primed today to what was primed yesterday, or to any other item in memory, including time and place and other (but not only) contextual information; he is functionally fixed in the semantic or procedural present. It is possible that being able to acquire new classically conditioned responses, such as withdrawing from a signal associated with heat, for example, could be of some service to the patient, but in adults such elementary pairings would most likely already have been established before the onset of amnesia, and preserved in the amnesic state. An amnesic child, on the other hand, might well benefit from the ability to acquire classical associations.

Similarly, the blindsight patient continues to fail to identify objects and to bump into them in his blind field. If he can detect a stimulus in the blind field, he does not know what it is. There may be some occasional benefit to him if he can duck as a rapidly zooming object approaches (although typically this is *not* a common response in blindsight subjects). The blindsight subject cannot image the stimulus, about which he has just guessed, in relation to other stimuli, or to their spatial setting, because it is not perceived. He can of course guess what it *might* look like if he actually were to see it, but that is a different matter, a matter of imagination rather than imaging. He may be able to discriminate wavelengths by forced-choice guessing, but he cannot relate the supposed colour of the current patch to the rainbow, the colour of his car, or the vase of daffodils, nor compare it with the colour he guessed about yesterday. And obviously a stimulus that is omitted in the half-field of a patient with unilateral hemi-neglect will suffer the same fate. And, the actual items being imageless, nor can they imagine them in relation to other percepts (although in blindsight, of course, this does not preclude a subject using the inputs to his intact hemifield for imagery in the normal way, and attempting to imagine the unseen in those terms, but the patients' descriptions suggest it may be difficult and strange). In addition, and perhaps crucially, the typical blindsight subject has an intact unilateral hemifield of vision with which to negotiate the world. For this question it would be helpful to study the relatively rare bilateral cases, and we are pursuing this at this moment— although for humane reasons one does not wish such patients to be common. One such case was studied by Perenin *et al.* (1980) with encouraging results, but not in great detail or longitudinally. These cases could tell us more about the capacity and potential of a total blindsight field, but no one imagines that such a patient would be able to negotiate the visual world with any great measure of success. Object identity, especially, is likely to be severely deficient, judging from the evidence from the effects of bilateral occipital lesions in the sub-human primate (Humphrey, 1974).

The prosopagnosic patient fails to recognize faces of members of his family, even though his autonomic nervous system does. The skin response does not overcome nor compensate for his social embarrassment, nor for his inability to use familiarity of faces as a guide to everyday events. The prosopagnosic is unaware of his ability to treat familiar faces as familiar in contrived test situations, and hence all faces, appearing unfamiliar, are merely isolated presentations unrelated to past associations or to each other. Again, the patient with unilateral neglect may covertly process visual information in his neglected field, but he himself ignores food on the left side of his plate!

Finally, perhaps the most severely disabled, the aphasic patient: there is a failure to comprehend and to communicate even though implicitly ('on-line') some patients can process both the semantics and syntax of spoken language. They would probably not even believe that they have this capacity, and even if they did it would be of precious little use to them.

In each of these domains, as mentioned, fortunately the deficit is specific. There are, of course, more complex compounds of deficits: the patient with advanced Alzheimer's disease combines more than one deficit in a cocktail that delivers a deadly punch. (However, even the Alzheimer's patient rarely exhibits cortical blindness: the striate cortex, and other primary sensory receiving areas of cortex seem to be largely impervious to this degenerative process.) But within each domain, what the patient cannot do is *think* or *imagine* in terms of the capacity or contents of which they are unaware. Of course, they can use their imagination; agnosic patients can trawl their memories for faces, or objects. In the next chapter a contrast is discussed, between the trawlings of two particular prosopagnosic patients studied by Andy Young *et al.* (1994). But within all of the domains we have considered, by definition none of these patients have negotiable knowledge of the material they cannot discriminate or detect explicitly, nor can they tell you about the contents of the material which they may be able to process covertly, nor can they talk to themselves about it either. Lloyd Morgan (1890) borrowed a phrase from Mivart that sums it up for me: 'If a being has the power of thinking "thing" or "something," it has the power of transcending space and time.'

On this view—perhaps not a startling conclusion—to be conscious is to be able to manipulate items in thought and imagery, to be conscious of the actual content of one's sensory experience. It does not necessarily mean being involved in strenuous or demanding thought, in everyday parlance, but it means that one's perceptions or ruminations must be cast in a form that would allow such manipulations. It is not only thought itself, in cold cognitive terms, that is lost, but also the associated emotional imagery that provides richness and affect to the contextual inter-weaving within the conscious stream, rightly stressed by Damasio (1994). The evolutionary value of thinking and imagery, in these terms, is somewhat easier to grasp than that of the value of consciousness, because it somehow appears not to venture beyond the traditional boundaries of psychological subject matter, and moreover, no one—short of the most extreme behaviourist—is apt to consider thinking or emotional content to be epiphenomena. But it is, in this view, the same domain—at least for the meaning of consciousness that is relevant to these particular clinical conditions. This is not awareness detached from behaviour, however; it is its powerful control of adaptive behaviour by which thinking lends substance to survival value.

On that basis, detections or other responses fixed in the immediate present in time and space, in the absence of an acknowledged awareness, are simply that—responses without awareness. In Rosenthal's terms, they are first-order thoughts without accompanying second-order thoughts (although I find it jars to talk of a *thought* of which one is unaware). If a creature were going to survive on such a basis, then the nervous system must be hard-wired so that the reactions necessary for survival and reproduction become automatic or 'instinctual'. And for many creatures, not excluding man, such hard-wired 'innate releasing responses' are well developed, including those involved in social interactions. Evolution restricted to such an arrangement occurs within populations of organisms, of colonies of individuals or their genes. Once commentaries can render the first-order thoughts manipulable, with the power of thinking 'thing' or 'something', evolution can be intra-individual, can be for what Richard Dawkins (1976) has labelled 'memes'.

However the jump occurred in evolution—whether it was gradual rather than abrupt (a first-order thought plus a half of a second-order thought?), whether it took a quantal leap with the evolution of language— it is not a jump that an individual can make occur by command or by practice. The teacher who implores, 'think, child, think!' can only have an effect if that child has the capacity (not to mention the desire) to do so, and even then it is characteristically an empty gesture! Similarly, the retraining of patients creates serious and seemingly almost intractable problems. Whatever else might be possible, one cannot go from the first-order to the second-order, from implicit to explicit, by 'trying harder' or by some kind of 'willed thought' prothesis. But is there some more principled route to functional prothesis?

Practice and retraining: can the covert be made overt?

There is not a large body of evidence bearing on the question of whether a patient's implicit capacity—that is, residual capacity without awareness— can be transformed into an explicit mode by training? Some modest progress has been made in the retraining of patients within some of the neuropsychological domains we have been considering, but much remains largely unexplored, despite the great benefits that would result were the efforts successful. Aside from such humane practical considerations, if the covert could be converted to the overt, we would learn much about the theoretical nature and boundaries of the two realms. Blindsight has received the greatest concentrated attention, perhaps because animal results have demonstrated quite positively that practice can help to improve sensitivity within field defects caused by striate cortex lesions.

Cowey (using a two-alternative key-press situation for a presence/ absence discrimination in a 'monkey perimeter') was the first to show this in a quantitative and systematic way (Cowey, 1967; cf. also review by Weiskrantz and Cowey, 1970). Striate cortex lesions in the monkey produce local visual impairments—visual field defects—lying approximately where they would be predicted from known anatomy and electrophysiology. The threshold for detection of a briefly presented target is markedly elevated within this defective region, most severely in its centre, but nowhere is it absolute. Strikingly, the ability of the monkey to detect a target with a given intensity of stimulation within the field defect improves markedly, by more than 2 or 3 log units (that is, from 100 to 1000 times), over several months of testing, and the field defect shrinks somewhat at its edges. But the improvement does not occur spontaneously: the animal must be engaged in repeated testing of this area of the visual field. Without such training, the shape and sensitivity of the field defect remains (as typically is reported for unpractised human subjects) largely static, even though *every* part of the animal's retina is being stimulated optically throughout the whole of its waking life in its everyday environment. Cowey found that a monkey's field defect remained unchanged for more than a year when the animal was not tested with stimuli within that field defect, but then showed a subsequent increase in sensitivity when such testing ensued. The pathways that are involved in the recovery have to be *pushed* into operation, *made* to be used, as it were, by repeated exercise, and not just passively stimulated.

This was shown dramatically in a study by Mohler and Wurtz (1977), using a testing situation in which monkeys were trained to make a saccadic eye movement to a visual stimulus projected into the small field defect resulting from a restricted visual cortical removal. These researchers, too, showed that there was a residual capacity, and that a gradual improvement of sensitivity occurred with repeated testing within the monkey's field defect. But when only *part* of the field defect was given such testing, that part recovered more than the remainder! They went on to show that the midbrain, more specifically the superior colliculus—which receives a direct projection from the eye—was involved in the recovery, because they could reinstate the field defect by making a lesion in that structure in the appropriate locus corresponding to the original field defect (determined by electrophysiological mapping). After that stage the field defect was static and showed no recovery. Also of significance was the fact that a superior colliculus lesion without the prior striate cortex lesion did *not* produce a field defect. That is, the superior colliculus had a critical sustaining and substitutive function in the absence of visual cortex, but not when it was intact.

The animal studies, however, do not tell us anything about recovery from blindsight *per se*, because we do not know whether these animals actually had blindsight, that is, whether their residual vision—either before or after the improvement—was discrimination without awareness. We now have reason to think that the monkey defect, indeed, can be that of blindsight, from the study by Alan Cowey and Petra Stoerig (see Chapter 4), but that was established in animals who were not studied for recovery with practice. Nor do we know anything (as yet) about the capacities of the recovered portion of the field for attributes other than those used directly in plotting the recovery, for example, for colour or orientation. The evidence for improvement with continued training does provide, however, at least a prima facie case for assuming that a training regime with human subjects might succeed in boot-strapping the residual function into more fully usable and 'conscious' vision. The challenge is especially striking because typically, as mentioned, field defects in man caused by cortical lesions have traditionally been described by neurologists as being remarkably stable and immutable. As this is often the message the clinicians also convey directly to the patients themselves, the likelihood that the patients will attempt any therapeutic regime is further reduced.

Sepp Zihl and his colleagues, more than any other investigators, have concentrated on examining the effects of practice and training on human subjects' field defects. Some of their studies were explicitly modelled on the Mohler and Wurtz procedure of measuring the accuracy of saccadic eye movements to targets in the blind field. (Control runs with 'blanks' were used, as a matter of course, to rule out unintended signals and other artifacts.) No feedback of results was given to the subjects. More recently, other researchers (Kasten and Sabel, 1995; Kerkhoff et al., 1994) have used similar methods and have reported encouraging results.

It is necessary to distinguish between two different types of outcome by this group of investigators. In some studies (Zihl, 1980), repeated practice (3 sessions per week for 3 to 5 weeks) with 3 subjects produced substantially improved accuracy, in one case to a virtually perfect level. But this improvement, it was said, remained within the blindsight mode. That is, it was reported that the subjects 'never reported seeing any targets during the test periods' (although it is also commented that 'after a few hundreds of trials two patients were sometimes able to "feel" the correspondence between target and eye position'). But this improvement in performance was said not to lead to a change in the size or shape of the clinically determined field defect with perimetry; the subjects simply became better 'guessers' (or possibly better 'feelers'). (N.B.: in the monkey, the methods available for determining limits of a field defect in a monkey perimeter (Cowey, 1963) would have led to a measured shrinkage of the field defect, even if the stimuli still remained not 'consciously seen' by the animal after the improvement; but Cowey's method of static perimetry involves many more trials—tens of thousands more—than is ever involved in clinical perimetry with human subjects.)

In the other type of outcome reached by Zihl and colleagues at the Max Planck Institute in Munich, there were elevations of visual stimuli, that previously could not be seen, into *seen* stimuli—consciously acknowledged as seen, with apparently normal attributes of colour, form, and acuity. Zihl and von Cramon (1985) carried out a training procedure closely similar to the one by Mohler and Wurtz described above, in which the subjects were instructed to move their eyes to the guessed position of a briefly flashed target. Some 80% of their group of 55 patients showed some enlargement of their visual fields, as clinically measured, most commonly by about 5° or less, but in some cases rather more. Even such a small increase, if it comes to include the region of high acuity near the fovea, can be very beneficial in enabling a patient to engage in fine-grained visual inspection and also to read. These results have been challenged by Balliett *et al.* (1985), who suggested that the shrinkage of the field defect was only found when the field was measured in a dynamic perimeter, that is, measuring the field limits with a moving target, but not with a static perimeter. However, Kasten and Sabel (1995) have used both types of perimeters and have reported positive findings with each. As with all regimes that depend upon practice, the length and persistence of the practice sessions are no doubt important.

Because the restored portions of the fields had form and colour, Zihl and coworkers concluded that in such cases the recovery must have been based on striate cortex surrounding the original source of the field defect that had not been irreversibly damaged. Indeed, their analysis of the aetiologies of their cases strongly suggested that vascular accidents, such as stroke (rather than closed head injuries, surgery, etc.), gave the best prognosis for training being beneficial. The median recovery of about 5° of radius of visual field is of the same order of magnitude as found with training in the monkey by Cowey. There, too, the argument for the enlargement *per se* (without regard to conscious perception, cf. Cowey, 1963) was also based on an assumption of laterally occurring inputs to striate cortex (e.g. as inferred from the phenomenon of lateral inhibition) that could be recruited through the training regime (cf. Weiskrantz, 1972); this finding was also supported by the animals having visual acuity appropriate for a visual field that extended 3 to 5° closer to the vertical mid-line than would have been predicted from a strict point-to-point retinal projection (Cowey, 1967; Weiskrantz and Cowey, 1970). This general argument is also in line with a variety of reports of a limited measure of plasticity of cortical 'wiring' when the balance of competitive inputs is changed (Merzenich and Kaas, 1980).

These accounts of improvements at the 'fringe' of the field defect probably do have a basis in the reorganization of the fringe of the damaged tissue itself, rather than any deeper boot-strapping from unconscious to conscious. The fact that it occurs in the monkey with surgical lesions rules out any exclusive aetiology of vascular accidents, as was the predominant case in the Zihl and von Cramon study. On the other hand, within the remaining 'unconscious' blindsight field, discriminative improvement occurs with training, but does not lift the improvement above a threshold for 'seeing' with acknowledged awareness (except perhaps to the level of 'feeling'). In the monkey Cowey found such an improvement with training, even when the striate cortex had been completely removed in one hemisphere, which caused a complete hemifield defect (Cowey, 1967). This improvement, therefore, *must* have been based on an extra-striate pathway. The evidence from Mohler and Wurtz (1977) referred to above implicated the superior colliculus for their particular response (saccadic eye movements), but there are a number of other extra-striate pathways that could be involved in residual capacity. We leave that matter to the next chapter.

One may wonder why such a simple procedure as requiring subjects to try to find a stimulus in the blind field as rapidly as possible, either by an eye movement or some other measure of detection, should be effective. The likely answer, especially for stimuli near the centre of the field defect, is that these procedures force the extra-striate pathways into use. Of course, if the subject is under no time pressure, he can move his eyes around randomly until the stimulus falls in the intact field. But with the subject trying to find the initially 'unseen' stimulus as rapidly as possible, the extra-striate pathways are put under pressure. And, as already indicated from the animal work, it is repeated pressure that apparently leads to the facilitated use of those pathways.

There is good evidence from other sensory modes, especially touch, that areas of cortex deprived of their normal sensory input can take over some responsibility for neighbouring regions (Merzenich and Kaas, 1980). Thus, a region of somatosensory cortex that normally responds when the thumb is touched may start to respond when an adjoining finger is touched. In the case of amputations, the effect can be dramatic. Ramachandran has shown that when regions near the missing arm are touched, the shoulder or the face, the subject reports a sensation *in the arm*. The regions of the body that yield this effect are the ones that are known to be adjacent regions of the arm area in the sensory cortex, the 'sensory homonculus'; that is, are brain areas next to the one that produces a sensation in the arm when electrically stimulated. Of course, in the situations we are concerned with in this book, it is not the sensory input that has been blocked, but the cortical targets themselves. Nevertheless, the evidence for plasticity just cited offers some encouragement for rearrangements at that level. In the case of recovery of fringes of the visual field, it could be argued that fringes of cortex either immediately adjacent to the damaged cortex, or even in a target served by a separate parallel pathway, are deprived of an input laterally from the damaged region, and thus are able to take on some of its functions. We have already noted that the visual acuity of a monkey with a macular visual field defect (i.e., placed in the centre of its visual field) is markedly better than might be expected from the map of the retina that projects to visual cortex. Because visual acuity falls off lawfully as a function of distance from the centre of vision, one can predict how much of a drop in acuity should occur with any given removal of the 'cortical map'. But the acuity shows less of a drop than it should (Weiskrantz and Cowey, 1970), as though the intact fringes of cortex can take on some of the capacity. (See Weiskrantz, 1972, for a further discussion of this finding.)

Because blindsight patients typically have a perfectly good half-field of intact vision, there is no particular pressure on them to press their blind fields into use. We could all negotiate the visual world remarkably well with just a half a field, especially if we learned to use eye and head movements more actively. Some patients, when legal licensing was more lax, drove automobiles with success (although with some anxiety to me as a passenger with one such patient, who could not always move his eyes or head rapidly enough to detect the single red light in the far left traffic lane of Magdalen Bridge in Oxford!). Fortunately for potential victims, bilateral occipital cases are relatively rare, and unfortunately for scientists, not to mention the patients themselves, are usually accompanied by other debilitating deficits when they do occur, although as mentioned there is at least one encouraging study of a bilateral occipital case (Perenin et al., 1980). Therefore we do not yet have a good idea about the properties of blindsight itself when the field defect extends over the whole visual field, nor about the recovery of function when there is an obvious pressure placed upon it to do so. The monkey, Helen, studied for so many years by Nicholas Humphrey, with a near total bilateral field defect produced by bilateral striate removal, came with time to have the ability spontaneously to avoid obstacles and to retrieve tiny visual objects, even specks of dust (although she was not able to identify them before touching or tasting).

These skills are greater than has been found for the affected half-fields of any of the blindsight subjects studied thus far, and suggest that under pressure the visual capacity may recover some of its sensitivity and ability to respond without prompting. For this and other reasons, blindsight investigators are obviously keen to study suitable bilateral occipital cases.

Dan Dennett (1991) offers more than a sneaking hope that confidence (plus feedback) will produce 'conscious' perception. He suggests an experiment that has never been done with a blindsight subject: suppose, he says, we give this person knowledge of results on each trial (this, as he rightly says, is typically not done in order minimize any unintended 'Clever Hans' cues from the experimenter). Let us tune up his 'guesses' to a maximum. 'Now suppose we start asking the subject to do it without cueing—to "guess when to guess", to guess "whenever the spirit moves you"'. Suppose the subject eventually becomes able to work without an external cue delivered by the experimenter, but cues himself and performs significantly above chance. If this were so, 'he could treat those experiences on a par with any conscious experiences. He could think about, and decide upon, policies that hinged on their occurrence as readily as on the occurrence of events consciously experienced.' (pp. 331–2).

Now, the crunch question: 'would this somehow *make* him conscious of the stimuli?' Dennett, along with people he says he asks about this, is open about the answer, but thinks it has a reasonable possibility of a positive outcome. This stems from his position that much of our normal vision is constructive and computational, based often on degraded inputs (such as we have in our peripheral visual fields). We can discriminate on the basis of patchy cues, and certainly the blindsight subjects can only glean paltry information from their blind fields—and their retina ganglion cell distribution might, indeed, be patchy. The question is whether there are some cognitive factors, like confident self-cueing, that would boot-strap the blindsight subject to a state of visual awareness of his encounters with visual events.

Dennett's experiment has not been carried out (as far as I know), but it seems to me unlikely to yield conscious perception on the basis of what we already know and what is to be found in our published research results. Subject D.B. often was tested with runs with stimuli that yielded high levels of confidence. When questioned after such a run, he would say, 'I got it right almost every time.' And he would be right about that. Yet, even so, he would firmly deny 'seeing'. In such a situation, it seems reasonable to assume that he assumed, or discovered, that he was in a good condition to guess, and also he somehow got his own feedback about his guesses, sometimes expressed in terms such as he 'felt' it, or 'knew' what was there. And yet I do not know of this ever graduating into acknowledged seeing. It might eventually happen, of course, but it is worth remembering just how many hundreds of thousands of opportunities for 'good guessing' these well-tested subjects have had in formal situations over several years, let alone the millions they have had in their daily lives.

The amnesic syndrome, being the first in which robust covert processing was uncovered through indirect testing, has been the focus of efforts to enlarge the repertoire of material that can be acquired by such a patient. It is the syndrome—amongst all of those we have discussed—for which perhaps the greatest benefit would be derived from therapy: blindsight and hemi-neglect patients still have a half-field of vision, but the amnesic patient is severely disabled in his everyday existence. Even the aphasic patient need not be deprived of the power to think and to reason (cf. evidence and discussion in Weiskrantz, 1988), whereas the amnesic patient is locked in the immediate present and is powerless to go beyond it in his thoughts about events. Moreover, the amnesic features are a conspicuous component of Alzheimer's disease and other degenerative disorders which are gathering such epidemiological momentum in the Western world's aging populations.

Peter Graf and Daniel Schacter (1985) have tried to discover whether new verbal associations can be acquired by amnesic patients using priming. Learning new pairings of words is a task that amnesic subjects find notoriously difficult to master when tested by being asked to recall each particular word that was paired with another particular word in the learning trial. But perhaps new associations can be acquired at an implicit level. Their subjects are given unrelated pairs of words, such as WINDOW–REASON and then tested for completion of, say WINDOW–REA vs. OFFICER–REA, with the inclusion of controls, of course, for pairs neither member of which had been presented (e.g. SHIP–CAS). The question was whether a new asociation would be demonstrated if subjects completed more stems in the same context (i.e., with WINDOW) and in the different context condition (i.e., OFFICER). Unfortunately, the results (Schacter and Graf, 1986) suggest that positive effects can be reliably found only in mildly amnesic patients rather than in the severe amnesics who, as we have seen, nevertheless typically show excellent priming for completion of single words.

On a more positive note, Schacter et al. (1991) and Gabrieli et al. (1990) have demonstrated successful priming in amnesic patients for drawings of novel objects or visual patterns (see Figs 5.5 and 5.6). We now know, as reviewed in Chapter 5, that a wide range of newly acquired materials is available to the amnesic patient via priming, including the learning of arbitrary semantic and syntactic rules. But these remain unavailable to the subject through recall or recognition. Heroic efforts have been made, with modest success, to use priming and particular mnemonic strategies to help amnesic patients guide themselves through their daily activities. They can be taught to use simple rules on a microcomputer, especially through the 'method of vanishing cues'. This method begins with the use of primes to acquire and access information but then the primes are gradually reduced and withdrawn. Severely amnesic patients have been taught the skills required for data-entry and word processing tasks. Electronic schedules, easily portable, offer other potential opportunities. In all these applications, of course, the demands of learning to use the device are by no means trivial, let alone the patient's knowing when and why to use them in a flexible environment. Excellent reviews, especially of the use of computers and other electronic aids, have been published by Glitsky (1995) and Kapur (1995). Barbara Wilson (1995) has also provided a very full and balanced account of various compensatory strategies, learning paradigms, group treatments, and external devices, set out in a humane and useful way for helping amnesic patients and their families. While a few successes can be documented with intelligent amnesic patients in the applied use of memory aids (e.g. patient J.C., described by Wilson, 1995), and other compensatory strategies, Wilson cautions that 'people with memory impairment and their families should not be led to believe that significant improvement in memory can occur once the period of natural recovery is over.' (p. 474).

In general, in fact, efforts to help the amnesic patient have provided crutches for support rather than success in healing the broken memory. Some subjects can be trained to establish implicit memories more efficiently. Thus, Baddeley and Wilson (1994) have shown that testing of retention by stem-completion is more efficient by amnesics using a procedure of 'errorless learning' designed to minimize false intrusions, and they suggest that the function of explicit memory—which the amnesics lack—is to correct such errors. Of course, this procedure helps the amnesic with implicit processing, but it still does not elevate him or her into an explicit processor. On a potentially more practical note, one amnesic subject was able to acquire complex new knowledge concerning the programming and operation of a microcomputer using the method of vanishing cues just described above (Glisky et al., 1986; Glisky, 1995) after several months of bi-weekly training sessions. The subject exhibited long-term retention with little forgetting across delays of up to 9 months (Glisky and Schacter, 1988). 'Nevertheless, when queried at the beginning of a session, K.C. could not remember any prior training episode and claimed that he had never worked previously on a microcomputer.' (Schacter, 1992, p. 183). No one has produced a breakthrough cure. It is possible that pharmacological and transplant treatments might one day find an application in the alleviation of the amnesic syndrome (either in its pure form, or as a major component of Alzheimer's disease), as they have in the treatment of Parkinson's disease, but so far results are not encouraging.

The evidence on memory disorders still favours the existence of relatively independent memory processing systems. When one of these is fractured, alas, the others do not step in to replace the injured system. Various taxonomic systems have been advanced to name these systems and their possible hierarchical ordering, but one practical, as well as theoretical, difficulty is that everyday demands draw on more than one memory processor. Thus, everyone agrees that the hallmark of the amnesic syndrome is the loss of episodic information, but acquisition of new semantic information is involved with a long-term semantic system, on the one hand, in which old semantic information (e.g. language, knowledge of who one is, where one grew up, the names of countries and addresses) is largely unaffected in amnesic subjects, and, on the other hand, with having to recognize and recall the new items, often repeatedly, as they are introduced into semantic store. Thus, it might be argued that, in principle, new semantic information might be acquired if such episodic demands were minimized, together with the repetition that is often a necessity for acquisition of new knowledge in normal subjects.

That acquisition of some new semantic knowledge in a usable form might be possible for amnesic subjects has been demonstrated by Tulving and his colleagues in their study of one severely amnesic patient, K.C. (Tulving et al., 1991; Hayman et al., 1993) (the same person, I take it, as the subject in the study by Schacter et al. just mentioned above). Such learning was slow and laborious, but once acquired, long-term retention, of newly acquired factual sentences, for example, was entirely normal. The results showed that the effectiveness of new semantic factual knowledge de- pended critically on the minimizing of interference, both for pre-task material and for items within the task itself. In the absence of episodic memory, interference can run rampant because one has no way of recognizing the relevant as being distinct from the irrelevant instance. K.C.'s 'newly-acquired knowledge,' they comment, 'represented ordinary facts of the world. . . . He thought other people would know "rays softened asphalt" [one of his learned sentences] as well as they would know that "dogs chase cats".' Even though he remained unable to recollect the learning episodes as such, it is possible that some new information might be acquired by amnesic patients which they could actually put to use. It is not clear whether K.C. is typical of the larger class of densely amnesic patients, or whether he is one of a minority group. Note that while K.C. can acquire new simple factual knowledge, he presumably cannot recall that he has done so, nor recognize it as newly acquired knowledge.

Sacks commented (1992, p. 60) about this study on K.C.: 'Could we give [an amnesic] patient not only "facts", but a sense of time and history, of the relatedness (and not merely the existence) of events, an entire (if synthetic) framework for thinking?' He urges us to come back in a year's time to get the answer! That deadline has now been passed by some years, and the answer, alas, is 'no', and is likely to remain so permanently. Tulving (personal communication, 1996) describes K.C.'s phenomenal world as being no different than it was five years ago. The amnesic patient can think about material in the immediate present, including short-term 'working memory' of up to a minute or so following an event (which remains intact in such a patient). He can also think about items in his semantic memory, his general knowledge. Indeed, typically there is no loss of the ability to carry out complex operations upon it, for example arithmetic, provided it is not lost with a break in the memory itself. But thinking for successful everyday adaptation requires not only factual knowledge, but the ability to recall it on the right occasion, to relate it to other occasions, indeed the ability to reminisce. The amnesic subject, by not knowing what he can remember, by not remembering what he retains, has lost precisely the evolutionary advantage that such knowledge bestows, and disappointingly seems doomed to remain in that state, as far as current evidence allows any conclusion.

As an aside, one can ask whether such a conversion ever occurs in normal subjects? It is, of course, the claim of psychoanalysts and other dynamic therapists to be able to bring this about—or least to use the overt to uncover the covert—but the evidence by its very nature is very fraught. Human subjects can be persuaded by skilful persuaders—who may not even realize that they are persuaders—to believe practically anything. Thousands of persons have 'uncovered' vivid memories of sexual abuse by alien visitors, and a Harvard Professor of Psychiatry has not discouraged the validity of such beliefs in the hundreds of cases he has treated. According to one survey, about one-quarter of a sampled group of American graduate therapists believe that it is possible to remember events from past lives under hypnosis (Yapko, 1994). It is not only in primitive cultures that animism can be so powerful.

But there is a practical question: if some implicit memories of traumatic events can be established, which may not be remembered explicitly because, say, of non-rehearsal over years or some other mode of normal loss, and if the stored implicit information is accessed via a prime (e.g. a fragmentary cue of the original event), can this *in itself* lead to an explicit 'remembering' of the event. This is what some so-called 'recovered memory' therapists claim is possible through the elicitation of 'body memories'. ('Body memories', as a term, is a terrible misnomer. It is not the cells of the whole body that retain information, but the brain; but—never mind—an implicit memory may be expressed, say, in an autonomic response in a patient undergoing psychotherapy in the same way that it can be elicited in an amnesic patient.) In fact, with recovered memory therapy the 'body memory' does not have to be *elicited*; the past trauma is assumed to be responsible for practically any personal or mental difficulty, be it arthritis, migraine, depression, obesity, bulimia, marital problems, or what have you; the check-list can be very long. From the existence of such a complaint, the therapist assumes that a corresponding 'explicit' memory of a causal traumatic event can be discovered, indeed *must* be discovered, if therapy is to succeed.

I have extreme doubts about whether such a conversion from implicit to explicit is possible, in normal, and even less so in brain-damaged subjects. But even if it were to appear to be, there is a powerful alternative explanation: the numbers of credible alternative explanatory scenarios being spun upon a psychological or physical problem are practically infinite—the more so if the client is desperately wanting to find such an explanatory scenario and is aided in this search by a therapist who is suggestive, sympathetic, and persuasive. It is no wonder that there are thousands of Western families who have been torn apart by therapists (or by friends or by a support group or by the media) who convince clients that they must have been abused by their parents 20 or 30 years ago. The scenarios can be genuinely believed—just as the memories of abuse by alien visitations are genuinely believed—even when they are historically false, which they can sometimes readily be shown to be. Just as one of the penalties of being able to think creatively is that it can generate social unease, prejudice, and paranoia—'why is he favouring someone else, is it to do me in?' or 'he is black, and therefore apt to be physically violent', so it can easily forge the construction of false scenarios of the past as an outgrowth of the effort to explain current problems. The pity is that with some therapies it is not only the client who may be misled and hence damaged, but the others upon whom the supposed blame falls. There is now a considerable literature on 'false' and 'recovered' memories in clinical practice, which cannot be reviewed here, but in that literature there has not been much focus or research on the specific relationship between covert and overt memory systems, although sometimes there is an all too easy appeal to implicit memory as somehow providing a valid basis for explicit reconstructions.

But in another domain, namely prosopagnosia, there have been a few promising reports of the successful elevation of the covert to the overt. The first was made by the late Justine Sergent together with Michel Poncet (1990) with a prosopagnosic patient, P.V. This patient characteristically was severely disabled in recognizing familiar faces. However, she was able to recognize some sets of faces when they were grouped and presented together (eight in each set) in the same occupational category. She could only do this when she herself could determine the appropriate category. When the same faces were then presented one at a time, in random order, she reverted to being unable to recognize any of them. Replication of such recovery has been reported by Diamond et al. (1994) and De Haan et al. (1991). In the latter study, their prosopagnosic patient P.H. was able to recognize pictures of faces if they were grouped (in a set of eight) in the same narrow category (characters of a TV soap opera, 'Eastenders'). The ability persisted in a test immediately afterwards when the faces were presented one at a time randomly (mixed up with other categories), although it dissipated after a longer interval. It is comforting to think that there might be therapeutic value, after all, in a soap opera.

Sergent and Poncet suggested that the deficit in their patient was a disconnexion between intact stored facial representations and intact semantic knowledge. Perhaps the simultaneous presentation of several members of the same relatively narrow class might have lowered the threshold for activation of the faulty 'connections'. The general approach fits in well with the perspective advanced here, that conscious processing requires a thought about a thought—a thought in isolation from the appropriate second-order thought will not do. It is tempting to speculate about possible extensions to other domains of covert processing in the absence of acknowledged awareness, at least for those that can be characterized as a disconnexion between intact domains. It would follow that providing simple knowledge of results, that is, 'correct' or 'incorrect', would be unlikely to suffice in elevating detection of events in blindsight, for example, to the level of conscious 'seeing' (although it might enable them to be able to improve in their ability to guess whether they were right or wrong). It provides feedback but is otherwise content-less, although it might help to provide a framework within which the proper connexions could be established, or even help lower the threshold for events that remain at the covert level. A procedure that would come closer to meeting the case in blindsight might be the presentation of a warning signal and a visual stimulus, followed by information that had genuine content, for example, 'square', 'a grating', 'red', etc., which is semantically and perceptually part of an intact system for blindsight subjects because they typically have a half-field of normal vision, as well as intact visual memory of seen events. Another interesting possibility might be to combine the presentation of stimuli to the blind hemifield, following immediately with the Torjussen procedure in which a complete stimulus is presented to both hemifields. Perhaps in such ways, especially if the category of such 'percepts' were kept narrow—all examples, say, of gratings with different spatial frequencies, or all colours, or all small sets of geometrical shapes— the 'feel' which some blindsight subjects acknowledge having under some conditions (or maybe even when they lack the 'feel'), might be joined to another intact system. In amnesia, perhaps, a link might be activated or exploited between new items (e.g. words or pictures) and *old* items (e.g. incidents or familiar pictures known from childhood) for which the amnesic patient still acknowledges having genuine recognition. The densely amnesic patient's retrograde amnesia, alas, can sometimes extends back over several decades. But even in very severe patients there are commonly at least some remnants of genuinely explicit recollections.

It has to be confessed that the trawl through the literature, incomplete as it is, does not yield a very optimistic outcome for potential boot-strapping of the covert to the overt, although there are some examples in restricted syndromes—and perhaps in restricted patients—that are more encouraging. These also may lead to suggestions that might be applied more broadly. We have already seen the partial recovery engineered in prosopagnosia by Sergent and Poncet, and others. In unilateral neglect, also, Marshall and Halligan's subject, who judged the 'burning house' (see Chapter 1 and Fig. 1.8) eventually could come to see the entire house, not just its right half. And in blindsight, as we have noted, there are examples of discrimination of movement and other transient events that are in overt mode if the stimulus parameters are right, and are covert if they are not; is it possible that in these conditions, especially, there is scope for graduation from one to the other using the practice? Moreover, there is the cited evidence of interactions between the blind and sighted hemifields in hemianopic patients (Torjussen, 1976; Marzi *et al.*, 1986; Rafal *et al.*, 1990). But while there are examples of grey areas, with some slippage between them, and some conversions of specific stimuli or subsets of stimuli from covert to overt, and some marginal improvement with practice, there is no encouragement that any wholesale cures can be effected by known behavioural engineering methods. No one has found a method that has cured amnesia, cortical blindness, neglect, or agnosia as clinical states.

If what is needed is a commentary that allows 'awareness of' or 'awareness that', depending on the category—or in Rosenthal's terms, a question of thoughts about thoughts—the underlying common difficulty in all of the disconnected awareness syndromes may have nothing to do with a specialized, or even a generalized awareness or monitoring system or module. Instead it might be a question of interrupting circuits that allow elaboration of thoughts in such a way as to permit commentaries (or higher-order thoughts) to develop and be sustained in each particular cognitive domain. In this sense, neural complexity may after all be an important feature in evolution that favours the survival of a system complex enough to sustain higher-order thoughts. But it is not complexity *per se* from which an emergent property springs, but the particular processing that it allows. And, as noted already, the specific and discrete loci in the nervous system that cause such disabling syndromes are not such as merely to reduce neural complexity, but rather interfere with the operation of the nervous system in quite particular ways.

Unawareness of what's wrong

There is a category of inappropriate commentaries that stands in apparent contrast to those that we have discussed thus far: anosagnosia—the failure to acknowledge the existence of a cognitive or sensory or motor impairment, or even resolutely to deny it. What we are asking of the commentary response for the putatively anosagnosic subject typically is not a commentary about a particular stimulus and response, but about a capacity. Anosagnosia is not a general dementia or loss of general judgment: it can be highly domain-specific, such that a patient may be unaware of one deficit but not of another, although they co-exist. It can occur even when the defect is severe and obvious to any observer, for example blindness or hemiplegia. It is a condition that can apply to the neuropsychological syndromes we have reviewed (which we dub as *unawareness of what is still o.k.*) or to other conditions in which there is no residual function, as in total paralysis of one side of the body.

Edoardo Bisiach (1988) describes the following examination of a anosagnosic patient with a paralysis of the left side of his body following a right cerebral stroke:

Examiner:	Do you know where you are?
Patient:	In a hospital.
Examiner:	Why are you in hospital?
Patient:	Something went wrong.
Examiner:	What went wrong [No reply]. Is your left arm all right?
Patient:	Yes.
Examiner:	Give me your left hand.
Patient:	Here you are [without performing any movement].
Examiner:	Where is it?
Patient:	[Still motionless] Here, in front of you.
Examiner:	Grasp my finger with your left hand. . . . Well, can't you move your left arm at all?
Patient:	[Hesitates] Just give me time to proceed from thought to action.
Examiner:	Why don't you need any time to proceed from thought to action when you use your right hand? Maybe you *can't* move your left hand?
Patient:	I can move it all right. Only . . . sometimes there are illogical reactions in behaviour; some positive and some negative.
Examiner	placing the patient's left hand in the patient's right visual field, asks: 'Whose hand is this?'
Patient:	Your hand.
Examiner	then places the patient's left hand between his own hands, and asks: 'Whose hands are these?'
Patient:	Your hands.
Examiner:	How many of them?
Patient:	Three.
Examiner:	Ever seen a man with *three* hands?
Patient:	A hand is the extremity of an arm. Since you have three arms it follows that you must have three hands.

Some prosopagnosic patients are apparently not aware of their deficit, deny its existence, and show no embarrassment where we ourselves would find it unimaginable that they should not know of it—as in not recognizing their close friends or children until they speak to them. Amnesic patients, similarly, show variable degrees of insight into their condition, especially the Korsakoff sub-group. The field has been well reviewed by Bisiach *et al.* (1986), McGlynn and Schacter (1989) (cf. also Young and De Haan, 1992, for a review of the anosagnosia in prosopagnosia; dare we invent a horrible term of anosoprosopagnosia, to make a super-normal incursion into the characteristically polysyllabic domain of clinical neurology?). In the next chapter we interpret the condition in terms of a highly rigid bias in the commentary system.

A graphic account of a blind anosagnosic can be found, as usual, in an article by Oliver Sacks (1992, p. 52):

> His eyes showed complete optic atrophy—it was impossible for him to see anything. But strangely, he did not seem to be aware of being blind, and would *guess* that *I* was showing him a blue ball, a red pen. . . . When I asked him about seeing, he acknowledged that his eyes weren't 'all that good', but added he enjoyed 'watching' the TV. Watching TV for him . . . consisted in following with attention the soundtrack of a movie or show, and inventing visual scenes to go with it (even though he might not even be looking toward the TV). He seemed to think, indeed, that this was what 'seeing' meant, that this was what meant by 'watching TV', and that this is what all of us did. Thus he had apparently lost the very idea of seeing.

Young *et al.* (1990) describe a skilled portrait painter who became prosopagnosic after a right hemisphere stroke. Despite being unable to recognize familiar faces, including those in her own paintings, she insisted that she had no problems in recognizing faces in everyday life, in paintings, on the television, in newspapers, and so forth. When confronted with a failure of recognition of the photograph of a familiar face, she would comment that it was a 'poor likeness'. Young *et al.* comment, akin to the description by Sacks (above) of the patient's having lost the 'very idea of seeing', that their subject appeared to have lost the idea of what it is like to recognize faces normally.

There is one feature of the anosagnosic condition that is different from the other unawareness states we have been concerned with; it would be difficult, if not impossible, to know whether or when it occurred in an animal. An animal that is paralysed but still attempts to initiate leaps from tree to tree may just be trying to make the best of a skill on which survival (or fun) previously depended. It would require a very particular and strange commentary message—and one established before operation—to show the existence of the condition of anosagnosia in an animal: it would have to signal that it 'saw' rather than just 'guessed' even for stimuli that occurred in a genuinely blind field. But we might first have to use a commentary arrangement to determine that the field was genuinely blind, unless there was unambiguous physiological evidence. But how would it respond when *no* stimuli were presented, that is, to 'blanks'? If it responded 'I saw' we would declare the animal to be hysterical, as indeed would frequently be the interpretation of an anosagnosic patient. But presumably (I do not know the answer to this) an anosagnosic patient would correctly deny seeing in the dark? If so, the patient would be dependent on his or her past knowledge of the contexts under which it is appropriate to 'see' and 'not see', which is very much in line with our interpretation of anosagnosia as a disjunction between current stimuli and an over-rigid organization of a commentary system. Perhaps we could obtain the same dissociation with a sophisticated animal—signalling 'I saw it', even if not entitled to do so in one context, and correctly signalling 'I did not see it' in another. But it is clear that we are dealing with a complex set of relationships, and I would not like my life to depend upon making such a demonstration in an animal. It would be a challenging enough task to design the appropriate gedanken experiment for a putatively anosagnosic animal, let alone carry out any such experiment.

Bisiach *et al.* (1986) argue that any particular anosagnosic condition (and as a class they can be, and typically are, highly domain-specific) reflects a failure of *monitoring* one's own performance in a particular domain and also, of course, of resting decisions upon it. Why, in neurological terms, it should occur remains something of a mystery, and in common with the other syndromes (of the 'unawareness of what is still o.k.' variety) does not, I believe, force one to invoke a common 'central' monitor; the monitoring can be 'decentralized' to use Edoardo Bisiach's term. This sense of the term 'monitoring' is somewhat different from the way I have used it to interpret blindsight, which I suggested might also be a disconnexion of a monitoring system (cf. Weiskrantz, 1986). But my earlier usage in the blindsight context (or in other syndromes of the 'unawareness of what is still o.k.' variety) is epistemologically rather different: in blindsight, by definition, there is no conscious perception of an event, and when there is (as is normally the case with all of us), we do not have to invent a monitor on top of a perceiver. In blindsight it is not necessary to argue that there is switched-off monitor, because there is not normally one switched on— unless one wishes to embrace the familiar homuncular infinite regress. I do believe there is a way in which it is reasonable to refer to a 'monitoring system' as a commentary system or a 'second-order thought' system in blindsight and other categories of covert residual capacity. But, as we have argued, the commentary is part of the awareness of perception itself; in the strong form of the hypothesis it has endowing powers, and is not a high-order observing system looking down on other activity.

In anosagnosia, strikingly, there most definitely *are* events to be perceived that would normally impress any normal perceiver, namely the deficit itself—the non-moving paralysed arm, or the non-appearance of a light when the switch is turned on—and it seems reasonable to apply a concept of a failure of monitoring to this condition. But I take this to be consequential, not causal. That is, we shall argue that anosagnosia represents a disjunction between a rigid commentary system and degraded stimulus inputs or response outputs. In the circumstances, as in unilateral neglect, the person may sample his environment or shape his responses in conformity with his beliefs, and the blind anosagnosic patient may persistently, resolutely, and unsuccessfully try to avoid bumping into objects whilst denying that he is blind. In one sense, he is *not* blind because he issues a commentary response even if there is no stimulus trigger for it. This need not be pretence; it can be genuine belief and perhaps even genuine experience, just as imagery can really be experienced. Like hallucinations, it is seeing in the absence of an external stimulus; but unlike hallucinations it is seeing based on a set of appropriate contextual cues rather than on having describable stimulus content. It may be that self-deception on such a convincing and self-consistent scale, like the clever rationalizations of the paranoic, is a skill confined to man or perhaps to the higher apes. If animals such as chimpanzees can deceive others, as has been claimed, or detect deception in others, perhaps they too would have the requisite capacity to deceive themselves.

The neuropsychological patients who have lost awareness *of* or aware-ness *that*, whilst retaining a robust capacity to respond in the domains in which they have lost such awareness, have lost the ability to use these capacities for thought and for imagery, and this loss typically is severe, disabling, and persistent. It is the loss of an ability to compare this with that, or this with what was, or what occurred at situation A or time 1 with what occurred at situation B or time 2, not merely to carry out standard and rigidly prescribed manipulations or procedures; it is the loss of ability to reminisce freely. It is this latter capacity, free and uninstructed reminis-cence, among others, that separates human thought from any computer that has yet been designed—although this is not to say that, in principle, no such machine could ultimately be designed. But like all capacities, there is a handicap and a price if over-developed or mis-used. In the social domain it can lead to paranoia, prejudice, and pre-emptive aggression; in the academic domain it can lead to obsession with verbal niceties and minutiae; in the psychotherapeutic domain, as with our everyday memories of events long past, it can lead to the construction of distorted and destructive narrative truths that are disjoined from historical truth; in the neurological domain—but not only in that domain—it can lead to denial. All of these handicaps bestowed by evolution must be worth the sacrifices and the risks, or else the capacities would not have survived. If the human race does not survive, perhaps some less endowed creature may draw some comfort from learning why.

8

The question of 'How?'

Triangulation

Having addressed some of the issues surrounding 'What?', 'Whether?', and 'Why?', and reviewed some of the evidence about blindsight and amnesia, assuredly to no one's complete satisfaction, we can turn to the question of 'How?' and extend that accomplishment. How does the brain generate conscious awareness? In fact, is 'generate' the right word? This is now a topic of intense interest, but with suggestions from two approaches that are traditionally polarized in addressing 'How?'-type questions. The contrast is sometimes described as the distinction between software and hardware. That is, how does the system work as a set of rules, algorithms, logical structure, and theoretical causal connections, on the one hand, and how are these implemented in terms of the actual neurones in the real brain, on the other? One can distinguish, that is, between the assertion that a power must be transmitted to something that will drive a train or some other device forward, and leave open the question of whether it is generated in the form of steam, electricity, or gravity, delivered in a host of possible ways that the engineers could harness and transmit in practical terms. Similarly, a set of rules must be obeyed for arithmetical calculations, but these could be effected in a pocket calculator, an abacus, scratches in the sand, flexed fingers and toes, or what have you. The distinction between hardware and software may be essential in computer technology, but I believe it can be seriously misleading in neuroscience. As a matter of fact, the software itself often implicitly reflects the hardware technology of the age, from Descartes' hydraulic statues to Cartesian 'animal spirits', from telephone switchboards to stimulus–response behaviourism, from video transmission to hypothetical scanning in brain circuits for visual shape perception, from parallel processing computers to some varieties of neural nets.

One result is that each new technological revolution tends to make the derived software of preceding ages obsolete. There may still be some psychodynamic or ethological schools that theorize about cognition in terms of hydraulics, but neural nets are the flavour of the month. And *this* month's flavour, as always, is assumed to be the final answer—the taste that gives ultimate satisfaction. But we can be quite certain that there will be another month ahead, and another flavour, in perpetuity. That is quite aside from the co-existence of two or more flavours both of which are satisfactory at the same time; psychologists are familiar with alternative theories which make equally reasonable predictions about the same phenomena, at least for a time. Indeed, it often turns out that the matter is decided in favour of both theories being correct, as in physics, each under a different set of conditions or assumptions.

But there is a more fundamental way in which the software/hardware distinction is inappropriate: the properties of the real nervous system themselves dictate the types of theories that can work. When I was a student, many models of pattern perception were based on the idea of transforming visual spatial arrays into temporal sequences of neural signals, as is done by television cameras. They were ingenious and credible. Quite clever predictions emerged, some of which were confirmed in animal studies. Such theories were decisively put to rest with Hubel and Wiesel's discovery (1962) that neurones in the visual cortex responded to particular features of visual displays, such as lines of particular orientations. This is not to say that we now have an adequate theory of pattern perception. But we can say that it is possible for a theory to make correct predictions and yet be fundamentally wrong because it ignores the internal properties of the organism. The c.n.s. (conceptual nervous system) of the theorists does not necessarily map onto the r.n.s. (real nervous system).

No one has yet designed computer software or any other complex machine that satisfactorily simulates human perception or thought or language, let alone human consciousness. Indeed, Penrose (1989) takes Gödel's theorem to mean that it could *never* happen, although never is a long time for such a confident conclusion. But complex structures that perceive, think, and are conscious *are* being made every day by the millions: they are living human organisms made of protoplasm. That is the stuff, with its intrinsic organization, that allows it to happen.

That being the case, why not abandon theory and go directly to the study of the nervous system—at whatever level one thinks appropriate, be it microtubules or synchronized neural firing? Indeed, why not also abandon the study of behaviour itself? If we had a complete understanding and unravelling of the operation of the nervous system, we would have a complete understanding of everything it controls and causes. Well, perhaps we would in principle. But it is not an ideal likely to be achieved in practice. The nervous system is not merely complex—it is fantastically complex. There are too many degrees of freedom to allow any practical constraint on the possibilities for our understanding. Horace Barlow pointed out many years ago (1961) that if we simply treat each of the 1010 neurones in the human brain as being a binary element, either firing or not firing—which itself is a vast simplification—then the brain as a whole can assume 2 to the power of 1010 states, which amounts to more possible states than there are particles in the universe as estimated by Eddington. It can be doubted that an exhaustive account could ever be made; indeed, it would be impossible even if we assigned a particle to each possible state! Even at the crudest level of understanding, indeed, who could ever say that, by a detailed and thorough description of brain anatomy as we know it, we could have discovered that the human brain contained in its organization a capacity, let us say, for language? If a Martian looked at the human brain and read every terrestrial textbook of physiology describing its intrinsic activity, he would never discover that the organ allowed comprehension and generation of speech. Only by first knowing that a person with that brain actually had the capacity for speech would he begin to learn where in the brain to search for its neural underpinnings, and to consider what kinds of brain activity might apply. Indeed, the Martian's first clue, if he were neurologically inclined, would probably come from the neuropsychological evidence that a brain damaged in certain places—notably Wernicke's area and Broca's area—interfered with that capacity.

And so studies of the nervous system restricted to it alone are bound to make major and fundamental errors of omission. This is not merely because of its complexity, but because the nervous system in isolation, like even much simpler man-made machines and other organs of the body, is opaque to revealing its functional capacities.

But there will also be errors of commission. The reason is that for every response within the body one not unnaturally seeks to find an antecedent stimulus and to build up chains of causal events. In so doing one often implicitly makes the assumption of a stimulus–response type of organism. But if man is a machine he is not *that* kind of machine, or at least not only that kind of machine. It is no accident that Pavlovian push-button notions of conditioning stemmed from the earlier work on the physiology of gastric reflexes, on which Pavlov first worked, or that the push-button mechanisms of the spinal reflex were taken by so many neuroscientists to be the building blocks for the rest of the nervous system. All that is needed is the substitution of one stimulus for another. A distinguished textbook of physiology written by a colleague of Sherrington has as the title of its final chapter: 'The nervous system as a whole—the conditioned reflex'.

Of course Pavlovian conditioning does occur, but we are controlled by predicted consequences of our behaviour as much as by the immediate antecedents. We are goal-directed creatures. In this sense we are response–stimulus machines rather than stimulus–response machines. Given a reliance on immediate antecedent events, some extra explanation is required to account for those aspects of behaviour that are patently not reflexive or wholly caused by immediate antecedent events. This has driven some scientists to dualistic explanations or to despair, or both. Sherrington (1940), the great physiologist of spinal reflexes, wrote 'The whole of human behaviour under what has been called "reflexology" might be taken to mean that the root organ of the brain reacts simply on the reflex plan. But that there is much that contradicts.' (p. 200). He comments wistfully, 'A purely reflex pet would please little even the fondest of us; indeed the fondest least.' (pp. 198–9). It is appropriate that he entitles a chapter in his *Man on his nature* (1940), 'Brain collaborates with psyche' and in it asks 'Will a day come when metaphor can be dispensed with?' He oscillates between an eloquent but mercurial dualism and an appeal to evolution.

It is ironic, in considering the history of psychology as a discipline, that Pavlov's work on conditioned reflexes had a very great impact on the subject, and was enthusiastically nurtured and integrated into behaviourism. And yet Pavlov himself was contemptuously dismissive of psychology. Sherrington's work on spinal reflexes, on the other hand, had practically no influence on the development of psychology, although he himself embraced the subject and supported its introduction into academic studies. Sherrington was prepared to accept the shortcomings of reflexes and struggled with the problem, whereas Pavlov appealed rather too easily to semantic solutions like the 'second signalling system'. These two great scientists, both deservedly Nobel Laureates, were fixated on immediate antecedent events for their scientific explanations, but in neither case are these sufficient. Of course, *somewhere* in the nervous system there must be immediate antecedent events that are related to, or 'represent', the future goals that behaving persons are bent on achieving, but the point is that without accepting the need to consider future goals those antecedent events will never be found!

And so where are we? I have argued that theoretical models that ignore the workings of the *real* nervous system are at risk of being irrelevant, that studying the nervous system is nigh impossible to do exhaustively, and that in practical terms such enquiries lead to serious errors both of omission and commission. Balanced progress, I believe, occurs in the activity, meta-phorically speaking, within the eternal triangle: psychology, theory, and neuroscience. The proper simile, I believe, is a spearhead. At the leading apex should be the empirical study of the behavioural phenomena we wish to explain, and which we must describe and understand in their own right—their properties, dynamics, and the conditions under which they are obtained. The apex should continue to lead, but an apex requires converging contours, creating two other supporting apices. One should be occupied by the theorists, the other by those with special knowledge of anatomy, physiology, neurochemistry, and allied disciplines. The theorists and the neuroscientists look to the leading apex for their direction, but it in turn gains force from the support of the other two, and the direction of its aim will reflect the mass and balance in the spearhead behind. But without the leading apex the spear will not penetrate at all. Nor can a spear be thrown sideways with good effect. There are some who maintain, indeed, that we do not need to do anything except study the leading apex, that the mustering and analysis of the behavioural evidence will suffice. Skinner was the leading advocate of the 'empty organism' approach, an approach that was empty (at least in overt form) of theory, and he performed a service (quite aside from his own empirical discoveries) in debunking what he called 'logical fictions': the use of theoretical jargon or meta-neurology simply to redescribe, or even mask, observable phenomena in the guise of explaining them. But for most, deeper understanding of how something works means looking inside and also having some ideas about it.

Even amongst those who take the results of brain damage seriously for theoretical purposes, there is a group of self-styled 'cognitive neuropsy-chologists' (dubbed 'ultra-cognitive neuropsychologists' by Tim Shallice, 1988) who believe that it is not necessary to know anything about the real nervous system, the 'hardware'—it is only the software they want to speculate about, not the hardware instantiation. I find this attitude astonishing for its anti-intellectualism, if for no other reason. It makes a virtue of self-imposed ignorance, a fetish of agnosia. They are not *neuro*psychologists but cognitive theorists parasitic upon neuropsychol-ogy. Knowledge of the pathways of the real nervous system, as they are organized in vision, for example, clearly is relevant to whether one adopts a modular view of visual disorders and, hence, of normal visual function. Or in the kind of connexionistic model one constructs. Or in understanding why there is experience of mis-assigned touch in persons with an amputated arm, and why it takes the pattern that it does. Such patients, as we noted in the last chapter, 'feel' that they are being touched in their phantom arm when someone strokes their face or their shoulder. Without knowing the electrophysiological map of the somatosensory projections onto cortex, this would remain totally mysterious, and indeed it is only recently that the mystery has been lifted (Ramachandran, 1993). No one could conceivably understand the contrasting details of vision in the light-adapted condition vs. the dark-adapted condition without knowing about photo-pigments in the eyes or different types of receptors. Within the metaphorical triangle, there ideally is continuous mutual interaction and flow; unlike other metaphorical triangles, it is an idyllically stable and romantic structure, neither bigamous nor adulterous—although no doubt subject to outbursts, selfishness, and incursions of jealousy. Those at one apex who try to dislodge those at the other apices, or patronizingly dismiss them, are the losers.

There is always a temptation for those working in the other two domains to assume, perhaps only implicitly, that the leading apex can be made to disappear as they gather more information or have deeper insights. Thus, it might be held that, with enough knowledge of the intricate structure of the nervous system, and when we delve deeper and deeper into smaller and smaller molecular mechanisms, there will no longer be a problem of awareness. Similarly, with adequate recourse, say, to the mathematics of quantum mechanisms, as applied to the properties of supposed neural structures, the meaning and operation of mind will be revealed. I take this to be a kind of arrogance—understandable, but arrogance nonetheless—if it is assumed that the entity one wishes to *explain* is no longer important once there is an explanation of it. That failing, at least, does not apply to cognitive neuropsychologists, with their other failings. The historical example is often given of the disappearance of 'vitalism' once organic chemistry provided a basis for life. But in no sense does life disappear as an interesting object of study because one understands some relevant chemistry. In the same way, the appreciation of seeing a lovely rainbow is in no way diminished (for me) by understanding that it is caused by 'reflection, twofold refraction, and dispersion of the sun's rays in falling rain or in spray or mist' (*The concise Oxford dictionary*). There is an implicit assumption, indeed it is often proudly made quite explicit, in some versions of philosophical identity theory (i.e., that mental states *are* physical states of the brain, and that every mental state is in some sense *identical* with some brain state or process), or more extremely in versions of eliminative materialism (i.e., that there will be no relation between brain states and common-sense mental concepts because the latter are themselves false misrepresentations of the nature of cognitive activity), that there will no longer be a question of awareness once we know the brain mechanisms. The problem will be solved either by sheer equivalence, or by a new grand cognitive scheme. And, at the same time, we will also be rid of crude folk psychological lingo (cf. the review by P. Churchland, 1993). The position adopted here, firmly and resolutely, is that the explanation *of* something does not eliminate that something. No lashings of identity theory can remove the characteristics of what it is that allows a blindsight subject to press the 'not aware' key for his blind field and the 'aware' key for his intact field, and why that is important both for science and for the patient himself. Once we have the explanation of this difference, then perhaps the *mystery* fired by our curiosity and our ignorance may diminish, just as the mysteries of life processes and sunsets diminish with explanation. Phenomena may become less puzzling or gripping, may even become less attractive aesthetically as a result, but that is quite another matter from making the phenomena themselves disappear. Psychology should beware of losing its consciousness.

Of the various syndromes we have been considering, blindsight offers the best opportunity for circulation within this romantic triangle. More is known about the physiology and neuroanatomy of the visual system in the brain than any other system, there has been no shortage of theoretical speculation about visual perception, and visual phenomena have been subjected to considerable quantitative examination. In none of these realms can it be said that an adequate state of knowledge has been reached: neurophysiological and anatomical information is much more complete for the cortical than the sub-cortical pathways, theorists still do not agree, and blindsight still requires much more detailed enquiry. The theoretical apex is perhaps a bit blunt if it covers the range from Marr to robotics, to connectionism, to frankly philosophical positions, but this increases our degrees of freedom. In any event, there is more than enough to get on with.

With blindsight, the leading apex of the triangle is visual awareness and its absence, studied in the practical context of the difference between successful residual visual discriminations accompanied by awareness and those without it, as measured operationally on the commentary keys or some other independent classification made by the subject. It is always easier to measure a difference between states than a stable state, and indeed this is not only the rationale of the subtraction method in brain imaging, but it is also intrinsic to the very concept of a control state. In terms of the real nervous system and visual capacity, there are two major questions: first, is it possible to identify the pathways that could mediate the phenomenon of residual vision, especially of the possible sub-types; and, second, is there any pathway *or organization of pathways* that seems critical for the occurrence and maintenance of conscious *awareness* of visual events? The first of these two questions is obviously much more amenable to direct empirical attack, and has been reviewed in Chapter 6, together with an introduction to the second question. But the reader who wants to get the idea of the general approach advanced here can carry on without back-pedalling. It will have become obvious, also, that the second question requires that we employ all three apices of our eternal triangle.

Awareness—back to the triangle

All of this means that we cannot put off grasping the most difficult nettle of all, namely, trying to understand how visual awareness can be generated— if that is the right word—by the nervous system. It will be obvious that we are in the realms of heady speculation, but it is also true that not only have we reached an interesting stage in neuroscience because of the development of new and more powerful imaging techniques, but also that scientists are now more willing to acknowledge that there is a real question. Beyond that, philosophers and scientists are addressing common issues, and even learning common facts.

Let's work back from instances of genuine blindsight, that is, processing in the absence of any acknowledged awareness. What is it that allows awareness to occur with an undamaged V1, and where might it be? One possibility we have already considered, namely that it is V1 itself, but this will not do for transient stimuli when accompanied by awareness in the absence of V1. V1 is not necessary for such awareness. Nor, it will be recalled, is V1 *sufficient* for visual processing: in the absence of *non-visual* cortex, monkeys are apparently blind, as found by Nakamura and Mishkin, and by Gazzaniga (and, within limits, by Sperry for the cat). These workers found that striate cortex in isolation in one hemisphere, with removal of all non-visual cortex, could not sustain *any* noticeable visually guided behaviour (the opposite hemisphere was intact so as to preclude paralysis, but was deprived of its visual input). Indeed, V1 alone will not do for *any* visual type of processing if the Nakamura and Mishkin, and Gazzaniga studies are taken to imply that the monkeys had no visual awareness whatever. Why, then, should V1 damage make it impossible for awareness to accompany successful discrimination (by forced-choice guessing) along dimensions of wavelength and orientation? Clearly, that is a question that must be answered.

Another possibility is that it is not striate cortex itself, nor indeed any other visual cortical area, but a particular and more distant region to which striate cortex projects, which may or may not receive a visual input over an extra-striate route. Daniel Schacter's 1989 DICE model ('dissociable interactions and conscious experience') was a box-and-arrow proposal that contained one box labelled the 'conscious awareness system', with specific connexions to 'knowledge modules', one of which could presumably be visual, an episodic memory system, among others. This could explain why disconnexion of the visual system from the awareness system yielded blindsight, but what is it that allows this, or any conscious awareness system, to generate its particular phenomenal property? Beyond that, no one has actually found the mysterious general consciousness module in the neuropsychological theatre, but this is not to rule out the possibility of there being one.

A third possibility is that there is some special and distinctive neural process which is necessary for all categories of visual awareness. For example, it may be a particular temporal rhythm that is generated under particular conditions of attention or discrimination. The 40 hertz synchronous activity seen between visual cells separated over some distance (Gray and Singer, 1989; Singer, 1993) has been advanced as a candidate (Crick and Koch, 1990), as has repetitive firing between thalamus and cortex (see Crick, 1994). For this type of hypothesis striate cortex would not be important in isolation but would be an important player in the orchestra, without whom no music could be successfully played.

A fourth possibility escapes to quite another level, namely to consider the application of quantum mechanics, rejecting any possible explanation at the level of systems, or at least at the level of systems that could be simulated by a computer, and arguing that one must go to the level of quantum states rather than neurones, or systems of neurones, to explain consciousness. 'On the view that I am tentatively putting forward', writes Roger Penrose (1994, p. 376), 'consciousness would be some manifestation of this quantum-entangled internal cytoskeletal state and of its involvement in the interplay . . . between quantum and classical levels of activity.' The structures he focuses upon at the cytoskeletal level are microtubules. I fail to see why this provides any specific explanation of anything we have been talking about, blindsight, for example. As John Searle (1995) comments about quantum mechanical accounts, 'the standard complaint is that these accounts, in effect, want to substitute two mysteries for one.' I do not understand, given the universality of quantum effects, and the ubiquitousness of microscopic neural features containing microtubules, why the spinal cord or the retina are not conscious? Consciousness, on this view, must at some point have an entrée into a relevant systems account. Penrose, the champion of this challenging position, considers his approach to be materialistic, but it verges on being a species of interactionistic dualism. It is not surprising that an open, self-declared interactionistic dualist such as Sir John Eccles, who postulates an interaction between 'dendrons' and 'psychons' (the latter of which are non-physical in any ordinary sense and may persist after death), finds the arguments from quantum mechanics so attractive.

There is yet another approach, namely to appeal to 'strong AI' (Artificial Intelligence); that is, to the assumption that if a complex machine could be made to do everything that we can do, to pass the Turing test (such that a human observer could not tell the difference between the machine and a human), then there would be no need for such folksy concepts as consciousness. Even accepting that no present-day computer or any on the visible horizon will overcome scepticism engendered by Gödel's theorem, who knows what engineering miracles lie ahead? If the complex species of software are stomped upon long enough, some may like to assume, the problem will disappear because they will allow any level of human cognitive complexity to be simulated. Beyond that, to follow Dan Dennett's line of argument, what we mean by consciousness is misleading if we assume it has a unity. Instead, he argues, there are really a whole complex set of states going on in parallel, 'multiple drafts' of plays instead of a single performance in the Cartesian Theatre. Searle has commented that, according to Dennett, we could not discriminate between human beings and mechanical zombies who behave as though they were human. It is not that sufficiently complex zombies would somehow have inner conscious states like us, but that in fact, says Searle (1995), Dennett's position is that 'we *are* zombies'. This stricture seems unduly severe if it implies that no one could ever, ever design a device that had all the properties of a human, but it is wholly justified, in my view, if it is assumed that awareness is not one of those properties that would have to be simulated, not to be bypassed using arguments based on the dreadful complexities of either our linguistic usage or our perceptual processing.

This by no means exhausts the various approaches to the topic. I choose not to have the neuropsychological problem—of performance with awareness as contrasted with performance without awareness—disappear by virtue of an appeal either to vagueness of language or to wait until we either have a simulation or a noncomputable quantum mechanics, in the false hope that they will make the phenomena disappear. I am prepared to consider that we might in fact some day succeed in simulating awareness, but I am not prepared to degrade the phenomena we wish to explain. The paraplegic has no difficulty whatever in telling you that he feels pain when he is pricked above the level of his spinal cut, and none whatever when it is below, even though his leg behaves as though he *does* feel. He will not readily dismiss the importance of the difference. Nor will the blindsight subject wish to have visual awareness dismissed as a byproduct of multiple drafts, or even as just one such draft. In that context he is likely to be a multiple draft-dodger. And even if he is not, how does his current draft, he might like to know, differ from the draft in which he knows that he *sees*? Nor am I happy with going to a level, perhaps because I cannot readily understand it, that seems as mysterious as the phenomena we wish to explain. I am prepared, just as I am prepared to accept a possible future for the strong AI approach, to be open about something marvellous emerging from the 'quantum-entangled internal cytoskeletal state', but it does not help us to know why pain is disconnected in the paraplegic patient, or visual awareness in the blindsight patient. Such an account, in any event, is going to have to interact with the neural systems as we conventionally study them, and will be constrained by their organization and their dynamics.

I wish to embrace the difference between successful performance, with and without awareness, to try to understand it in terms of the operations by which we decide that someone is or is not aware, to map these onto a general theoretical stance and, at the same time, to map them onto the known, or potentially knowable, nervous system. We know too little for this to be more than a general and simplistic approach, but it might stimulate further thought and research.

Commentary keys and beyond the 'oil refinery'

I start with commentary keys. They provide, metaphorically, the means by which we decide whether someone is or is not aware of an event. I am not concerned here, although it is important, with whether the person may be lying. That decision is based, as it is in all psychophysics, on the consistency and lawfulness with which the person responds in relation to a systematic range of stimuli, including the usual liberal sprinkling of 'catch' trials, not on directly knowing the person's experience. The commentary keys also, again metaphorically, allow us to say whether we ourselves have awareness of an event. I take them to be the *sine qua non* of consciousness of a sensory event. It is an open matter, as we have discussed earlier, as to whether they are actually *endowing* of a state of awareness, or more conservatively are *enabling*, that is, whether being able to make a commentary about an event is the same as—what we mean by—having awareness of that event, or whether it simply allows us to communicate that one is aware, with the property of awareness having arisen at some earlier stage through an (as yet) unknown mechanism.

One might say, in passing, that there are those who may adopt the enabling position all too easily, without considering further just which structures might allow this property to be produced and why. Thus, it is argued that 'activity in visual areas outside the prestriate cortex, without a parallel activity in V1 or indeed any activity in V1, is sufficient to lead to a correct discrimination and one, moreover, of which the subject is consciously aware.' (Barbur *et al.*, 1993, p. 1301). Must the 'visual' structures be cortical structures? Can they be any 'visual area', and in fact what is a 'visual area' in this connexion; for example, must it be *exclusively* visual? Do visual structures include areas relatively far removed from V1, such as frontal eye fields, inferotemporal cortex, cerebellum, not to mention the whole set of sub-cortical structures? But however defined, why and how are these areas capable of enabling 'conscious' awareness to occur such as to activate a later commentary stage? Or is 'awareness' attributed simply by fiat, such that activation of *any* area that lights up in a brain image during visual discrimination is assumed to contribute to conscious awareness by some curious but marvellous boot-strapping? Does this include the cerebellum, the superior colliculus, the insula? Or, broadening the assumptions, is 'visual discrimination' simply made synonymous with 'visual awareness'. If so, we are back to the original dilemma caused by blindsight evidence—in which there is good discrimination without awareness—not to mention the perfectly good visual discriminations made, for example, by insects.

It will be evident that the *endowment* view is a species of the same type of position advanced by David Rosenthal (see above); in his terms, that it is a further operation required before a 'thought' is rendered 'conscious', in his terms, a higher-order thought. For present purposes we can leave open the matter of whether the commentary is endowing or enabling. If it *is* endowing, I do not necessarily take this to be an easy solution to the question of how qualia—the particular experiences of colour, say—arise. But we can proceed with the development of the theme with the assumption that being able to make a commentary about an event is the same as deciding whether a subject has awareness of the event. (It could be argued, for example, allowing speculation to run riot, that the neural system in which the commentary operates is the skeletal organization within which Penrose's quantum phenomena somehow generate qualia.) This is not to argue, obviously, that the commentary must actually *be made* explicitly or overtly. It is the capability, the report*ability*, that is critical. It will also be obvious from our discussion of animal consciousness that the commentary need not be verbal.

If generating a commentary is an essential operation, where and how in the brain might it take place, and how does it interact with the visual inputs? The important point is that not only V1 but its neighbouring 'visual cortices' were left intact in the studies (reviewed in Chapter 6) by Gazzaniga, and Nakamura and Mishkin in which they removed all or much of 'non-visual' cortex, resulting in total visual non-responsiveness. Clearly, from such evidence, the striate cortex is not sufficient, although it *is* necessary for *awareness* of colour, orientation, form, and perhaps even for *all* attributes and dimensions under given certain critical stimulus conditions (for example, low velocity, low contrast, or high ambient illumination for moving events). Therefore, we are tempted to look for targets lying well outside the constellation of visual cortices, V2 to V5 (MT) directly connected to V1, together with their *oil refinery* sets of complex inter-connexions (I am indebted to Alan Cowey for the label), as displayed in the well-known diagram (Fig. 8.1) prepared by Felleman and Van Essen, (1991) emanating from their connexions with V1. The anatomical disposition in the monkey brain of some of these areas can be seen in Fig. 8.2.

The evidence by Nakamura and Mishkin/Gazzaniga, however, that removal of all or most of non-visual cortex rendered monkeys behaviourally visually non-responsive (although the neurones in V1 still continue to function) antedates the oil refinery diagram, which is based on more recent electrophysiological and anatomical studies. Therefore, it is necessary first to consider whether the earlier definition of non-visual cortical areas might have included visual structures now included in the oil refinery. And before that another question has to be sharpened: how far do we allow the oil refinery constellation to extend? It is sometimes said that with just 4 or so synapses one can reach anywhere in the whole brain from any other

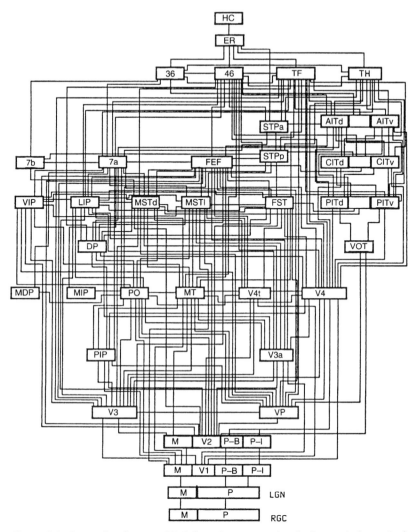

Figure 8.1. Connexions between V1 (where they emanate) and other cortical areas in the monkey brain, the oil refinery. (Adapted with permission from Felleman and Van Essen, 1991, Oxford University Press.)

point in it! It will be noted that the structures in Fig. 8.1 go to cortical regions physically quite remote from V1, for example the entorhinal region, the hippocampus, structures in the frontal lobes such as the 'frontal eye fields', and areas 36 and 46. (On the other hand, other structures, such as the amygdala, which have a direct connexion with V1, are not included.) One way to try controlling the colonial greediness of the oil refinery complex is to restrict the definition to include only those

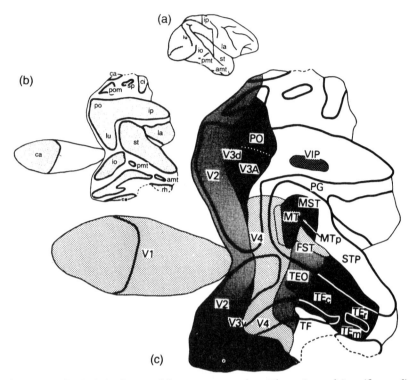

Figure 8.2. Cortical visual areas of the macaque monkey. The various sulci are 'flattened' to show the topology. The portion of the cortex flattened is shown in grey in (a). The major sulci are shown in grey on the flattened map in (b). Visual areas are labelled in (c). (From Desimone and Ungerleider, 1989, with kind permission from Elsevier Science—NL, Sara Burgerhartstraat 25, 1055 KV Amsterdam, Netherlands.)

structures that have a direct connexion with V1, and one further connexion beyond them. This, however, eliminates only a few of the structures in the oil refinery, namely, AITd, STPa, STAp, and area 7a (the abbreviations do not matter just here). But even subtracting these few areas, we are still left with a rather formidable tangle of inter-connexions.

Malcolm Young has suggested another very helpful way of structuring the cascade of connexions based on the degree of anatomical 'connect-edness' between the visual cortical areas. It is a mathematical optimization procedure, itself based on the functional 'proximities' between various points in the oil refinery (Young, 1992). Fig. 8.3 provides a useful information-rich summary of the known connexions between different visual cortical areas, which are utilized in his mathematical procedure. (In a more recent paper (1993) he has reviewed the connexions not only for the

Figure 8.3. A summary of the connexions between various visual brain regions. 1 indicates a one-way connexion, and 2 a reciprocal connexion. Loci of some of the posteriorally located areas can be found in Fig. 8.2. (Reprinted with permission from Young, 1992, *Nature*.)

	V1	V2	V3	Vp	V3a	V4	VOT	V4t	MT	MSTl	FST	PITd	PITv	CITd	CITv	AITd	AITv	STPp	STPa	TF	TH	PO	PIP	LIP	VIP	DP	A7a	FEF
V2	2																											
V3	2	2																										
Vp	0	2	2																									
V3a	2	2	1	2																								
V4	2	2	2	2	2																							
VOT	2	2	2	0	2	2																						
V4t	1	1	0	1	2	0	0																					
MT	2	1	2	2	2	2	0	2																				
MSTd	0	2	2	0	2	2	0	2	2																			
MSTl	0	2	2	0	2	2	0	1	2	2																		
FST	0	2	0	0	0	2	0	2	2	2	0																	
PITd	0	1	2	0	2	2	0	0	0	0	2	0																
PITv	0	0	1	0	0	2	1	0	0	0	1	2	0															
CITd	0	0	0	0	2	2	0	0	0	0	1	1	1	0														
CITv	0	0	0	0	2	2	0	0	0	0	1	1	2	2	0													
AITd	0	0	0	0	2	2	0	0	0	0	0	2	1	1	1	0												
AITv	0	0	0	0	2	2	0	0	0	0	0	1	1	1	1	2	0											
STPa	0	0	0	0	0	0	0	2	2	2	2	0	0	0	0	0	0	0										
STPp	0	0	0	0	0	0	0	2	2	2	2	0	0	0	0	0	0	2	0									
TF	0	0	0	0	2	2	0	0	0	0	0	2	2	2	2	2	2	0	0	0								
TH	0	0	0	0	0	0	0	0	0	0	0	0	0	0	0	0	0	0	0	2	0							
PO	2	2	2	1	1	0	0	1	1	1	0	0	0	0	0	0	0	0	0	0	0	0						
PIP	2	1	2	1	1	0	0	2	2	2	0	0	0	0	0	0	0	0	0	0	0	2	0					
LIP	0	0	0	2	1	0	0	2	2	2	2	0	0	0	0	0	0	2	2	0	0	2	2	0				
VIP	0	1	0	1	0	0	0	2	2	2	2	0	0	0	0	0	0	2	2	0	0	1	2	0	0			
DP	0	0	2	1	1	0	0	2	2	2	1	0	0	0	0	0	0	2	2	0	0	2	2	2	0	0		
A7a	0	0	0	0	0	0	0	0	0	0	0	0	0	0	0	0	0	2	2	0	0	0	0	2	1	2	0	
FEF	0	0	0	0	0	0	0	1	2	2	2	0	0	0	0	0	0	2	2	0	0	1	1	2	2	2	2	0
A46	0	0	0	0	0	0	0	1	2	2	1	1	2	2	2	2	2	2	2	2	1	0	1	2	2	2	2	2

visual areas, but also for the auditory and somatosensory–motor systems.) Malcolm Young has summarized the situation for visual cortical areas in Fig. 8.4, which confirms that the main organization of connexions leaving V1 is along two streams, a dorsal stream along the top of the figure, and a ventral stream along the bottom, with inter-connexions between them. (Note, incidentally, that the areas eliminated by the 'one synapse beyond V1' definition above, are now replaced.)

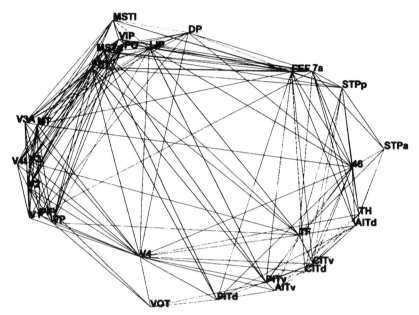

Figure 8.4. Organization of connexions, derived mathematically by Malcolm Young, depending on their 'closeness'. Note the segregation into a dorsal route, shown along the top of the diagram, and a ventral route, shown along the bottom. (Reprinted with permission from Young, 1992, *Nature.*)

If we use this set of inter-connexions based on degree of 'connected-ness', then we can ask whether any of the visual structures in the chart were also included in the Nakamura and Mishkin, and Gazzaniga studies and considered by them to be non-visual cortex. The answer is that there are three such areas, namely area 7 and its closely proximal structures lying in the dorsal stream, and two regions placed dorsolaterally in the frontal lobes: the frontal eye field (FEF) and another area (46) lying in front of the FEF on the dorsal–lateral surface. Of these various structures, the FEF is the most intriguing in the present connexion. It gets its name because electrical stimulation of this region in the monkey produces highly reproducible contralateral conjugate eye movements, the precise direction depending on the locus of stimulation. (Note, however, as we will discuss soon, that this definition of the FEF is not necessarily the same as another definition, based on the assumption that the FEF is identical to Brodmann's area 8.) A lesion of one FEF causes 'neglect' of visual stimuli on the side contralateral to the lesion. The defect is in many ways exactly like the defect caused by unilateral striate cortex removal! Like the latter, it may be difficult to detect in the animal's gross everyday behaviour, but it is perfectly evident when measured carefully in a 'monkey perimeter' (Latto and Cowey, 1971). And, as with occipital lesions, the defect is not absolute but is characterized as a relative loss of sensitivity. Bilateral lesions of the FEFs cause bilateral neglect, that is, the threshold for detecting visual stimuli is elevated over the entire visual field. The effect cannot be put down to an inability of the monkeys to make eye movements (Latto and Cowey, 1971), although the FEFs may be involved in monitoring or in calculating the paths of anticipatory eye movements. Alternatively, the defect may involve deeper visual processing, of which eye movements are just a reflection or an index. The severity of the 'field defects' caused by FEF and occipital lesions are initially of the same severity but with time there is more recovery of function following the former.

That a lesion can so closely simulate the effects of striate cortex lesions themselves makes it a very attractive candidate for the commentary-system focus. But there is a difficulty, namely that the FEF (and the other frontal area, 46) was left perfectly intact in one monkey in the Nakamura and Mishkin series, and yet the animal was rendered behaviourally unresponsive to visual stimuli. We should not dismiss its candidacy out of hand simply on this one case, however, because possibly the connexions between other visual areas (e.g. area 7a and MT, see Fig. 8.1) and the FEF were severed in this one animal. The structures in the dorsal stream, area 7, etc., damaged by Nakamura and Mishkin as non-visual cortex, however, were left perfectly intact in the two animals studied by Gazzaniga. Area 7 lesions can cause temporary unilateral neglect, but more striking are the temporary directional effects in visually guided reaching and in visuospatial discrimination tasks.

The contralateral field defect caused by unilateral FEF lesions has been seen often in monkeys, but only rarely in humans despite many patients with leucotomies, gunshot wounds, and other pathologies, although a few cases have been recorded (see Latto and Cowey, 1971). In this context, it may be that a few true positive results may be more significant than a larger number of possible false negatives. The anatomical connexions displayed in

Figs 8.1 to 8.4 are based entirely on monkey. The connexions may be different in detail in humans, and the FEFs apparently have migrated anteriorally and medially relative to the monkey.

If we define the oil refinery along the lines proposed by Malcolm Young, then we can see that there are at least two regions within it of some interest as possible commentary-key targets, namely the FEF and area 46, despite, as we have mentioned, their having been left intact in one Nakamura and Mishkin monkey without changing the picture. More broadly, Young summarizes a global view of the organization of sensory systems in the brain in Fig. 8.5, in which the oil refinery (and its counterparts in the auditory and somatic systems) feed into a 'fronto-limbic' complex. The FEF and area 46 are perhaps just at a junction point, that is, they may belong both to the visual processing system, as indicated by Young in Fig. 8.4, and also be part of the fronto-limbic complex of Fig. 8.5. However, there are other structures that have relatively direct connexions with V1 that can be identified (cf. Young, 1993), namely the entorhinal region and the amygdala, both of which are no more than 1 synapse removed from V1, although they are not exclusively visual. Their involvement in the so-called non-visual cortical removals of Nakamura and Mishkin, appears to have been somewhat variable; the amygdala typically was included in the lesions but the entorhinal area was left intact in most, if not all, of the animals. Amygdala lesions in isolation do not alter an animal's responsiveness to visual stimuli, although they do change their repertoire of emotional significance.

On the assumption, after this long excursion, that not only V1 but the whole oil refinery, as defined either by Felleman and Van Essen or by Malcolm Young, is not sufficient to sustain visual awareness, then we must look outside it to find the commentary-stage target. The oil refinery might do the equivalent, metaphorically speaking, of addressing the envelope, enclosing and summarizing the visual material, but unless it is posted and received, it is entirely without impact. There are two different possibilities as to how the commentary stage is reached, how the letter gets delivered, so to speak. The target may itself receive a visual input through a route that bypasses the oil refinery completely, or it may receive a visual input via the oil refinery.

There are numerous possibilities for visual information to reach non-oil refinery cortices, for example, via the superior colliculus, which projects not only to the LGN and pulvinar (and thence to the oil refinery) but also to a constellation of thalamic nuclei which in turn project widely to a large number of more anterior cortical areas, including, for example (via the

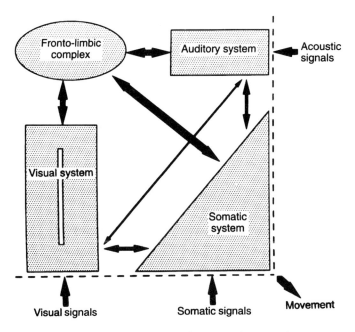

Figure 8.5. Schema of general organization of visual, auditory, and somatic processing systems connecting with the fronto-limbic complex. (Reprinted with permission from Young, 1993, The Royal Society.)

medial dorsal nucleus) a large extent of the frontal lobes (cf. Hverta and Harting, 1984). The colliculus also projects to other midbrain structures and downstream to the pons, by which information can reach the cerebellum. In short, the oil refinery complex of visual cortices can be snubbed by the retina if it so wishes. We can refine oil elsewhere. I shall invent a horrible but convenient acronym for a visual oil refinery bypass: a VORB. (I have eschewed inventing new terms in this book, although some would argue that the subject sorely needs to escape from the layers of ambiguity in folk psychological language. But I also know how new terms impede intelligibility in the guise of pretended precision.) Visual information can also reach—and this could turn out to be very important—regions of the brain that receive *both* an indirect projection from V1 via the oil refinery, and a VORB, such that there is convergence of influences arriving via V1 and via a V1 bypass.

With modern imaging techniques we can explore whether there are regions that 'light up' during a particular behavioural task or mental state. There are two major contrasting possibilities about a brain region that lights up in a PET or fMRI scan in association with visual awareness.

Suppose there is a region of the non-oil refinery cortex, as defined above, that lights up in a blindsight subject when he is *aware* of a visual event, but not when he is unaware (call such a region 'C'). We have already seen how this might be identified—and undoubtedly it will be tested soon—in a blindsight subject using moving stimuli with different parameters of speed, contrast, size, etc. But we also have the *intact* hemifield of such a subject at our disposal, in which he will typically be aware of those stimuli of which he is unaware in the blind hemifield, but which could be further reduced or altered to fall outside a window of awareness. If the same region lights up in either hemisphere when, and *only when*, the subject is aware, that makes it a strong candidate for playing a key role in generating visual awareness. The contrasting possibility is that a region of non-oil refinery cortex also lights up reliably to a visual signal when the subject is not aware, but more strongly when the subject *is* aware. In this case we are drawn in the direction of concluding that it might be involved in the commentary activation, but that it must exceed a given threshold of activity. That threshold itself can be tested, via the intact hemifield, to determine what level of intensity (or speed, or contrast, etc.) is required for the subject to report awareness in that intact hemifield. In other words, the two major possibilities are that there may be an awareness signal in an area that does not normally respond to visual events but which is uniquely active when, and only when, the subject reports visual awareness, or alternatively, that there is an analogue response in an area that fires to visual events but does so with increasing signal strength (for the relevant visual parameters) and at some level reaches a threshold at which awareness is acknowledged by the subject. There is a variation of this latter alternative that is also possible, namely that the area lights up for any adequate visual event, but its response is not analogue but instead is discontinuous; that is, it becomes *abruptly* stronger when awareness is expressed. Such a region would still signal a clear difference between awareness and unawareness but would also always have a chronic level of responsiveness to visual events, and therefore would function like C. There is still another possibility, namely that there is a C that lights up only when the blindsight subject is aware, but not when he is unaware, and cannot be reproduced by any manipulation of parameters in the intact hemifield. In other words, the hotspot is limited to the blindsight phenomenon, and perhaps is only seen in the hemisphere in which the V1 damage itself occurs. In that case, we will have found out something of great interest about the state of blindsight awareness, but which perhaps cannot be generalized more widely.

Of course, finding any of these main outcomes experimentally would be exciting, and would not only lead to further active research but would also serve to distinguish a degradation from a non-degradation hypothesis of blindsight. But we could be unlucky: there could a region lying outside of the oil refinery which has to be intact for awareness to be expressed, but which does not light up as such during such an expression. In other words, responsibility is transferred elsewhere. 'Elsewhere' could, in fact, be the quantitative level of activity in a visual region within the oil refinery; for example, activity in area MT might increase with increasing velocity of a moving target, but still require the intactness of another area—one that lies in the large complex lesioned in the Nakamura and Mishkin preparation— for awareness to be expressed. And that other area may itself respond non-differentially to visual events with respect to awareness or may even be wholly non-visual.

There are various areas of the brain that receive inputs from wide regions of cortex and from more than one sensory modality. Curiously, given how doggedly and insistently visual physiologists have pursued the oil refinery part of the visual complex, there are regions that are still virtual no-man's lands. One of these is the *claustrum*, a thin sheet that separates part of the basal ganglia from the *insula* (a quite large island of cortex), with which it is co-extensive; both regions are buried deep in the Sylvian fissure. The insula is also called the Island of Reil, and I rue the fact that Reil is not spelled Ryle in order to tease those who would confuse it with the philosopher, who would not have welcomed the way in which the name is being considered here! Both of these neighbouring regions are difficult to study physiologically because of their inaccessibility and because they are covered by a maze of branches of the cerebral artery. But they *are* perfectly accessible, if one aims for the right 'slice', with computer tomography in brain imaging.

One recent PET study (Bottini *et al.*, 1995), in fact, implicates the insula in *conscious* experience—this time, of tactile stimulation. It is known that loss of tactile sensitivity on one side of the body caused by some forms of stroke can be temporarily overcome by squirting cold water into the ear opposite the side of the body that has lost the sense of touch. How marvellously counter-intuitive and surprising that is! And what, one wonders, would our so-called cognitive neuropsychologists make of that? The recovery can last 30 minutes or so. It is called 'caloric vestibular stimulation' because cold water stimulates the vestibular system, and normal subjects report transient dizziness and vertigo. A host of areas light up in normal subjects with combined calorific stimulation and touch to the hand. But when the sense of touch is temporarily restored in a patient by the calorific stimulation, the insula and immediate neighbours light up (and also one other area, the prefrontal cortex at the base of the frontal lobe on the side opposite to the caloric stimulation and to the hand being touched). The insula itself receives an input from the tactile system, which it apparently shares with a projection from the vestibular system. The vestibular stimulation (which was given prior to the actual tactile testing) may heighten the sensitivity of this region in the insula. It is not possible to determine, from the report of this PET study, whether the insula was active before the caloric stimulation, when the patient was not aware of being touched. But, in other words, the effect of the calorific stimuli is to stimulate a region of the brain, the insula, that normally receives both vestibular and tactile information. In the stroke patient, one target of tactile input is destroyed, and presumably the projection to the insula is too weak by itself to reverse the tactile anaesthesia. But vestibular stimulation increases the sensitivity of the insula to the tactile stimulation, or perhaps actually summates with it.

There is one other PET study, this time of a blindsight subject, G.Y., being tested when he was *aware* of visual motion (Barbur *et al.*, 1993), which we have already discussed in Chapter 6. Areas within the oil refinery lit up, except of course for V1, which is destroyed in this subject (apart from a remnant at the occipital pole, corresponding presumably to his small region of 'macular sparing'; the visual stimuli in this study were, of course, placed outside this spared region, cf. Chapter 6). These were principally V3 and V5. But if one looks forward on the map there is also another hotspot in the anterior temporal lobe, not commented upon by the authors, whose interest was apparently focused on the oil refinery, and especially because of the association of area V5 with visual movement (Zeki, 1993). (There is, in fact, a danger, in the enormous statistical complexities in imaging work, of condemning genuinely active areas to being 'false positives' because they were not predicted. And, once condemned, they become 'false negatives!') I am not a radiologist, but this anterior hotspot is suspiciously close to the depths of the temporal lobe wherein lies the insula. In fact, the comparison between the hotspot in patients with caloric stimulation, who recovered awareness of touch, and the hotspot in G.Y. while he has visual awareness, shows apparent overlap.

We must await the more crucial experiment with G.Y. in which we can compare, within the same subject, his performance when aware and when unaware, for the same type of visual discrimination and for matched high levels of performance. But the point is that imaging studies may be on the brink of revealing structures that may have a unique role to play in conscious awareness of sensory events.

Of course, the possibilities I outline above for a special area C or a differential lighting up of a VORB are by no means the only ones. Even if we get a successful lighting up during awareness, it may involve a whole constellation of areas—perhaps even the entire region that was lesioned in the Nakamura and Mishkin study, although this does seem unduly pessimistic. And we cannot stop there: even if a C area lights up, it will feed back into the oil refinery region, and awareness may depend on that interaction. On the other hand, perhaps, after all, there will be no discernible difference with brain imaging between aware and unaware states. Such a result would swing speculation away from the hypothesis that conscious sensory awareness might reflect a change in the spatial distribution of activity in different structures, and towards the possibility associated with a change in temporal activity within the same structures, such as the 40 hertz synchronous activity linking separated visual cells. Such temporal changes would be unlikely to be made visible by functional brain imaging. But we could be even unluckier. As discussed in the next chapter, it could be that when the subject is guessing in the unaware' mode, a commentary system is involved which overlaps, or may even be co-extensive with, the aware mode.

But my own bet, which is the best we can do in these days of lottery addiction, is that there will be a discernible difference in the brain images between the aware and the unaware modes, and I plump for the outcome being a region that receives a converging input as a VORB and also receives a clear but indirect input from V1 via the oil refinery. Given the qualitative differences that are suggested in blindsight research between the parameters that control awareness and those that control unawareness, if these hold up I hope for the sake of parsimony that the answer will turn out to be not just an analogue threshold device, but one of the two varieties of C that were outlined above. There are many theorists who would find the threshold outcome more to their liking. Note, however, that in either case we are not talking about one of the visual processing areas lying in the oil refinery, but of activity some distance removed from it. The insula, in fact, as well as being well placed in humans for both Wernicke's area and Broca's 'language' areas, has a further attraction in lying near to the region of the primate brain that appears to be specialized for visual memory, namely the anterior inferotemporal cortex. An awareness commentary will typically occur in association with, and in terms of, already established visually stored categories and, while a commentary need not be verbal, in humans it often will be.

Having focused on regions outside the oil refinery of visual cortices, we must remind ourselves that blindsight arises because of damage to V1, its major input! Why is this? Why, when we must assume, for example, that there must be some activity in the remaining parts of the oil refinery for wavelength discrimination to be possible in a blindsight subject? And why, in contrast, can movement discrimination give rise to a form of awareness in the very same subject? The glib answer, of course, is that there may not be a good connexion from those particular isolated parts of the oil refinery to C (and/or back) that are involved, say, in processing wavelength differences, or orientation, whereas there are still good connexions from those processing movement directionality, or spatial location. But clearly this is *too* glib. First, the meaning of 'seeing' almost invariably entails object perception. We do not see orientations in the raw, and rarely do we see colour in the raw, unattached to objects. Colour is an attribute of an object, and orientation is both an attribute of a whole object and also of components within it. When a blindsight subject says that he is 'aware', but does not 'see', part of what he is trying to convey, I believe, is that there is no object as such of which he is aware, and that there is nothing in normal 'seeing' that is movement in the absence of 'something'—be it an object, a line, a spot—that is moving. For full-blown, organized perception, we clearly need the striate cortex, which feeds the entire complex of targets involved in object perception. A position I find appealing is to assume that, in normal perception, we may well be tuned to select for particular attributes in advance, such as the colour of a traffic light, and we do not have to involve the entire V1 apparatus on such an occasion. We might bypass V1 and depend directly on those regions that are specialized for a particular attribute or category. There is a very recent claim, in fact, that in normal subjects visual information can reach areas such as V5 *before* it reaches V1 (ffytche *et al.*, 1995), although this is bound to remain controversial without replications. Were it suddenly to start to fire, we would then want the full perceptual works. In that case there is a back projection from the relevant parts of the oil refinery to V1, which in turn can engage the entire perceptual apparatus. In the blindsight condition the subject lacks both imagery and visual thought. If we assume that in blindsight information can reach the relevant cortical areas involved in specialized processing, such as wavelength or movement, it is still the case that in the absence of a back projection to striate cortex such specialized processing remains isolated and unattached to any meaningful object.

I take such a back projection—from 'higher' visual cortex in the oil refinery back to V1—to serve a crucial role in *normal* perception in engaging the entire visual system after a particular relevant attribute has been noticed or selected. It is tempting to consider the back-projecting activity itself to be involved in the origin of awareness, and for V1 to be its ultimate source. After all, along the lines of speculation of a commentary generation, an *additional operation*, and not one which is simply an increment in signal strength, is required to lift a visual input to the aware mode. The back projections to striate cortex are anatomically rich and they have been invoked by others (e.g. Edelman, 1989) as having an important integrative function via 're-entry' of information. There are two reasons, however, why the idea of the striate being the locus of the commentary, or of Rosenthal's 'higher-order thought', will not work. The first we have already considered, namely that V1 and the back projections to it from within the oil refinery still are intact in the Nakamura and Mishkin preparation, and yet awareness apparently does not emerge. And the second is that visual information arriving at V1 from the retina is cast in retinotopic coordinates—the scotomata caused by striate cortex lesions are, after all, cast in 'retinal map-space'; they move as the eyes move. If we are seduced by the literal idea of a visual awareness as it normally occurs, it won't be cast in *those* coordinates—it will be in object coordinates, not retinal coordinates (Marr, 1982). The striate cortex, on this argument, is not the locus of the *origin* of the commentary, but the *funnel* (and possibly switching apparatus) that allows further identification and analysis to take place, as appropriate. And we make the further assumption that either a C or a VORB will require activation for awareness to accompany this identification and analysis.

It may be that the back projections to V1 are not essential for certain isolated fragments of awareness to arise, such as 'pure movement'. Perhaps they can have direct access to a C or a VORB. Perhaps in blindsight the strength of activity in more specialized visual circuits is not great enough to make adequate contact. This is a logical possibility, but not compelling when one remembers that a blindsight subject can perform at very high and sustained levels of success: 90–100% correct, by forced-choice guessing, without any acknowledged awareness. Activity strong enough to sustain such performance ought to be capable of finding a route to a commentary stage.

The idea is that if a subject is tuned to attend to a particular visual attribute, perhaps the specialized area in question receives the information first. But this would normally be followed by the back firing to V1 further to engage the whole complex of visual processors. Object perception is commonly assumed to be the job of the ventral stream flowing out of V1, and it is for this reason that David Milner and Mel Goodale suggest that genuine blindsight—discrimination without awareness—occurs with damage to the ventral stream. On the other hand, those capacities involved in perceptual action—reaching, locating, etc.—are the province of the dorsal stream, which they consider can function, in any case, without *perceptual* awareness, without 'percepts', as the term is usually used. And so, they argue, if the dorsal stream is damaged, perceptual action will be lost, but if the ventral stream is still intact it could allow 'perceiving' to occur, even if there is poor control of action by visual stimuli, as in cases of optic ataxia. This is a provocative hypothesis, but as the authors point out, the two streams are hardly hermetically sealed from each other. Quite aside from that, wavelength discrimination is usually considered, from electrophysiological evidence in the primate, brain imaging in persons, and human clinical evidence, to be processed by structures located in the ventral stream. If the fact that some blindsight subjects can make wavelength discriminations by forced-choice guessing implies that the ventral stream must be intact, then why is there no awareness of colour as such?

The case of detection of movement and sharply transient stationary stimuli *with* awareness of their occurrence and their spatial location in blindsight subjects is considered in Chapter 7, in terms of their having a priority in evolutionary terms for detection of danger signals and orienting to them. Paraphrasing William James, the role might be 'of sentinels which, when beams of light move over them, cry: "Who goes there?" and calls the fovea to the spot.' (1890, p. 73). But if we consider it now in terms of circuitry, one possibility is that the superior colliculus, which we know responds sensitively to such stimuli (but has poor sensitivity to differences in colour and orientation) and has a retinotopic map, could therefore give rise to a strong projection (via the thalamus) to a VORB. It might be sufficient to increase the VORB's sensitivity such that *directional* information from regions within the oil refinery could be processed with awareness, where these still are preserved, as they evidently are in G.Y., judging from his brain scan.

It is worth bearing in mind that there is a deeper midbrain system, involving the ascending reticular formation, which might provide another route of convergence with striate cortex outputs. It is more usually considered to be a setter of tonic levels of general vigilance rather than to contribute a specific role in visual experience *per se*. But this possible line of thinking should not be dismissed too quickly. It could be that conscious awareness of a complex sensory input requires an integrity of the complete system of visual inputs via striate cortex and/or VORBs *plus* a commentary-key stage or higher-order thought *plus* confirming or antecedent evidence of an incremental change in vigilance through the ascending reticular system. It could also be the case that various specialized regions within the oil refinery are sensitized through 'attention' and 'anticipation' via the ascending reticular system; serving as William James' 'sentinels' for specific categories of visual events before engaging the larger system for further analysis and identification.

Leaving such modulating influences aside, our main argument can be summarized as follows: sensory awareness entails the activation of a commentary stage. Because of the outcome of experiments that isolate, but leave intact, the visual oil refinery, yielding apparent total and enduring blindness, it is postulated that this commentary stage involves a critical locus outside the cortices that receive direct connections from V1 or are strongly connected to them (the oil refinery), but there can also be feedback into the oil refinery from that stage. Blindsight arises because a major distribution centre of visual inputs is disrupted (V1); however, because of multiple parallel pathways from the retina to other targets in the brain, visual information can still reach other regions of cortex to which V1 would normally project, as well as regions far removed from them via visual oil refinery bypasses (VORBs). Most of these regions do not have adequate direct access to the commentary stage, which is normally reached via back projections to V1 and thence over further projections forward that allow integrated visual information, especially of object representations, to access the commentary stage, possibly in tandem with VORBs. In the absence of V1, of course, this further stage cannot ensue. Rapid movement and sharp transient stimuli, however, because of their evolutionary importance as signals of danger, may have an independent route to a commentary stage via the midbrain and the further thalamic projections. (It is possible, in principle, that other areas of the oil refinery might also sometimes achieve direct access to the commentary stage in the absence of V1 in some patients.) Given the highly variable disposition of the lesions in naturally occurring brain damage, the range of potential dissociations is very large (cf. Weiskrantz, 1980). Possible candidates (e.g. insula and claustrum, prefrontal cortex) for the commentary stage, among others, may have remained unexplored physiologically and neuropsychologically because of their relative inaccessibility, but no such problem exists with modern imaging techniques. Finally, because blindsight (performance without awareness) can be contrasted with discrimination with awareness for the same class of discriminations in the same subject, and for a matched level of performance, a possibility exists for identifying structures that may be uniquely involved in visual awareness.

Another candidate that must considered seriously is the frontal eye field, (FEF, commonly placed in area 8). It not only gets a relatively direct input via the oil refinery (via MT) (cf. Figs 8.1, 8.3, 8.4), as well as via a VORB, but as we have noted, lesions of the FEF also simulate those of striate cortex itself in the monkey. It has tended to be linked to control or prediction of eye movements, but the functional hemianopia induced by a FEF lesion occurs even with eye movements intact.

It is important, however, to distinguish the FEF from area 8. A recent review (Paus, 1996) makes it clear that the FEF and area 8 may overlap but are not co-extensive, both in the human and monkey brain. If the FEF is defined in terms of its involvement in tasks involving saccadic control, it lies posterior to area 8 in humans and even in the monkey is found at the most posterior border of area 8. 'It is conceivable that, although neurons in area 8 play a role in processing of visual information, the eye-movement field proper lies in Brodmann's area 6 (Paus, 1996, p. 476). In man, area 8 occupies an extensive area of prefrontal cortex. The evidence suggests that it is area 8, or other regions anterior to the FEF, rather than the FEF proper, that is involved in cognitive aspects of visual oculomotor tasks, such as memory-guided saccades or inhibition of saccades.

Even if such structures as insula, claustrum, or dorsolateral prefrontal cortex do emerge with imaging techniques, a cautionary note is called for. It cannot be assumed that such structures are the place where all of the actual work goes on, or that visual awareness would be destroyed were these structures to be removed. As will be discussed in the next chapter, a 'hotspot' on a brain image is almost certainly part of a larger system. In the history of neurology no one has yet found a lesion—even a very large lesion—that completely removes awareness from vision in the way that striate cortex lesions do for certain classes of visual stimuli (i.e., non-transient stimuli), with the possible exception in the monkey, as just noted, of the FEFs (overlapping with area 8 at the latter's posterior border) in the prefrontal cortex. But the emergence of a hotspot for the visually aware mode would be an exciting finding, because it would point the way for analysing the anatomy and operation of the network within which it is involved.

Blindsight is performance in the absence of acknowledged awareness. But, as reviewed in Chapter 1, it is but one of a whole spectrum of dissociations between performance and acknowledged awareness. Some of these bear a logical similarity to blindsight in that there is an apparent disconnexion between independent but normally interacting systems. But others appear to reflect a bias within a commentary system itself.

One such example—anosagnosia—contrasts sharply with blindsight; it is a denial or a failure of acknowledgement of a severe deficit caused by brain damage. An anosagnosic person may be cortically blind, and yet deny it (Anton's syndrome). Or be severely paralysed or insensate on one side of the body as a result of stroke, and yet deny it. All kinds of verbal circumlocutions are emitted when they are confronted with situations which expose their deficit, such as 'I am too tired to lift my left arm today'. Here we have an over-developed and rigid commentary system, which simply cannot divorce itself from the performance with which it is normally integrated. Some varieties of unilateral neglect might be an example of an asymmetrical bias of a commentary system towards one side of space, even though it may be possible to demonstrate that intact processing remains throughout the whole of space. In the classical, ingenious 'Cathedral of Milan' experiment of Bisiach and Luzzatti (1978), they demonstrated that this bias can extend not only to real scenes but also to imagined ones. They asked their unilateral neglect subject to *imagine* the familiar view of the Cathedral Square from one particular vantage point, and to describe it. The subject reported a description of the right side of the imagined scene. They then asked him to imagine the same scene from the exactly opposite vantage point. His description again reported the right side of the imagined scene, the portion that had been neglected before. Because, as argued in the previous chapter, the commentary system itself feeds back upon the control of both ongoing behaviour and thought and imagery, which in turn are closely linked to various memory systems, severe failure of adaptation to the primary deficit in anosagnosia or unilateral neglect can further compound the patient's problems. There is a host of other interesting issues in neglect, such as why it occurs more commonly with right-sided rather than left-sided parietal lesions, an issue that has attracted a great deal of speculation. Indeed, it seems likely that there is a wide spectrum of different varieties of unilateral neglect.

Other dissociations are closer to blindsight in the sense that there is a failure of the commentary stage, rather than a biased commentary system. The extensions to 'blind touch' (Paillard et al., 1983) or 'numbsense' (Rossetti et al., 1996) and 'deaf hearing' (Michel and Peronnet, 1980) are clear enough; there are multiple routes to regions of the brain involved in tactile and auditory processing that can still be patent after damage to the primary receiving area, and the other parallels with blindsight, such as the failure of the back projection to a primary distribution centre, are also clear.

Can we apply such a general scheme to the other neuropsychological deficits in which there is residual capacity in the absence of acknowledged awareness? It is important to note that obviously the commentary stage will not necessarily be the same as that invoked in sensory awareness. In prosopagnosia, aphasia, amnesia, etc., what is lacking is not awareness *per se*, but acknowledgment in each case that the residual performance, indeed, is itself *residual*. The distinction is between awareness *of*, as in blindsight and blind touch, and awareness *that*, as in amnesia and prosopagnosia.

The extensions to such non-sensory cognitive types of deficits— prosopagnosia, aphasia, amnesia—are more problematical than the sensory varieties, and we are forced to speculate in even more abstract terms. In the case of amnesia, Warrington and I (1982) have already suggested that this syndrome arises from a disconnexion between intact storage of associations, events, and the enduring facilitation of old stores, on the one hand, *and* cognitive elaboration and manipulation of them, on the other, which we called the 'cognitive mediational system'. (cf. Chapter 5). In present terms, it is that elaboration which provides the experiential attribute of acknowledged recognition, of a memory being an acknowledged 'memory'. Where this disconnexion actually is in neuroanatomical terms is the subject of much current research (although not usually cast in these disconnexionistic terms). One possibility is that the incoming information has an entrée to the nervous system along any of the appropriate routes of cortical (or sub-cortical) elaboration, for example along the ventral visual route for elaboration of object identification. It must be the case that the entorhinal, parahippocampal, and hippocampal structures are not necessary for storage, but they *are* necessary for recognition and recall. The hippocampus and its neighbouring structures both receive and deliver connexions widely to the same regions of cortex that, one assumes, serve as the substrate for storage. It is the connexion between the current input, via entorhinal structures, and its wide distribution to cortex, converging upon the parallel input along specialized circuits, that is blocked in amnesia and that blocks 'cognitive elaboration' or 'cognitive mediation'. In Chapter 5 the notion is more fully developed of the amnesic syndrome being a failure of a joint interaction between current and stored information. In our original paper in 1982 Warrington and I speculated that it was a disconnexion between medial temporal lobe structures and prefrontal cortex that precipitated the amnesic syndrome. It is of considerable interest that recent PET imaging studies of normal subjects (Grasby *et al.*, 1993; Shallice *et al.*, 1994; Nyberg *et al.*, 1996) implicate the dorsolateral prefrontal cortex in the encoding (left prefrontal) and the retrieval (right prefrontal) of episodic memory. Shallice *et al.* propose that episodic memory involves frontal control of hippocampal function.

Prosopagnosia has received little focused attention in the present context except for the suggestion by Wallace and Farah (personal communication) that it is merely a form of weakened normal face identification (cf. Chapter 2). Most serious efforts to account for *normal* face recognition, however, have either not addressed the problem (e.g. Burton *et al.*'s interactive activation model, 1990, restricts itself to an account of priming), *or* in other models (e.g. Bruce and Young, 1986; Young, 1988, Burton *et al.*, 1991; Young and De Haan, 1992; Young, 1994) have dealt with the problem by assuming that a certain level of activity in a 'face recognition' unit, or a 'personal identity unit' will be accompanied by an acknowledged experience of recognition. (Face recognition units in these models, incidentally, do not refer necessarily, or even conveniently correspond, to the 'face neurons' studied physiologically, Rolls *et al.*, 1987, but to a theoretical structure that contains stored representations of every familiar face. The face neurons reported so far do not have a mnemonic component, but simply respond to any face or subpart of a face, new or old, that contains the requisite stimulus features.)

Andy Young (1994) argues that 'preserved priming effects without explicit classification of face inputs can be simulated quite simply with the Burton, Bruce, and Johnson (1990) model by halving the connections between FRUs ['face recognition units'] and PINs ['personal identity nodes'].' But labelling the face units as face *recognition* units may be finessing the issue. The evidence from covert processing in prosopagnosia *must* imply that face recognition units can be activated strongly without *recognition* as such. (Perhaps it would be better call the units face 'identity' units instead of recognition units, or just face 'stored ensemble' units. In amnesic research, fortunately, those two different meanings of recognition have been kept reasonably well apart.) And normal face perception can occur with *experienced recognition*, but without any experience of personal identity or associated semantic information. Indeed, this is a problem that confronts all of use from time to time—'I know that face but who the devil is it!'

Based on network simulation, Young asserts that the 'problem of how covert responses can be preserved when there is no overt discrimination may thus be less intractable than it first appears', but acknowledges that 'this type of simulation does not provide any solution to the more philosophical problems concerning awareness; we do not claim that the computer is *aware* just because it passes an arbitrary threshold.' (1994, p. 163, italics added). But it is not just a philosophical question, but a psychological and neural question as well. What are the mechanisms that allow recognition and awareness to flow from activation of certain circuits, and why do they *not* flow when there nevertheless is good covert processing of faces without awareness in prosopagnosia? It cannot be settled by fiat, any more than awareness or recognition can be said to flow simply from a definition of 'episodic memory' as consisting of events that have the attribute of being experienced as remembered, as memories.

Not all cases of prosopagnosia necessarily show covert processing of faces (cf. Young, 1994), and there are lots of individual variations, as in all neuropsychological syndromes. Pure cases of prosopagnosia are relatively rare, and the proportions that do or do not show it are difficult to assess. But, as in all of neuropsychology, it will be the fine details of the lesions, in conjunction with imaging of normal subjects, that will potentially lead to inferences about where the critical processing systems lie. Interestingly, there can be loss of face recognition without the loss of the ability to conjure up images of remembered faces. Thus, patient H.J.A. can accurately remember *details* of famous faces, for example hair length (but not their general 'configural' appearance) although he no longer recognizes pictures of them (Young *et al.*, 1994). This patient also does not show covert identification of faces. Thus, his deficit appears to lie at an input stage prior to wherever face identity units may occur, which is consistent with his other visual perceptual impairments; both percepts and images may be similarly fragmented. In contrast, another patient, P.H., has good covert identification of faces but severe difficulty in evoking imagery of faces. As Young *et al.* comment, 'these observations are inconsistent with the idea that face recognition impairments have a unitary underlying cause and vary only in severity. Instead, they imply multi-stage causation', in contrast to the argument advanced by Levine and Calvano (1989) of a unitary perceptual impairment in prosopagnosia. While this seems a reasonable gloss on the findings, the results reinforce the view that in patient P.H. both the perceptual and the imagery stages are impaired in terms of overt processing, and stand in striking contrast to the intactness of the covert processing of faces.

Is there an approach that can be developed along the lines of the blindsight argument? Perhaps a parallel can be drawn as follows: the lesion that is commonly associated with prosopagnosia lies at a fairly early stage in the visual cortical nervous system, in the lingual gyrus. In fact, it is often associated with upper quadrant field defects because of its proximity to the lower bank of the calcarine fissure, in which the striate cortex is buried. (It is also close to the region in which a lesion that causes achromatopsia occurs.) Indeed, patient P.H. of Young and De Haan's had a 'severely constricted visual field' and also an apparent reduction in acuity. On the other hand, the prosopagnosic deficit is not typically visual-field specific (although there may be such cases of which I am unaware). Even though it appears that the critical lesion lies in the right hemisphere, the syndrome itself applies to familiar faces wherever they fall in the visual field. In this regard, therefore, the lesion—while relatively early in the visual pathway serial cascade—is beyond the point at which it is retinotopic with regard to face processing.

Let us assume that the major visual input to the face recognition units postulated by Bruce and Young, is via the lingual gyrus (in turn receiving a striate cortical input). Let us assume that the face recognition units, when deprived of their major input, can nevertheless receive visual information over an indirect parallel route, in much the same way as we have postulated for blindsight, except that in prosopagnosia the striate cortex can still be intact. Assume further, that the coupling between face recognition units and personal identify units could still be intact, although this is not a necessary assumption—it could depend on the subtype of prosopagnosia.

The position, then, is that the face recognition units receive an input, not necessarily of full strength or of all features of a complete face, which generates the first response (the 'first thought' in Rosenthal's terms, if you will). Normally there is a back projection to the region that serves as the distribution point in the network that can attach the relevant meaning at the moment, be it semantic (e.g. the type of conference one might be attending), associative (a chance dinner companion at this conference), mnemonic (when did I last see *him*?). In the absence of the major distribution point, the further elaboration cannot be generated. It is this further elaboration (Rosenthal's second-order thought, if you will) that is a precondition for the commentary stage to be achieved.

Prosopagnosia, like cortical blindness, aphasia, or unilateral neglect, of course does not always yield evidence of residual functioning through indirect testing. There are patients who cannot recognize familiar faces overtly and also have nothing going on covertly. In these instances, we assume that the lesions have indeed invaded the critical face recognition units. Equally, there may be a critical blockade of the *visual* input to these units, even though the stored information might still be accessed mnemonically. We have just referred above to the contrast between two different patients studied by Young *et al.* (1994). The study of lesion locus, therefore, could help to differentiate 'centres' (more strictly, small networks) from a major distribution point to the networks. PET scanning and other functional imaging methods might help to validate such a view, as well as elucidating it. In general, there will be as many subspecies of deficits as pathological vagaries will allow, but we are not committed to explaining *all* of them in detail (any more than the physicist must be expected to be able to predict the precise path of a falling leaf on a windy, but unseasonably warm, March day, or any other day).

And so, the *general* proposal for a prototypical deficit with preserved function in the absence of acknowledged awareness is: (a) that the lesion which characteristically causes it is a major distribution point for a network capable of mediating and processing a variety of attributes and components; (b) that a subpart of this network can still be stimulated over a less direct route; (c) that the normally important back projection to the distribution region now is without effect because of the lesion, and (d) that in the absence of such further elaboration, an output to the commentary stage cannot be generated. That last stage is a *sine qua non*, not only for the expression of awareness but, in the strong form of the hypothesis, also for its generation. The commentary stage may well differ for different dissociations, and especially between the 'aware of' and the 'aware that' types of deficits. It follows that the lesion (such as V1) causing preserved function without awareness does so by a disconnexion, as often assumed: it is not itself the centre for the awareness or the commentary. It is not a disconnexion from 'an awareness system', however, but is a blockade of a route to an elaboration that in turn allows a further progression to a commentary stage.

We are still at a loss as to the identity of structures in the commentary stage, and its different forms in different types of processing. We do not know if there is just one stage, covering all processing, or whether there are dedicated systems for different forms of processing. The fact that the neuropsychological domains we have been considering are domain-specific might suggest that there are separate systems, but this is not a logical necessity—there can be domain-specific disconnexions from a common system. But if there are independent systems, there also may presumably be a superordinate system that allows transfer of commentaries from one mode to another.

The commentary stage may involve the entire fronto-limbic complex (in which I include not only prefrontal cortex but also insula and claustrum), or there may well be specialized regions within it dedicated to, and wired for, different cognitive and sensory demands. My guess is that the fronto-limbic complex will increasingly turn up in imaging studies of 'awareness of events' vs. 'non-awareness of events' nevertheless processed, as in blindsight or in memory or in neglect. It may be that different regions of the complex serve as quite different points of entrée to it, depending on the modality and the nature of the processing, or that the fronto-limbic complex is itself a collection of dedicated commentary stages. Any finding in brain imaging, however, of a supposedly unique hotspot need only indicate a connecting point, rather than the entire body of the commentary system itself. And given the profusion of parallel pathways, which we have emphasized throughout, it will be very difficult to disconnect any process from the commentary stage by a single isolated lesion, perhaps even by a quite large one. Finally, the commentary stage is not assumed typically to be a simple 'yes—aware' or 'no—not aware' state. An affirmation of awareness also entails the accessing of a large storehouse of relevant, contextual knowledge that is implicit in the affirmation.

Whether or not any of these speculations will turn out to have survival value, one point is clear and exciting. It is that we are on the verge, given new technologies, of being able to identify whether there are critical structures in the human brain that are uniquely involved in various kinds of conscious experience. If none emerge that show any differential activity, then hypotheses based on temporal coding will be given an impetus. But if some structures *do* emerge, as seems likely, then a new frontier will no doubt attract its posse of scientific scouts. But neither of these possible alternatives is simply a frontier on the localizationistic horizon. Our triangle has plenty of material at all of three of its apices to ensure interaction and integration. Examples of performance without awareness—at the leading apex—will no doubt continue to be pursued and refined. In our view, the commentary system plays a critical role, on a theoretical level, at one of the trailing apices, and at the third apex lies the potential body of information, regarding neural activity outside the oil refinery, that plays a critical role in its instantiation (together with, of course, the oil refinery itself which distributes and processes the combinatorial aspects of visual features). Whatever the outcome, we can be certain that we will never be short of apical alternatives.

9

And so. . . .

And so, where are we?

It is time to pull some strings together. This is the position: first, in every area of cognitive neuropsychology there are preserved capacities of which the patients remain unaware. These range from perception to attention, meaning, long-term memory, and language, and within each of these categories there are several different varieties. The blindsight patient can discriminate visual stimuli without seeing the stimuli; the blind touch ('numbsense') patient can locate the position of a tactile stimulus on the arm which has lost the sense of touch. The amnesic patient can store information that can be retrieved by the experimenter but is not acknowledged as a memory by the patient. In prosopagnosia there is loss of specific memories of familiar faces, but the patient demonstrates through indirect means that this information is retained. In unilateral neglect, information can still be processed in the left side of visual space even though the patient not only denies seeing it, but behaviourally ignores it. And a patient who has lost the ability to comprehend language can nevertheless demonstrate through 'on-line' reaction-time testing that there is an intact capacity to process both semantic and syntactic information, of which the subject remains ignorant and which cannot be used in his or her discourse. A complementary condition occurs: anosagnosia, in which a patient denies the existence of a deficit such as cortical blindness or hemiplegia: we argue that a rigid commentary stage has taken control. This by no means an exhaustive list. In all of these conditions the type of brain damage that causes them is either known or, in principle, is knowable.

Next, the argument is that in every instance the subject has lost the ability to render a parallel acknowledged commentary. It is not necessary that the commentary actually be made overtly, but it should be capable of being made. In the case of loss of sensory awareness, it is the loss of being able to acknowledge awareness *of* an event. In the amnesic syndrome, it is the inability to acknowledge awareness *that* retrieved information can be accessed, or that a residual capacity is retained. In all of these examples, were we to try to assess the condition directly during testing, we would require on every trial that the subject not only make the response that indicates the retained ability, but also that they indicate, quite independently, whether that response is or is not an example of such an ability. The clearest examples are with deficits of sensory awareness, as in blindsight, where on every trial a subject can be required to make a visual discrimination, by guessing if necessary, and to indicate independently with separate responses whether or not he or she had any visual awareness of the event.

The next step in the argument was to posit that the commentary plays a key role in the experience of awareness as such. A minimal condition is that it normally *enables* an acknowledgement of awareness to be made, and then to be further communicated, that is, that awareness arises at an earlier stage than the commentary, and as a precondition for it. A strong position is that it is not only enabling, but is actually *endowing*: it is what is meant by saying that one is aware. The position bears some similarities to, and might be mapped onto, a philosophical position that awareness is a matter of 'higher-order thoughts,' that is, that to be aware implies that one has a thought about a thought. Regardless of terms used in the argument, the assumption is that a two-stage operation is a minimal requirement for awareness.

Regardless of which of these positions is adopted, and probably they cannot be distinguished experimentally as yet, one can proceed to consider the brain mechanisms that allow commentaries of awareness to be made. Even if they are assumed to be just enabling, the question of the type of information that feeds into a commentary stage would be of interest, although the enabling assumption bypasses the question of what *earlier* mechanisms bring awareness to the point of allowing a commentary to be made. To repeat my own preference, it is for the strong form of the hypothesis—that the ability to make a commentary is what is meant by being aware and what gives rise to it. The theme that is developed rests largely on evidence about blindsight because the anatomy and physiology, on the one hand, and the psychophysics, on the other, are the best known. The argument is that neither primary visual cortex, nor the neighbouring visual cortices to which it is connected, are sufficient for visual awareness, because when these are isolated from non-visual cortex no visual behaviour takes place. As primary visual cortex still continues to be electrically active, the assumption is made that the isolation has, indeed, made it impossible for a commentary stage to be reached, and hence for visually initiated behaviour to occur. Various possible routes over which this would normally take place are discussed. It is argued, in addition to such forward transmissions, that back projections from this stage to visual cortices (the oil refinery) are of vital importance. And within the network of visual cortices, as well, back projections from 'higher' visual association cortex to primary visual cortex are also important, especially for fully implemented processing of attributes such as colour and shape. On the other hand, stimuli of especial importance for detecting danger, such as moving and rapidly transient events, may have an independent and older system that can have access—perhaps even have privileged access—to a commentary stage independently of the visual cortices.

Next, it is argued that, in principle, animals as well as humans may possess the same ability to indicate whether or not they were aware of the stimulus to which they have responded. The recent evidence from research on blindsight in monkeys indicates that, indeed, they classify visual stimuli which they can detect and locate in the same way as a human blindsight patient can. That is, when asked to classify a flash of light they treat it as equivalent to a non-light, even though they can detect it and locate its position. The question of animal consciousness depends, if one is to make a judgment of its existence dependent on a commentary response, on first training the animal to validate its ability to discriminate the two states of awareness (e.g. a light) vs. unawareness (e.g. a blank). But this involves one in a circular argument, and thus one is drawn back to a dependence on arguments from analogy. But, this analogy can be strong if changes in awareness, as in blindsight, follow similar courses in animals to those in man, as we have seen actually happens, and if the brain systems revealed by brain imaging also show such parallels. Other approaches to the question, in the absence of commentaries, are also available by tests designed to study intentionality and changes in preference by animals.

Finally, the evolutionary question is broached by asking what penalties follow from the loss of awareness in neuropsychological cases. And the evidence suggests that it is severe and deeply incapacitating within the particular category in question. It is by no means a mere subtraction of an epiphenomenon. The challenging issue of rehabilitation in such cases gives rise to mixed expectations. In blindsight there are positive indications that if the remaining extra-striate visual pathways are exercised and put under pressure of use, some return of visual function is possible. In the realms of memory deficits, especially of the amnesic syndrome, the evidence is less encouraging, although improvements through establishment of implicit functioning may be helpful for custodial arrangements. In more specific memory deficits, as in prosopagnosia, there are more encouraging, if limited, signs.

That, in summary, is the position, the details of which are spelled out in the preceding chapters.

And so, what might be wrong?

Well, of course, practically everything. In terms of our romantic triangle, with a relevant neuropsychological syndrome at the leading apex, and with theory and neurosciences at the two trailing apices, one can certainly find stumbling blocks in the treatment of the two trailing apices, and also, indirectly, of the leading apex. First, the definition of awareness itself, and the varied usages employed in the argument (Allport, 1988). Awareness of the occurrence of a sensory event will probably be accepted as having ostensive validity without demur. Most persons will have no difficulty in grasping, say, the difference between seeing and not seeing, or feeling and not feeling (as, say, when an arm or a tooth is anaesthetized), and will consider it reasonable, even challenging, as I do, to try to understand the basis of the difference. When one ventures into the question of being aware of attributes, such as colour, one might encounter traditional philosophical favourites such the inverted qualia problem, but even here most persons can accept the difference between seeing a colour and not seeing any colour. But the use of the term awareness, in connexion with entire *capacities*, such as the ability to recognize or to recall in the amnesic syndrome, extends it to much more complex levels of discourse. This is especially the case because those capacities are themselves often described in everyday language with much ambiguity: just note how varied and inconsistent is the use, even by specialists, of terms such as short-term memory, long-term memory, and implicit memory. Even memory experts disagree about definitions of, say, semantic memory and declarative memory. An amnesic patient may well *say* that he can recall information about an event, not because he can provide any recallable details, but because he knows from semantic knowledge that he should be able to do so. That is, he may know that he has a wife, or even perhaps that most men do have wives, and therefore *should* be able to remember various events of married life and of possible offspring, even if he cannot recall them when tested. Lumping all the various neuropsychological syndromes together masks the very great differences not only in their putative mechanisms but also in the stress that is placed upon the term awareness. Nevertheless, I believe it is fair to say that all of them involve a critical loss of a commentary stage, different in character, of course, in each of the syndromes. Because sensory awareness is the easiest to grasp, most of the detailed argument in the book has been of blindsight. Whether the arguments or potential evidence to be revealed about brain mechanisms of visual awareness (awareness *of*), will readily generalize to other more linguistically complex syndromes (awareness *that*) remains to be seen, but I am optimistic.

The discourse has deliberately kept close to folk psychological terminology. I recognize the value of inventing new formal definitions to free oneself of accumulated baggage—a large set of lightweight carrier bags instead of a cluttered, heavy rucksack—but I believe that the folk psychological terms about awareness relate precisely to the nettles to be grasped, the issues hopefully to be illuminated, rather than explained away by appeals to complexity, or by escaping to other domains that are even more ineffable, or by the use of neologisms so devoid of connotation as to require complex exposition themselves. Refinements of meaning and of laws follow from empirical evidence and discovery rather than from them being obligatory fore-runners. Using folk psychological terminology does, after all, make it easier for sceptical folk, if they so wish, to criticize the arguments advanced here: for example, that there is a close connexion between awareness and commentaries. They may have the same objection that the Man on the Clapham omnibus has to philosophical identity theory, that awareness *is* the brain state associated with it, in this case the brain mechanisms associated with commentaries. He may hold that being aware of a sensory event is *just that*. No commentary is needed to endow it. The argument, this intrepid bus traveller may say, is just circular, although cast in somewhat elliptical shape in the book. The man on the Clapham omnibus (and a good many others, even some Nobel laureates accustomed to more elevated modes of travel) remains resolutely a dualist, and this is firmly embedded in our use of everyday language.

I do not wish to stomp over ground that has been thoroughly ploughed by countless discourses on the philosophy of mind. At some stage one has to take a position. It is obvious that states of awareness are radically altered by brain damage and, therefore, that this leads directly and swiftly, if not inevitably, to a materialistic position. I am a materialist determined to give due regard to the phenomena that make some people dualists (a non-eliminative materialist, if you will). We depend on the issuing of a commentary to know whether someone, animal or human, is aware. It is closely linked to what we mean by being aware, and it is a bold but possible assumption to argue that it *is* what we mean by it. But even if this is rejected, the close association holds out the hope that studying the brain systems involved in the issuing of commentaries about events might reveal important evidence about mechanisms of awareness, if only to identify the structures that are uniquely and, possibly, invariably implicated. And studying those examples where the commentaries yield differences in reports of awareness vs. unawareness (science always deals best with *differences* in states) offers a promising entrée.

But what of the empirical neuroscientific evidence itself? An important plank in the argument is that visual cortex (V1 plus its immediate connexions, the oil refinery) is necessary but not *sufficient* for visual awareness. This evidence derives from rather complex experiments (by Sperry, Gazzaniga, and Nakamura and Mishkin, reviewed in Chapters 6 and 8) intended to isolate the oil refinery without turning it off or paralysing the animal. The result is that the animals display no visual behaviour whatever, despite the continuing electrophysiological activity of the visual cortex. This evidence was provided not by making a surgical disconnexion (an impracticality), but by removing all non-visual cortex in one hemisphere and preventing visual signals from reaching the other hemisphere. It can be argued that the definition of non-visual cortex itself is ambiguous. For example, the so-called dorsal stream was affected in some of the experiments, and this in itself might be expected to influence what Milner and Goodale describe as the system involved in visual action. The matter is discussed in some detail in Chapter 8, in the light of more recent classifications of visual cortex', which do not alter the main conclusions. This is not to say, in passing, that the definitions of visual or non-visual cortex do not need tightening up. Visual cortex, especially, even if defined 'V1-fugally', can sometimes take on generous dimensions in flow diagrams. Beyond this, it might be claimed that the procedure of ablating all non-visual cortex is so extreme as to affect the visual pathways themselves as well as other sub-cortical structures. Nakamura and Mishkin address this latter question, among others, and reject it. Nevertheless, some critics of my own use of their evidence may argue that these complex experiments, although yielding results that are unquestionably dramatic, are being made to carry too heavy a burden. My reply is they are highly instructive and, load-bearing arguments aside, they serve as a weather vane pointing to a hypothesis. Regarding possible 'non-visual cortical sites' that may be involved in the commentary stage, we draw particular attention to the FEF lesions (or more likely, area 8, which lies anterior to it and with which it overlaps in the monkey) that in some ways, mimic those of striate cortex itself, to prefrontal area V6 and also to deep structures in the anterior temporal lobes. The evidence from brain imaging, and from increasingly refined suggestions that emerge from that source as well as from parallel experiments, will reveal whether that hypothesis has anything going for it.

It might be argued, not unfairly, that I have given less attention than they deserve to possible specialized processing 'modules' within the oil refinery. Exciting and important results have emerged from research on apparently specialized systems for, say, colour and directional discrimination of movement, and will not doubt continue to attract further exploration. But if the previous argument about their being necessary but not sufficient is correct, then excitement alone will not suffice to solve the problem of awareness, although each of the several modular components—if indeed they really are modular—will of course make its own contribution to perceptual processing. How such a contribution feeds into the picture that we have drawn is a challenging theme for the future. Nor will re-entry over recurrent pathways confined entirely within the oil refinery work. Also, as mentioned in the Chapter 1, it appears that the degree of specialization suggested by electrophysiology is less clearly supported than predicted either by clinical work or animal neuropsychology. The danger of modular thinking for future work on imaging research is that only those regions that happen to fit a modular view, such as V3 or V5 for motion, V5 for colour, will be taken as supportive evidence, ignoring temporal lobe, area 7, cerebellum, prefrontal cortex, etc., when we are dealing specifically with signals of which the subject is aware. This is precisely what led to the downfall of phrenology, which remained popular with leading scientists and the public alike for several decades: bumps that conformed with the phrenological maps continued to be taken as confirmatory evidence, but counter-evidence was ignored. Such is one of the deep temptations in all scientific hypothesis testing, and indeed in everyday thinking about women, blacks, Pakistanis, Oxbridge dons, or what have you—we notice confirmatory evidence in favour of a hypothesis but not that against it. All imaging entails setting criteria for what is taken to be activation among a complex set of changes in levels of activity, the subtractive procedure not withstanding, and a priori assumptions figure importantly in such criteria. One person's excitement is another person's false positive. It would be a pity if we extend phrenology from bumps on the head to regions inside the brain.

Turning to the neuropsychological evidence itself, the temptation to offer interpretations in terms of degradation is very great. Just as it might be said that I have placed too heavy a burden on the experiments isolating visual cortex, it might also be said that I have made too much of the claim that the intact residual function is dissociated from acknowledged awareness, rather than that a function merely has been weakened to the point where normal subjects would also be unaware when dealing with such impoverished signals. This objection is not, please note, a difficulty or weakness in the empirical phenomena as such, in the data, but with their interpretation, and so this is a matter of theory rather than of fact. In Chapter 2 I argued against such a degradation interpretation applying universally to all of the syndromes with which we have been concerned, and it would be redundant to rehearse the argument here again, but it is so strongly embedded in thinking about cognitive function as having strength along an analogue scale that it can be predicted to be offered in practically any discussion of any of the syndromes. There may well be instances of neuropsychological syndromes in which degradation is a reasonable interpretation, and it may well be that dysfunction can sometimes be simulated by stretching the demands on normal function, although that still does not logically require that the simulation is a correct characterization of the underlying deficit. But it is folly to try to take such an approach generally in pathology. Paralysis is not just having weakened muscles. Blindsight is not just having weak eyesight. Agnosia is not just having weakened 'meanings'. Unilateral neglect of the left part of the visual field is not just having greater difficulty in moving the eyes in one direction rather than the other. And given that there are multiple visual pathways arising in the retina, it seems a curiously inefficient arrangement, evolutionarily speaking, for these to be thought to summate their activity along a single dimension of strength, all of them emptying their contents into a single bucket, as it were. The existence of multiple pathways arising early, at the very origins of the input stage, suggests differing processing modes, each making a different contribution to the final visual product. In the field of memory disorders, although the amnesic syndrome was early suggested to be just weak memory, it is now widely accepted that there is a multiplicity of memory systems, or, at the very least, of processing modes. Fortunately, however, the issue of degradation vs. dissociation is open to empirical attack, at least in some circumstances. Double or multiple dissociations of memory disorders are what led to a view of multiple memory systems, and the same strategy is available across the board. Beyond that we can, for example, compare brain imaging for weak signals in an intact system and contrast it with the results of residual function using stronger signals; for blindsight we can actually do this within the same subject because typically only one hemifield is impaired. We have time to wait and see.

Whatever interpretation turns out to be correct for residual function, the patients themselves are severely disabled in the domain in which that function is found; this was the theme of Chapter 7. But what has not received discussion here, or indeed very much in the literature, is the value of *these* residual functions? If we appeal to evolution to speculate about the value of being aware, what is the evolutionary value of possessing functions without awareness? Of course, we can point to the myriad of bodily processes that operate automatically and autonomically, which maintain metabolic homeostasis, muscular tone, and which underlie practised skills, and so forth. It can argued that it would be a waste of neural space to be aware of such processes when awareness is not necessary for their functioning. These not only operate in the absence of moment-by-moment awareness, but awareness can get in the way. Stephen Potter, the famous gamesmanship expositor, was well aware of this in concocting his ploys. Take, for example, his recommendation on how to triumph over a golf opponent: that one should praise the victim profusely after a good stroke, and express the wish that one would like to mimic the stroke exactly. At that point a copy of the chart of the muscular system from *Gray's anatomy* is presented, and the opponent asked to point to each and every muscle that was used for the stroke, and in which precise sequence. That is enough to destroy the opponent's skill and composure when he tries to demonstrate!

However, not all of the residual capacities in the syndromes we have discussed submit readily to such a neat functional interpretation. Admittedly, in the amnesic syndrome skilled, learned habits do persist, and in blindsight and prosopagnosia autonomic responses can be found. We know, as was set out in Chapter 1, that there are instances of brain damage, for example to the basal ganglia, that yield deficits in learned skills, and these are powerful examples for demonstrating double and multiple dissociations. One could also point to deficits in autonomic functioning with hypothalamic damage. But what is the value of discriminating without awareness in blindsight, or of priming in amnesia, or in the isolated autonomic response to a familiar face? Clearly, as we have seen, they are apparently of little value to the patients themselves. What we would need to reach a judgment on the matter would be to see the neuropsychological complementary conditions for the very cognitive functions under consideration—all memory functions intact, but with priming destroyed, visual discrimination with awareness intact, but no discrimination without awareness, normal face recognition but no autonomic response, and so forth. And, of course, we do not have such conditions available for scrutiny for all of the syndromes, and when we do have a claim for a specific loss, say in priming, as with the benzodiazapine drug lorazapam (Brown *et al.*, 1989), the wide spectrum of effects of such drugs is hardly restricted to priming, although there may be clues that might potentially arise from such a treatment. There are hemianopic patients who apparently do not have blindsight but, as discussed in Chapter 6, the most likely explanation of such cases is that they have suffered more extensive brain damage than those who do exhibit blindsight, and so a direct comparison is not possible. The general picture suggested is that the so-called implicit functions, aside from those involving specific identifiable skills for which, as mentioned, awareness would actually get in the way, are background supportive functions rather than being vital for survival—as the overt, explicit functions assuredly are. In blindsight they may well be involved in phylogenetically old-established mechanisms of detection, systems that serve as William James' sentry who gives the initial warning.

Whatever their status, the implicit residual capacities are not easily described as being functions of the 'unconscious mind' of psychoanalytic writers. As we have seen, the characteristic of the capacities we have discussed is precisely that they are devoid of mentation, of thinking. Nor is there any credence to their having a status as suppressed or repressed forces being held in check, or as making devious intrusions into conscious life. The evidence that we have considered does demonstrate that there are unconscious capacities, but these are not Machiavellian or mischievous or condemned players in the unconscious theatre of the analysts. Whether or not one considers that there are any such players lurking in some dark dungeon is another matter, altogether, but not for discussion here.

The issue is related, of course, to the large and somewhat contentious topic of putative dissociations that occur in the psychiatric domain, although the criteria for deciding between a theoretical mechanism of repression leading to amnesia, on the one hand, and normal forgetting through lack of rehearsal or inadequate retrieval cues, on the other, are very difficult to satisfy. It is of interest that when they tried to find experimental evidence for repression in a large literature search, Pope and Hudson (1995) could not locate a single instance that satisfied reasonable but rigorous criteria. Of more interest in the present context are the dissociations between performance and awareness induced by hypnosis, which have been investigated for many years by Hilgard (1977) and others. This, indeed, would make an interesting link to forge with the syndromes reviewed in this book.

As we are still rehearsing omissions in the book, it should be mentioned that we gave little attention to the dynamic balance between the aware and unaware modes. This is not so much an omission as an admission: that there is still much to be discussed in future treatments. It would be wrong to give the impression that, in blindsight, for instance, there will never be acknowledged awareness for a moving stimulus travelling at, say, 5° per second, and that there always will be awareness at, say, 15° per second, which were the values in one of the examples we cited in Chapters 3 and 6. Undoubtedly the balance will shift somewhat depending on states of arousal, time of day, length of testing session, and so forth. I hope G.Y., for example, will forgive me for saying that there is little point in testing him for any visual discriminations before 10 am; in fact he does not willingly make an appearance before then! In our experience the shifts in the balance are not great, but it would be misleading to suggest that the two modes are rigidly bounded, or that there is not oscillation or shading at the boundaries. But, as argued in Chapter 2, this is not the same boundary that exists in standard threshold-setting determinations in psychophysics because, as mentioned, the levels of performance are well above those found in that shadowland. (A more interesting parallel with psychophysics using normal subjects may lie in the approach adopted by Kolb and Braun, 1995, of using stimuli suggested by electrophysiology, and generating blindsight without brain damage.)

Another omission in my treatment of residual function—another topic for future consideration—concerns the effect of the type of response employed in testing for residual function. There have been claims, for example, that verbal responses are less effective in detecting residual function than non-verbal responses (Zihl and von Cramon, 1980; cf. also, Dennett, 1991, p. 248, for an account of related experiments by Marcel). For example, in blindsight, it could be important that the subject responds verbally 'yes' or 'no' rather than by blinking or pressing a key. I have never been so impressed by the topography or type of response making much of a difference, but I have not really pursued the subject. But it seems to be that the distinction lies not so much with the response typography or musculature as with whether it is voluntary or not, and I see little difference in this regard between a key press and a verbal utterance.

Finally, some will undoubtedly think I have played fast and loose with my slipping into the use of a 'commentary *stage*'. We may all think we understand what it means to make a commentary, but what is the *stage* at which this is reached? I acknowledge some slippage in the way in which I use this term. What I mean to convey is that once a commentary can be made about an event, a larger encyclopedia of knowledge and interests can be brought to bear, including what is sometimes called self-knowledge or self-awareness, which I take to be a complex concept. It also means that one can infer the commentary from the content of the verbal communication that accompanies an event. Beyond that, just as we do not normally see red, for example, divorced and isolated from an object and a context, so we do not issue commentaries as isolated nods of the head or presses of a key without also conveying just what it is that is being commented upon. Whether we are aware of a patch of purple, or a moving spot, or a face, will not only be context-bound but will alter the way in which further visual analysis takes place. I do not know how such complex integrative and attentional phenomena find expression in brain activity (although the cingulate gyrus keeps insisting on making its appearance in brain images dealing with attention; cf. Posner and Rothbart, 1992) but there is no doubt that these are powerful accompaniments of what one consciously detects, with powerful behavioural consequences. We have suggested that back projections into the oil refinery may change the directions along which visual processing itself is carried out. But the actual *content* of experience is another matter. I do not know why red is red, but the nature of the knowledge that is elicited by the commentary stage is obviously of relevance to the content of experience.

The prime entry in the '*and so what might be wrong?*' category is that the brain simply may not work with systems that are *spatially* distinct in coding the differences between aware and unaware states. Consciousness may be a matter of temporal organization, as other authors have suggested, for which there are several candidates, for example thalamo-cortical reverberatory firing, or cells that can fire synchronously at 40 hertz, and so forth. If so, our whole line of speculation here will be wrong, at least in terms of there being a hope of finding brain images with spatially distinct areas of activation corresponding to aware vs. unaware states of discrimination. But that is also one of its strengths—the view is testable. If it is entirely a matter of firing rates, there will be no commentary stage that lights up differentially in a brain image. Instead, the same structures will fire more or less actively as states of awareness change. Those who are sceptical of a commentary-stage approach may still interpret specific regions lighting up differentially as being byproducts of a change in temporal activation, although that too is testable by means of lesion or cooling experiments in animals. But it could also turn out that *both* spatial and temporal properties are involved in brain mechanisms of conscious awareness.

There is, however, a dire way in which searching for brain images based on aware vs. unaware modes in blindsight could lead to a dead end, simply by virtue of the Heisenberg uncertainty principle; that is, that the method of measuring the phenomenon alters the phenomenon itself. When a blindsight subject is forced to guess whether, say, a spot is moving vertically or horizontally, and then to press a commentary key about his or her accompanying experience, the subject will presumably be aware of that situation and of his/her responses. And the brain mechanisms involved in *that* awareness may be co-extensive (e.g. perhaps in the fronto–limbic complex) with those that are involved in being aware of a moving spot. And so the lack of a difference between aware and unaware modes in blindsight may simply be equivalent to 'aware of guessing and pressing keys' and 'unaware of moving spot and pressing keys'. The implication of this line of argument is that a negative result will be inconclusive, whereas a positive result will be informative. Such a situation is not uncommon in science. We are very fortunate when we have that rare experiment that will prove to be conclusive no matter what the result. If absolutely no differences appear in the brain images in association with awareness, we return to the drawing board.

But even if differences do appear in brain images between the aware and unaware modes of discrimination in blindsight, one must exercise caution in thinking that we are home and dry, that the hotspots are where it all goes on. We are reaching the point in imaging and electrophysiological research where it is clear that the hotspots can sometimes be lesioned with impunity without removing the behavioural capacities with which they correlate for example, as already mentioned earlier (Chapter 1), the colour hotspot; V4, can be removed in a monkey without causing achromatopsia. In such a case, the hotspot may be part of a larger system, perhaps even the most important part, but in which there is sufficient redundancy and parallelity as to make it insensitive to a restricted local intervention. But the hotspot may be a region that mirrors activity elsewhere that itself may be too distributed for focused detection. For example, the frontal lobes may be involved in the 'planning' or 'effortful' aspects of many disparate psychological processes. A prefrontal hotspot in an image may reflect the effort involved in the task rather than reveal the site of the underlying processing itself.

And so what?

Well, even if the current line of speculation turns out to be incorrect, hopefully it will lead to further empirical progress and conceptual analysis. No matter what, some important nuggets do remain. The first is that the evidence at the leading apex—the evidence that there are *residual capacities of which the subjects lack awareness*—still leads. If the support arising out of the other two apices is the wrong sort of support, then some others will have to be sought. This is not to say that the empirical phenomena are not subject to strictures that apply to all empirical enquiries regarding proper control, repeatability, and so forth. Nor is it to deny that the actual ways one chooses to study the empirical phenomena do not themselves influence the types of theories and neural evidence one seeks at the other apices. That, indeed, is part of the dynamic within the spearhead which is so fruitful. But if the approach that is suggested here turns out to be unprofitable or just wrong, other theories and neuroscientific evidence will have to be brought to bear on the phenomena under consideration. There is no way in which these phenomena can be dislodged from their apical position, nor bypassed by efforts from the armchair or from the physiological laboratory. Nor, I would add, by computer simulation or artificial networks, nor by molecular analysis. The road to understanding may be long and twisting, but a goal is not reached by taking a detour that bypasses it.

Second is the corollary that the topic of *awareness itself*, no matter on what basis it may be studied or analysed, also will not go away despite all of the difficulties. It cannot be dodged by drafts. In the end there is a transparently clear distinction in experience between being aware and not being aware, whether this arises through brain damage, anaesthesia, spinal section, attention, practice, or what have you. One may demonstrate that the psychological phenomena are complex, that the criteria for demonstrating awareness in others may be difficult, and that these various phenomena do not have the same explanation, but in the end the paraplegic or the blindsight subject knows to what one is referring in distinguishing between performance with and without awareness, and the same applies to normal subjects in all of the other categories. And when one or more explanations are found, the phenomena may become less astonishing, but the phenomena as such remain. To repeat my pontification in the Introduction and Chapter 3: one's explanations should be elevated to the phenomena being investigated, rather than that the latter should suffer reduction—or worse, disappearance—by explanation. When they actually do disappear, not by philosophical discourse, but by brain damage, the effects are dire.

The third point should be evident from the discussion in the previous section. The view put forward here, despite its acknowledged inadequacies, is testable, or at least leads to tests. Either brain circuits are recruited when a subject becomes aware, or they are not. Linking the search to a subject's commentary not only provides an operational criterion but also a hook on to which to hang one's brain imaging findings. This is, of course, not the only testable hypothesis about brain mechanisms of consciousness, far from it, but its fate, like those others, rests on empirical enquiry rather than on rumination.

Finally, it is clear that not only is there an upsurge of interest in the general topic of the scientific basis of consciousness—an upsurge that itself is astonishing compared to its dismissal not long ago—but also that the new brain imaging technologies and other neuroscientific methods offer inroads into that question that even a few years ago would have been considered a creation of the wild fantasies of science fiction writers. These technologies are absolutely bound to illuminate this topic, as indeed they are illuminating other psychological questions of some depth, but they do so only if the questions are posed appropriately. In that case, the answers will astonish. If the questions are not, we may end up with internal phrenology no more revealing than the external bumps on the head. And among the phenomena that allow appropriate formulation and unique opportunities are those that arise out of the neuropsychological syndromes which demonstrate the difference between performance with and without awareness.

Even if this, or any other particular approach regarding conscious awareness, is disconfirmed by imaging results, empirical data, or any other conceivable development, the contribution and role of neuropsychology to our understanding of the mind will remain. There is an interesting metaphor that emerges from a technique sometimes used in neuroanatomy: freeze-fracture. If a bit of neural tissue is deep frozen, and then tapped, it may fall apart in a way that reveals and preserves the separate independent anatomical structures. Similarly, the injury that the mind suffers from brain damage can sometimes produce freeze-fracturing of its cognitive functions. This does not always, or perhaps even often, happen—just as freeze-fracturing in anatomy does not always work. But the results, when it does work, offer penetrating and fascinating insights into the structure of the mind itself. For we can establish, with considerable richness of detail, just which capacities can remain intact when others are damaged, and in turn which are invariably affected consequentially and hierarchically. And these results, in turn, can foster further lines of research into the structure of the mind in normal individuals. As the associated brain systems themselves inevitably become better understood, more refined prospects for rehabilitation and physical treatment also may develop. Understanding has always been in the debt of the study of damage.

Postscript

Research moves quickly in this area, and it could readily be anticipated that there would be fresh evidence after submitting the manuscript. Oxford University Press kindly agreed in advance to allow me to add a piece at the page-proof stage to bring matters a bit more up to date.

The argument was advanced in the book that a promising possibility stemmed from the distinction between the aware and unaware modes in blindsight: that brain imaging which allowed the identification of brain structures critical to each mode, and especially to visual awareness, could be carried out. In April 1996 such a study was conducted by John Barbur, Arash Sahraie, and me, at the Institute of Psychiatry, London, with the collaboration of the fMRI team there, Dr Steve Williams, Dr Andy Simmons, and their colleagues. The tests were modelled on the paradigm in PNAS (*Proceedings of the National Academy of Sciences, USA*, in Weiskrantz *et al.*, 1995), and with the same subject, G.Y. It was necessary to construct a portable battery-operated laser projection system and a new screen to fit into the confines of the magnetic imaging environment, and then to repeat the psychophysical determinations to ensure that they still held up with the new equipment and new screen. They did—the original data were closely replicated (Sahraie *et al.*, in preparation).

In the unaware mode we used a low velocity, and in the aware mode a high velocity, as derived from the psychophysics. Each mode had two levels of contrast. We also tested the sighted hemifield with both speeds and contrasts. In addition, a subthreshold control was run in the blind hemifield, set below the level of successful performance as determined psychophysically (which generated nothing of interest in the brain image). A conservative threshold was applied, based on minimal values of two statistical indices, Total FPQ and Max FPQ (Bullmore *et al.*, 1996), and also on the cluster size of areas of activation. The results must be considered provisional, given the single subject and complexities of statistical inferences; further studies are needed. But here, as far as it goes, is a brief summary of the salient features of the combined results for aware vs. unaware modes in the affected hemifield, irrespective of contrast level, as well as for the sighted hemifield. A full multi-authored paper is in preparation.

In the aware mode, dorsolateral prefrontal activity was seen in area 46 (right hemisphere), as well as area 47 (both hemispheres). There was also activity in area 18 in both hemispheres. The sighted hemifield also produced increased activity in prefrontal areas 46 (right) and 9 (right) and left frontal pole. In the unaware mode, and only in this mode, there was activation of the superior colliculus. There was activation of the right medial and orbital frontal areas, but none in dorsolateral regions. There were two other features of note. In the unaware mode increased activity was seen in the left occipital lobe (area 19, ipsilateral to the lesion). This implies that activation of such a visual cortical region is not *sufficient* for phenomenal visual awareness. In addition, in the aware mode in the blind field, as mentioned above, activity was seen in area 18 *contralateral* to the lesion. It would appear that the intact hemisphere may have been recruited, via callosal connexions. Cross-field interactions may well be of some significance for residual visual function, as seen in visual completion phenomena reviewed in Chapter 4. It is of interest that Ruddock and colleagues have recently reported that particular values of moving visual stimuli in the intact hemifield actually produce an experience of phenomenal 'seeing' in G.Y.'s blind hemifield (Finlay *et al.*, 1997).

In the terminology of Chapter 8, it would appear that prefrontal areas may well qualify as a 'C' given that areas 46 and 47 were activated in both the aware mode of the blind hemifield and the intact sighted field. It is of some interest that area 46 lies at an anterior point of rich convergence of many of the pathways, both ventral and dorsal, emanating from visual cortices, as seen in Fig. 8.4. Area 8, with which the FEF is usually identified, was not activated in any condition, but the area immediately anterior to it (area 9, right hemisphere) was activated—but only during stimulation of the sighted field. Given the ambiguity of the anterior border of the FEF (Paus, 1996; see Chapter 8) and the errors that can intrude in plotting onto an 'average' brain map, area 9 may well implicate the FEF, which is also inter-connected with area 46. If so, the FEF would serve as a candidate for distinguishing between 'awareness without seeing' (i.e., in the affected field) and normal phenomenal seeing within the intact visual system. Area 46 and the FEF (and possibly areas 47 and 9) would also qualify as VORBs. Speculations about other possible candidates did not gain support. The insula was active in both the sighted hemifield and the unaware mode (albeit in opposite hemispheres). The cingulate was active in all modes, although there may be potentially finer differences along its anterior–posterior axis.

The major outcome, however, of the imaging results is not so much an isolated 'centre' or C for visual awareness—although area 46 is certainly of interest in this regard—but a shift in the pattern of activity between the aware mode (both in the affected and intact hemifields) and the unaware mode, from dorsolateral to medial prefrontal cortex, and from cortex to superior colliculus. The role of the latter fits in well, of course, with the evidence from recovery of function in monkeys following V1 lesions, as reviewed in Chapters 6 and 7.

Just before our own fMRI study was finished, Colin Blakemore and Hank Spekreise in Amsterdam (in preparation) carried out SPECT (single photon emission computed tomography) brain imaging on G.Y. using the same aware and unaware parameters employed in our PNAS study. They, too, found a prefrontal aware focus, when the unaware imaging results were subtracted from the aware results. They also found evidence of activity in an occipital area contralateral to the damaged V1, with visual stimulation of the blind hemifield. The SPECT analysis only permitted one subtraction, but it is reassuring to find some measure of overlap, and the findings will be compared in further publications.

Recently, I gather, it has been claimed by Semir Zeki, of University College, London, in several lectures, that he cannot repeat our PNAS findings. Replicability is, of course, at the heart of scientific progress, and so the matter is of some concern. The background, as far as I can recount it without having been present, is as follows: our young post-doctoral collaborator, Arash Sahraie (both Barbur and I were abroad at the time) was requested to view Zeki's set-up because of difficulty in replicating our findings. Arash pointed out a number of difficulties with the particular visual display on a PC monitor (among them, a moving line artifact, highlights, limited excursion, discontinuous movement) and also explained why we found it preferable to use a smoothly moving, red laser stimulus projected onto a wide screen. Zeki apparently then tried a red laser stimulus, still without positive results. He kindly sent me the particular stimulus parameters of the laser set-up. It is evident that a number of serious problems remain, which also make it clear why a replication was almost bound to fail. Firstly, his velocity was very far outside the range we used. For the particular experiment of ours that he tried to replicate, we used a velocity of 15°/sec with an movement excursion of 20°. Zeki used 280°/sec. The resulting brightness of such a target is likely to be very low because of spatiotemporal integration: at 280°/sec a target only takes 70 msec to move 20°. I doubt that G.Y. could detect or discriminate anything at all at such a high velocity (and he has since confirmed to me that, in fact, he could not). Parametric details are as crucial to psychophysics as electrode diameter, impedance, anaesthetic level, cortical depression, etc., are to the electrophysiologist. In Chapter 6 there is an account of how even a small difference in a stimulus parameter (50 msec) can switch results from chance level to virtually perfect performance in the blind field. Here, instead, we are dealing with a difference of more than an order of magnitude. Secondly, Zeki did not actually study the same discrimination as we did. Ours was a directional movement task; that is, the subject had to judge (by guessing, if necessary), whether the spot was moving horizontally or non-horizontally. His task was a movement *detection* task, a moving spot vs. non-movement, quite a different situation from a differential discrimination, and one that also has characteristic problems of response criterion. Thirdly, as far as can be judged, only 300 trials were administered for the laser condition, which is a flimsy basis on which to draw any firm conclusions, especially to report a disconfirmation to a large audience. Fourthly, Zeki has suggested publicly that our results should be set aside until someone outside our group repeats them. He was apparently unaware that Colin Blakemore (working in collaboration with Miroslav Kubna and Zuzans Kulbova) had, in fact, already repeated our major PNAS finding, and reported his evidence to a large audience in Tucson in April 1996 at the 'Towards a Science of Consciousness' meeting. This confirmation was carried out, not in Oxford, but in Prague in an electrophysiology laboratory. Since that time, Blakemore and Benson have been analysing the effect of different types of instructions for the commentary responses on movement discrimination, an eminently reasonable follow-up.

In the end the data must speak for themselves. We repeated our PNAS findings, as already mentioned, in order to carry out an imaging study. More recently we have replicated them again for another reason: it was suggested to us, quite reasonably, that perhaps a binary commentary decision, aware vs. unaware, may be too gross, and that even when the subject reports unaware there might be a smidgen of awareness unreported by him. And so Arash Sahraie and I (in preparation) re-ran the PNAS study with a six-point awareness scale, zero to 5 levels of awareness. The pattern of results was unchanged: for G.Y. zero really means zero whether it is contrasted just with 1 or with 1 to 5 (Fig. P.1). We also explored the use of a six-point 'confidence' rating instead of, or together with, an awareness scale. We found conditions under which G.Y. could perform well even with zero confidence. We found as well, not surprisingly, that the more questions one asks the subject the poorer is the discriminative performance. We also found that G.Y.'s sensitivity for directional movement discrimination had improved, a point to which I will return soon.

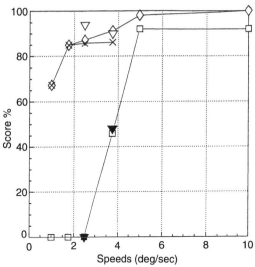

Figure P.1 Results for directional movement discrimination with awareness commentary responses in G.Y.'s blind hemifield. See caption for Fig. 6.5. The open triangles show discrimination results using the six-point awareness scale. The solid triangles refer to percentage of trials on which G.Y. signalled awareness, using the six-point scale: zero for no awareness, and 1 to 5 for degrees of awareness. The squares show results using binary awareness scale, either not aware or aware. Crosses show discrimination performance when zero or no awareness was signalled. Note closeness of results with six-point and binary awareness scales. Note, also, increased sensitivity as a function of velocity, as compared with Figs 6.4 and 6.5.

Over the past year, other demonstrations of the validity of the distinction between aware and unaware modes for G.Y. have emerged. One was combined with a direct test of the hypothesis advanced by Gazzaniga and colleagues (Fendrich *et al.*, 1992, see Chapter 6), which was found not to apply to G.Y.'s condition. In a variation of the test of the Gazzaniga hypothesis we added a commentary key to the detection task with which G.Y. signalled his awareness or unawareness. We were able to find several points in the blind field in which he performed well above chance in the signal detection task (even reaching 100% correct) while signalling no awareness (Kentridge *et al.*, in press).

Another example emerged from considering the question of whether unaware signals or targets in the blind field can direct a subject's attention. There were plenty of hints that if a blindsight subject knew *where* a target was likely to occur, he could perform more efficiently than if he did not, but it has never formally been put to the test. The results of a study at the University of Durham by Kentridge and Heywood (in preparation) are striking and show both the positive capacity and the limitations of the blind field. If the cueing stimulus's contrast is lowered so that awareness is degraded, it can nevertheless render the reaction to the target (also of degraded awareness) quicker if the signal is a valid rather than an invalid cue to the position of the target—provided the cueing signal is in the same location as the target. But if the cue requires a shift to a different target location, then there is no such advantage bestowed by a valid cue. (Of course, with cueing signals of which the subject was fully aware, there was no such limitation.) Hence, a cue can serve as a *prime* for an event in the same locus but not as a signal for a *shift* in attention to a different locus. (This fits with other evidence, for example that subject D.B. could not make a same/different judgment for two stimuli within his blind field, whereas he had no difficulty in doing so between the intact and the blind field; see Weiskrantz, 1986, Chapter 14). It was amusing that, in the phase of the experiment (August 1996) when both the cues and the targets had both been set at contrasts in the unaware mode, but he was nevertheless performing very well, G.Y. actually interrupted the testing, saying that 'these are very difficult', and suggesting to Bob Kentridge that he check the data to see 'whether it is even worth collecting any more!' Fortunately, his advice was not heeded.

Another example of good performance, either with or without aware-ness, again with G.Y.'s blind field, was recently found by Cowey in a colour substitution task. The subject was instructed to indicate the locus on the screen at which a *change* from a white to a colour patch occurred. In switches from white to blue or from white to red, there was no value of luminance of the coloured stimulus that ever reduced the discriminative performance to chance. Even when G.Y. claimed it was pure guesswork, discrimination was well above chance. As luminance differences between white and colour increased, G.Y. then reported awareness, as expected (but not of colour, as such, or of normal seeing). Conversely, with a switch from white to green, the performance did drop to chance when the white and colour stimuli were of equal or near equal luminance. The result is not only an indication of differential responses to wavelength in blindsight (see below), but also makes it clear that G.Y.'s commentary responses are not based simply on a different response criterion between aware and unaware modes, as otherwise all wavelengths should be affected similarly.

The wavelength composition of the target has also turned out to be important, not only in psychophysical determinations in blindsight, but also for pupillometry. Barbur, Sahraie, and I (in preparation) find that stimulation of G.Y.'s blind hemifield triggers a small but significant pupil constriction in response to a briefly presented red target, given appropriate size and other parameters. This is less so, if at all, when the same target is presented in green light. Red has also been seen to be important psychophysically for G.Y.'s blind field by Ruddock and colleagues (Brent *et al.*, 1994) and by Barbur *et al.* (1994b). In none of these examples (see Chapter 6) does the subject acknowledge any awareness of colour, *per se*, although discriminative performance is good. Interestingly, in a recent fMRI brain image study (Barbur, Sahraie, and myself, with Dr Steve Williams, Dr Andy Simmons, and colleagues at the Institute of Psychiatry) the superior colliculus was seen to be activated by the same red target, presented to G.Y.'s blind field, that generates a small, but significant pupillary response. This was not the case for the green target. Such differential responses in the superior colliculus probably reflect a bias in a broad band response to wavelength, rather than colour opponency, but even this is uncertain given the evidence by Stoerig and Cowey (see Chapter 6) in their spectral sensitivity determinations in the blind fields of hemianopes. It certainly would be helpful to have dedicated electrophysiological studies of midbrain neuronal responses to wavelength, with and without the integrity of V1.

Pupillometry, it was argued in Chapter 3, offers a precise indirect non-verbal method of assessing the capacity of the blind fields of human subjects, circumventing the need to engage in curious instructions to a subject to guess about something that could not be seen. Being non-verbal it could be used with animals and with human infants. Cowey and I recently have made a direct comparison between monkeys with total unilateral V1 removal and G.Y., using pupillary constriction to sinusoidal gratings in the same apparatus and the same environment, and employing identical recording methodology. The results of the monkeys and G.Y. map onto each other very closely, and clearly reveal the existence of a narrowly tuned, spatially structured channel, with a peak sensitivity at 1 cycle/degree, and with an acuity of about 7 or 8 cycles/degree (See Fig. P.2). Interestingly, when we examine the channel for G.Y., previously determined psychophysically (Barbur *et al.*, 1994a), it shows a similar shape and acuity, as shown in the figure. This is a clear demonstration that V1 damage in human and monkey yields closely similar results, and reinforces the evidence for a narrowly tuned spatial channel. Even though the channel is clearly defined by the spacing of the bars in the grating, G.Y. never reports any experience of the bars as such, although he typically has an awareness that 'something has happened'; that is, a response, no doubt, to the transient onset/offset of the presented stimulus. Whether there is a spatiotemporal channel measured with the pupil response for which he would have no awareness whatever (see Chapter 6) remains to be determined. We also know that, psychophysically, there is a luminance channel (Barbur *et al.*, 1994a), but we have no pupillometry determinations for that as yet.

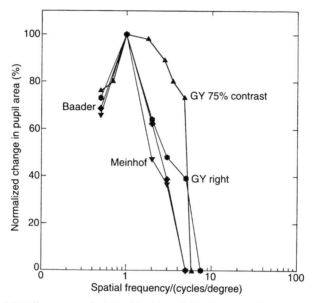

Figure P.2 Pupillometry results in the blind hemifields of two monkeys (Baader, Meinhof) with unilateral V1 lesions, and for G.Y. Also shown are the psychophysical results for G.Y. with gratings, labelled 'GY 75% contrast', from the study by Barbur *et al.*, 1994a. (The pupillometry gratings had a contrast of 80%.) All values have been normalized such that their peaks are set at 100%.

It has become evident, in the last six months or so, that G.Y.'s visual performance in his blind field has improved markedly. Not only are his velocity thresholds reduced, but the same is true for signal detection thresholds in successive attention studies carried out in Durham by Kentridge and colleagues, and has also been found by Petra Stoerig (personal communication) for G.Y.'s recent spectral sensitivity determination as compared to the curve measured about 4 years ago in the same testing apparatus. It may be that earlier results, such as we published in PNAS, could be more difficult to replicate because of a smaller psychophysical range within which to work, and for this reason it is a pity that Zeki's recent test was not carried out with the appropriate parameters—it could have been of interest. Within the last year or so, G.Y. has been heavily tested in Oxford (by 3 different groups), in London (by 3 different groups), in San Francisco (at least twice), and in Birmingham, Durham (several times), Prague, Amsterdam, Frankfurt, Munich, and Tübingen.

Long ago it was shown by Cowey (1967), as reviewed in Chapter 7, that if monkeys with V1 lesions are given lots of practice in their blind fields, their sensitivity also increases. It can be substantial—as much as 3 log units (as shown in Fig. P.3). But it only occurs if the animal is required *to make use of* the extra-striate pathways. Passive stimulation of the visual field, which occurs throughout daily life, does not work. As also mentioned in Chapter 7, similar evidence for improvement also occurs in hemianopic human subjects. Of course, typically such subjects do not bother to practice with visual stimuli presented to their blind fields. They do not need to, because they have a perfectly intact half-field with which they can negotiate their everyday world. It would be hard to tell them, or their monkey counterparts, apart from their normal peers in everyday behaviour. (It is for this reason that rare cases with bilateral damage would make interesting comparisons because they have no such visual crutch and any residual

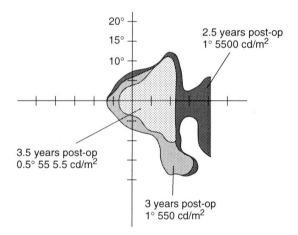

Figure P.3 Field defect of monkey 'Squib' at various times postoperatively. Luminance values refer to peak intensity of a 50 msec flash, subtending an angle of either 1° or 0.5°. 2.5 years postoperatively the animal had a field defect shown by the total area covered by all the stippling. Gradually, with training, the animal completely recovered with the parameters of light stimulation used. When light intensity was reduced by 1 log unit, the field defect could be demonstrated but the area of defect had decreased (medium and light stippling together). Again, with further training the animal gradually recovered completely and the field defect could be demonstrated only by decreasing the light intensity another 1 or 2 log units and decreasing the diameter of the flash stimulus. Even so, the size of the residual field defect had shrunk still further (light stippling alone). Redrawn from Cowey (1967), reprinted from Weiskrantz (1972) with permission.

function must depend on the use of extra-striate pathways.) If G.Y.'s increased sensitivity derives from the heavy testing of his blind field to which he has been subjected recently (in contrast to the previous 18 years, when testing was much more spaced and infrequent, and over which period he remained relatively stable), it would be a fascinating and gratifying outcome for what is, in a sense, a Heisenberg effect—the phenomenon being measured changing as a result of the measurement!

Finally, some critical tests of particular hypotheses concerning residual function turn on evidence from hemispherectomy; for example, whether remaining extra-striate cortices are necessary for particular residual visual functions, or whether the midbrain nuclei (or their projections to contralateral cortex) can suffice. As mentioned briefly in Chapters 2 and 6, earlier evidence of positive visual function in the blind hemifields of hemispherectomized patients has been put in doubt by more recent control experiments suggesting that there may have been stray light entering the intact hemifield (King *et al.*, 1996; also reinforced by a recent paper, Stoerig *et al.*, 1996). These studies found no evidence of positive function when constraints on stimuli in the blind field were imposed so as to guard against such an artifact (but in the course of doing so they may not have used stimuli sufficiently salient to be effective). Recently an alternative and indirect approach has been used that avoids such difficulties. It depends on interactions between the intact and the impaired hemifields. In two hemispherectomy patients Tamaiuolo *et al.* (in press) have demonstrated a visual spatial summation effect across the vertical meridian despite the subjects' lack of awareness in one hemifield. That is, the reaction time to stimuli presented to both the intact and the blind fields was shorter than to the intact field alone. No response was made to stimuli in their blind hemifield. Their findings cannot be explained in terms of light diffusion: quite dim LEDs were used, and there was an optic disc control. The evidence is a clear demonstration that simple detection phenomena can be subserved by subcortical mechanisms, and without the subject's awareness. It remains to be seen whether more complex cross-field interactions, for example of the Torjussen variety (cf. Chapter 3), would also work in hemispherectomies. In any event, the evidence by Tamaiuolo *et al.* reopens the hemispherectomy question.

No doubt further evidence will have emerged even since this postscript was written (31 December 1996). But there is a limit to how many PPSs can be tolerated by the publisher or the reader.

Appendix: terminology and other boring matters

Tasks, knowledge, and processes

The common feature of all of the clinical material considered in the book is the dissociation between performance and the subject's awareness. The general category is one that can be dubbed 'Lack of awareness of being able to do something of which one normally *would* be aware'. Because of the diversity of syndromes and methods, a variety of terms have been used that do not necessarily translate from one study or commentator to another. As we also wish to be able to apply terms both to humans and animals with some degree of consistency, an attempt at definitions is in order. Terms commonly used can be classified in terms of their application to tasks, knowledge, and processes.

Tasks

Only one distinction is required, that between *direct* and *indirect* tasks. A *direct* task is one in which the subject is instructed or trained to respond to the dimension that is of particular interest to the experimenter. For example, in blindsight it is to respond to stimuli (whether or not it involves guessing or reaching) in the blind field, even though the subject does not see them, the point being that it is about material in the blind field that the question is being directly addressed. Similarly, in an animal study we can guide the discriminative response directly to stimuli delivered to the putatively hemianopic field. In prosopagnosia, it would be asking the subject whether he does or does not recognize the face, and in amnesia it is to ask questions about whether or not an item is recognized. An *indirect* test is one in which the relevant information is derived incidentally; for example in a priming task, which seeks to determine whether an amnesic subject has incidentally stored information about an item without questioning him about his *memory* for that item. Or in a blindsight experiment, in which the sensitivity of the blind hemifield to visual information is inferred from its indirect effect on the subject's processing of stimuli delivered to the *intact* hemifield. This distinction is sometimes the same as 'explicit' or 'implicit', as they apply to instructions. But I do not use explicit and implicit to apply to tasks, because it implies a dependence on verbal instructions and I wish to make no distinction between animal and human subjects with regard to task demands. The distinction between implicit and explicit also is related to a contrast that is more specifically relevant to memory research and to language, namely, intentional vs. unintentional, when it refers to how or whether the subject is instructed to retrieve or to reflect on items, but again this pair of terms is not easily applied to non-speaking animals (although, of course, putatively homologous tasks can be proposed) and so will not be used here.

Knowledge

Whether the subject can provide evidence of knowledge of successful handling of material in the particular category in question is independent of the type of task. If he can, the knowledge can be said to be *overt*. If the subject has no such knowledge or insight, the knowledge is *covert*. Thus, in blindsight, discriminating by pure guesswork, when successful, is covert. When it is tested by cross-field interaction the subject's knowledge of the perceptual outcome is overt, even though the task itself is indirect, but it remains covert with respect to stimuli in the blind field. In memory research, priming is typically overt in the sense that the subject has knowledge of the stimuli to which he is responding at any particular moment, but as a phenomenon of priming *per se*, or as knowledge of its prior exposure is covert in amnesic subjects.

It might be assumed that the distinction cannot be applied to animals, and hence that it violates the original intention of only using terms that can. But it has been argued in Chapter 4 that there is a real sense in which it is not only valid, but also that there are experimental approaches to its application.

The distinction between knowledge of a procedure or of stimuli, on the one hand, and knowledge of an outcome, on the other, is an important one for consistency of usage. We are assuming that, in all cases under consideration here, the knowledge of an *outcome,* in some deep and complete sense, will be covert when the procedure is one that generates evidence of function without awareness ('lack of awareness of what is still o.k.'). On the other hand, knowledge of the stimuli in the task in question may or may not be covert; for example, it is covert in blindsight but not in amnesia.

Processes

A host of theoretical inferences are drawn from the evidence, and terms vary from one investigator to the next. We restrict the terms implicit and explicit to refer only to processes. These overlap but are not synonymous with 'automatic' and 'conscious'. As used by some, for example Jacoby and Kelley (1992), conscious comes close to meaning 'overt' knowledge of the *task demands* plus *control*, built into and sustained by the instructions to the subject, instructions which the subject can obey; for example: 'ignore all stimuli in the current test that you recognize as having been in the test that last occurred'. Automatic is taken to refer to aspects of the task over which the subject has no control (even if he wanted it). In one important sense, processes at the level of explanation are *always* unconscious. What subjects are aware of are test conditions (including the test stimuli in question), procedures, and some of their own responses, not how the nervous system allows any of these to take place (or, if you prefer, of the weights of nodes, hidden or otherwise). But one needs *some* sets of terms to distinguish between those theoretical processes that give rise to 'lack of awareness of what is still o.k.' and those that allow such awareness. There is bound to be variation in preferential terms for processes, but the hope is that they will not be terms that can be confused with those used to classify tasks, or with subjects' knowledge. This is especially the case because tasks are *never* process-pure (cf. Weiskrantz, 1989; Jacoby and Kelley, 1992). Knowledge of underlying processes I take to be always unconscious, whereas knowledge, in the sense of accompanying thoughts or experiences of control, or experiences of sequences of stages (e.g. of drawing a logical inference or forming a concept), might help illuminate underlying processes, but still requires explanation in terms of process, *per se*.

At the animal level, the distinction between conscious and automatic may be admissible at a theoretical level of processes, but hardly at the level of instructed control by the subject. It is equally difficult to know what is an implicit or explicit *process* for an animal. In this sense, theoretical terms are best used as they emerge from specific explanatory accounts of each of the syndromes in question, except where some common account can be given. One such general account is offered, in fact, in Chapters 3 and 8, combining neural processes with a particular characterization derived from folk psychology, but the terms used there should not be confused with any just referred to, although they may well reveal or lead to other grounds of confusion.

Dissociations

So much has now been written about the power and powerlessness of dissociations in neuropsychology that little need be said here beyond brief summary and reiteration. The reason for saying anything at all, beyond what was said in Chapter 2, is to preserve the supply of adrenalin in those readers who might think that more (or less) is being claimed when there are references to dissociations referred to in this book, as for example in the field of memory disorders or visual disorders, including the double dissociation between intact and blind hemifields in blindsight.

We will assume, and sometimes assert, that double dissociations of functions are powerful sources of inferences about possible *independence* of processes or systems. If one treatment affects one type of task and not another, and another treatment affects the second but not the first, we are in a position to speculate about underlying differences in process. We are also in a position to rule out explanations that claim the outcome is due to simple differences in difficulty between the two types of tasks. And, in any experimental paradigm, it is a *necessary* condition that double dissociations be obtained to infer independence of functions. However, and this is where the disputatious make their entrée, it is never a *sufficient* condition. Patterns of double dissociations can be obtained where we have good reason not to accept independence, for example when task difficulty and performance are not monitonically related. We assume in this book nothing more than that double dissociations are powerful and useful, but not omnipotent.

Double dissociations can be absolute or relative (Weiskrantz, 1968, 1989, 1991b), or what Shallice (1988) defines as 'classical' or 'trend' dissociations. That is, the difference between the outcome of the treatments on the two tasks in question can be a matter of degree, or all or none. Shallice surmises that trend dissociations could be produced by lesions in a hypothetical single network (e.g. of the parallel distributed processing variety), whereas this is not possible with classical dissociations. But even relative double dissociations can be rich sources of inferences about independence and should not be prematurely discarded (cf. further discussion and examples in Weiskrantz, 1989).

Single dissociations are those in which one treatment affects one type of task and not another, but in which a treatment that affects the second will also affect the first; or, as an alternative way of stating the relationship, one type of task is affected *only* when another type of task is also affected by the same treatment, but the second task can be affected without the first being affected by another treatment (e.g. deafness causes slurred speech, but a treatment that slurs speech—returning from the dentist with an anaesthetized mouth—does not cause hearing difficulties; blind people have trouble recognizing faces, but you can be bad at recognizing faces without being blind). Single dissociations are useful for drawing inferences about hierarchical structures, but also signal when there may be confounding differences in task difficulty (e.g., as an analogy, raising the bar to 3 metres in a high-jumping task will cause a deficit in jumping in both tall and short persons, but a lower height may allow tall persons to manage, while still leaving a deficit in the short). Again, a single dissociation is a *necessary* condition for an inference of hierarchical structures, of superordinate and subordinate arrangements, but it is clearly not sufficient.

With both types of dissociations, evidence is provided on which to base inferences, but not on which to draw inescapable logical conclusions. The strategy will always be pragmatic and will depend on converging approaches from sets of related tasks and related treatments, from theory and theoretical background, and from physiological and anatomical evidence; that is, in terms of 3 sets of approaches and activities forming the triangle promoted in Chapter 8.

Glossary

Agnosia: a condition, caused by brain damage, often diffuse, in which subjects no longer appreciate the meanings of words, objects, places, concepts, or faces (see prosopagnosia), depending on the specific form of agnosia. In associative agnosia, there is no disturbance of sensory function as such. In apperceptive agnosia (a difficult concept) the subject has a problem in achieving coherent perception.

Amnesia (amnesic syndrome): loss of recognition or recall of events beyond a short interval, usually of a minute or so (anterograde amnesia). It is also associated with loss of recall of events that occurred some time before the onset of brain damage (retrograde amnesia), often from several years earlier.

Anosagnosia: a condition in which a subject denies the existence of a deficit clearly visible to others, such as paralysis of one side of the body, or blindness.

Aphasia: deficit in language caused by, usually, damage to the left cerebral hemisphere, especially in right-handed persons. In pure (rare) form, either of speech (Broca's) or of comprehension (Wernicke's).

Blindsight: loss of phenomenal seeing in the contralateral half of the visual field caused by damage to V1, but with residual capacity still present.

BWCS: British weather commentary syndrome. The capacity to discuss the weather at length in a state of complete and unknowing unconsciousness.

C: a hypothetical area of the brain that becomes active when a subject is aware of visual events, but remains inactive when a subject is unaware but able, nevertheless (as in blindsight), to discriminate these events.

Claustrum: a thin band of cortex, co-extensive with the insula, lying deep within the Sylvian fissure. It has not been extensively studied, but is thought to have connexions with large regions of cortex, including visual cortices.

Dorsal stream: projections from V1 proceeding dorsally into occipital–parietal cortex. It is thought to be especially involved in processing of visual space and/or with visually guided action.

Entorhinal cortex: cortex lying on the medial–ventral aspect of the temporal lobes, in the region of, and below, the rhinal sulcus.

Episodic memory: memory for individual events.

fMRI: functional magnetic resonance imaging. A method of detecting activity in regions of the brain by measuring changes that result from delivering brief magnetic pulses, and displaying these as images via tomography.

Frontal eye field (FEF): the region situated anteriorly in frontal lobes, so named because electrical stimulation causes contralateral conjugate eye movements, the precise direction depending on the locus of stimulus. Lesions in monkeys cause visual field defects/neglect very similar to those caused by lesions of V1. The FEF is often equated with Brodmann's area 8, which overlaps with, but mostly lies anterior to it.

Ganglion cells (retinal): the cells in the retina which give rise to the optic nerve fibres. In the primate they are of 3 main types, alpha, beta, and gamma. Following striate cortex lesions, there is differential partial loss of beta cells— which code for colour and have high spatial resolution—in relation to the other two classes.

Hippocampus: a structure buried within the medial surface of the temporal lobe (which looks like a sea-horse in cross-section, hence the name). It is implicated in the amnesic syndrome, in episodic and spatial memory.

Inferotemporal cortex: a region of cortex lying on the inferior surface of the temporal lobe which, in the monkey, is especially concerned with complex visual processing and also with visual memory for objects. It is situated in the ventral stream.

Insula (Island of Reil): a large area of cortex buried deep within, and at the base of, the Sylvian fissure.

Lateral geniculate nucleus (LGN): the principal nucleus of the thalamus receiving fibres originating from retinal ganglion cells. The LGN in each hemisphere receives fibres from half of each retina, corresponding to the opposite visual half-field.

MT: the same region as V5, originally given these initials because in the owl monkey (but not in all monkeys, including the rhesus) it lies on the medial temporal surface of the brain.

Neglect (unilateral): a condition, typically caused by parietal lobe damage in the right cerebral hemisphere, in which patients fail to detect events on the left half of space.

Oil refinery: a short-hand for the extensive inter-connexions within cortical areas closely associated with V1, shown in representations by Felleman and Van Essen (1991) and Young (1992).

PET: positron emission tomography. A procedure for evaluating changes in blood flow to specific regions of the brain by measuring emission of radioactive particles following injection of labelled metabolites.

Phantom limb: the continuing perceptual experience of the presence of an arm or a leg even though it has been amputated (or denervated).

Prestriate cortex: the complex of cortical areas in close proximity to striate cortex (V1).

Procedural memory: acquired skills, both perceptual–motor (e.g. mirror drawing) and conceptual (e.g. arithmetic rules).

Prosopagnosia: a loss of recognition of familiar faces caused by damage in the posterior and ventral part of the brain. Very rarely seen in absolutely pure form (without other agnosic disturbances).

Pulvinar: a nucleus in the thalamus which receives inputs from the retina and the superior colliculus, and sends fibres widely throughout posterior regions of cortex.

Retrograde transneuronal degeneration: after damage to nerve fibres there is degeneration back to the cell of origin (retrograde degeneration). In some tracts, unusually in the nervous system, there is also degeneration back to the cell bodies that give rise to the fibres projecting to the site of retrograde degeneration. In the primate visual system, striate cortex damage leads to degeneration in the LGN, followed by transneuronal degeneration back to the some of the ganglion cells in the retina.

Scotoma: a visual field defect, such as is caused by damage to V1.

Semantic memory: stored acquired knowledge of the world.

SPECT: single photon emission computed tomography. Similar to PET, but using a different radioactive emission agent.

Striate cortex (see V1): primary visual cortex, so named because of the conspicuous stripe that can be seen in anatomical cross-sections.

Superior colliculus: a region in the midbrain which receives a direct projection from the retina via the optic nerve. It is part of the tectum. It sends connexions to thalamic nuclei which have a wide distribution to cortex, and it also receives connexions from several cortical areas.

Tomography: a mathematical procedure for deriving 3-D images of the brain with a scanner. Individual 'slices' can then be displayed on a computer screen.

Ventral stream: projections from V1 progressing ventrally in the brain, with connexions to inferotemporal cortex and other areas en route. It is thought to be especially concerned with processing of visual object perception.

V1 (striate cortex): the first cortical area, and principal target of inputs from the retina via the optic nerve. The optic nerve first terminates in the LGN, from which fibres proceed to V1 (and it is now known, also thinly to other cortical areas).

V2, V3, V4, V5: areas of cortex with direct connexions (reciprocal) with V1. V4 is thought to be selectively involved in colour discrimination and colour constancy, and V5 in visual directional movement.

VORB: visual oil refinery bypass, referring to a route by which visual information arising in the retina can reach regions of the brain without travelling via the oil refinery (see above).

References

Andjus, R.K., Knopfelmacher, F., Russell, R.W., and Smith, A.U. (1955). Effects of hypothermia on behaviour. *Nature, Lond.*, **176**, 1015–1016.

Allport, A. (1988). What concept of consciousness? In *Consciousness in contemporary science,* (ed. A.J. Marcel and E. Bisiach), pp. 159–182. Oxford Univ. Press, Oxford.

Baddeley, A. (1995). The psychology of memory. In *Handbook of memory disorders,* (ed. A.D. Baddeley, B.A. Wilson, and F.N. Watts), pp. 3–25. Wiley, Chichester.

Baddeley, A. and Wilson, B.A. (1994). When implicit learning fails: amnesia and the problem of error elimination. *Neuropsychologia*, **32**, 53–69.

Balliett, R., Blood, K.M., and Bach-y-Rita, P. (1985). Visual field rehabilitation in the cortically blind? *J. Neurol. Neurosurg. Psychiatr.*, **48**, 1113–1124.

Barbur, J.L. and Forsyth, P.M. (1986). Can the pupil response be used as a measure of the visual input associated with the geniculo-striate pathway? *Clin. Vis. Sci.*, **1**, 107–111.

Barbur, J.L. and Thomson, W.D. (1987). Pupil response as an objective measure of visual acuity. *Ophthal. Physiol. Opt.*, **7**, 425–429.

Barbur, J.L., Ruddock K.H., and Waterfield V.A. (1980). Human visual responses in the absence of the geniculo-striate projection. *Brain*, **102**, 905–928.

Barbur, J.L., Thomson W.D., and Forsyth P.M. (1987). A new system for the simultaneous measurement of pupil size and two-dimensional eye movements. *Clin. Vis. Sci.*, **2**, 131–142.

Barbur, J.L., Forsyth P.M., and Findlay J.M. (1988). Human saccadic eye movements in the absence of the geniculocalcarine projection. *Brain*, **111**, 63–82.

Barbur, J.L., Watson, J.D.G., Frackowiak, R.S.J., and Zeki, S. (1993). Conscious visual perception without V1. *Brain*, **116**, 1293–1302.

Barbur, J.L., Harlow, J.A., and Weiskrantz, L. (1994a). Spatial and temporal response properties of residual vision in a case of hemianopia. *Phil. Trans. Roy. Soc. B*, **343**, 157–166.

Barbur, J.L., Harlow, J.A., Sahraie, A., Stoerig, P., and Weiskrantz, L. (1994b). Responses to chromatic stimuli in the absence of V1: pupillometric and psychophysical studies. In: Vision science and its applications. *Optical Soc. Amer. Technical Digest*, **2**, 312–315.

Bard, L. (1905). De la persistance des sensations lumineuses dans le champ avengle des hemianopsiques. *La Semaine Medicale*, **22** (May), 3–255.

Barlow, H.B. (1961). The coding of sensory messages. In *Current problems in animal behaviour*, (ed. W.H. Thorpe and O.L. Zangwill), pp. 331–360. Cambridge Univ. Press, Cambridge.

Barlow, H.B. (1987). The biological role of consciousness. In *Mindwaves*, pp. 361–381. Basil Blackwell, Oxford.

Bauer, R.M. (1984). Autonomic recognition of names and faces in prosopagnosia: a neuropsychological application of the guilty knowledge test. *Neuropsychologia*, **22**, 457–469.

Bender, M.B. and Krieger, H.P. (1951). Visual function in perimetrically blind fields. *Arch. Neurol. Psychiatr.*, **65**, 72–79.

Benevento, L.A. and Yoshida, K (1981). The afferent and efferent organization of the lateral geniculo-striate pathways in the macaque monkey. *J. Comp. Neurol.*, **203**, 455–474.

Beninger, R.J., Kendall, S.B., and Vanderwolf, C.H. (1974). The ability of rats to discriminate their own behaviors. *Canad. J. Psychol.*, **28**, 79–91.

Berry, D.C. and Dienes, Z. (1993). *Implicit learning. Theoretical and empirical issues.* Erlbaum, Hove, UK.

Berti, A. and Rizzolatti, G. (1992). Visual processing without awareness: Evidence from unilateral neglect. *J. cogn. Neurosci.*, **4**, 345–351.

Bisiach, E. (1988). Language without thought. In *Thought without language,* (ed. L.Weiskrantz), pp. 464–484. Oxford Univ. Press, Oxford.

Bisiach, E. (1992). Understanding consciousness: clues from unilateral neglect and related disorders. In *The neuropsychology of consciousness*, (ed. A.D. Milner and M.D. Rugg), pp. 113–137.

Bisiach, E. and Luzzatti, C. (1978). Unilateral neglect of representational space. *Cortex*, **14**, 129–133.

Bisiach, E., Vallar, G., Perani, D., Papagno, C., and Berti, A. (1986). Unawareness of disease following lesions of the right hemisphere: anosagnosia for hemiplegia and anosagnosia for hemianopia. *Neuropsychologia*, **24**, 471–482.

Block, N. (1995). On a confusion about a function of consciousness. *Behav. Brain Sci.*, **18**, 227–247.

Blythe, I.M., Bromley, J.M., Kennard, C., and Ruddock, K.H. (1986). Visual discrimination of target displacement remains after damage to the striate cortex in humans. *Nature, Lond.*, **320**, 619–621.

Blythe, I.M., Kennard, C., and Ruddock, K.H. (1987). Residual vision in patients with retrogeniculate lesions of the visual pathways. *Brain*, **110**, 887–905.

Bottini, G., Paulesu, E., Sterzi, R., Warburton, E., Wise, R.J.S., Vallar, G., Frackowiak, R.S.J., and Frith, C.D. (1995). Modulation of conscious experience by peripheral sensory stimuli. *Nature, Lond.*, **376**, 778–781.

Braddick, O.J., Atkinson, J., and Hood, B. (1996). Striate cortex, extrastriate cortex, and colliculus: some new approaches. In *Infant vision*, (ed. F. Vital-Durand, J. Atkinson, and O.J. Braddick), pp. 203–220. Oxford Univ. Press, Oxford.

Brent, P.J., Kennard, C., and Ruddock, K.H. (1994). Residual colour vision in a human hemianope: spectral responses and colour discrimination. *Proc. R. Soc. Lond. B*, **256**, 219–225.

Brindley, G.S. (1960). *Physiology of the retina and visual pathway*. Edward Arnold, London.

Brindley, G.S., Gautier-Smith, P.C., and Lewin, W. (1969). Cortical blindness and the functions of the non-geniculate fibres of the optic tracts. *J. Neurol. Neurosurg. Psychiatr.*, **32**, 259–264.

Brooks, D.N. and Baddeley, A.D. (1976). What can amnesic patients learn? *Neuropsychologia*, **14**, 111–122.

Brown, M.W., Brown, J., and Bower, J.B. (1989). Absence of priming coupled with substantially preserved recognition in lorazepam-induced amnesia. *Q. J. exp. Psychol.*, **41A**, 599–617.

Bruce, V. and Young, A. (1986). Understanding face recognition. *Brit. J. Psychol.*, **77**, 305–327.

Burns, J.E. (1990). Contemporary models of consciousness: Part I. *J. Mind behav.*, **11**, 153–172.

Bullmore, E.T., Rabe-Hesketh, S., Morris, R.G., Williams, S.C.R., Gregory, L., Gray J.A., and Brammer, M.J. (1996). Functional magnetic resonance image analysis of a large-scale neurocognitive network. *Neuroimage*, **4**, 16–33.

Burton, A.M., Bruce, V., and Johnston, R.A. (1990). Understanding face recognition with an interactive activation model. *Brit. J. Psychol.*, **81**, 361–380.

Burton, A.M., Young, A.W., Bruce, V., Johnston, R., and Ellis, A.W. (1991). Understanding covert recognition. *Cognition*, **39**, 129–166.

Byrne, R.W. and Whiten, A. (1988). *Machiavellian intelligence*. Oxford Univ. Press, Oxford.

Campion, J., Latto, R., and Smith, Y.M. (1983). Is blindsight an effect of scattered light, spared cortex, and near-threshold vision? *Beh. Brain Sci.*, **6**, 423–448.

Casagrande, V.A. and Diamond, I.T. (1974). Ablation study of the superior colliculus in the tree shrew (*tupaia glis*). *J. comp. Neurol.* **156**, 207–237.

Cermak, L.S., Butters, N., and Moreines, J. (1974). Some analyses of the verbal encoding deficit of alcoholic Korsakoff patients. *Brain Lang.*, **1**, 141–150.

Churchland, P.M. (1993). *Matter and consciousness*. M.I.T. Press, Cambridge. Mass.

Claparède, E. (1911). Recognition et moite. *Arch. Psychol. Geneva*, **11**, 79–90.

Cochrane, K.A. (1995). *Some tests of residual visual functioning in humans with damage to the striate cortex*. D.Phil thesis, Radcliffe Science Library, University of Oxford.

Cocker, D., Moseley, M.J., Bissenden, J.G., and Fielder, A.R. (1994). Visual acuity and pupillary responses to spatial structure in infants. *Ophthal. Vis. Sci.*, **35**, 2620–2625.

Cohen, L.B. (1988). An information-processing approach to infant cognitive development. In *Thought without language*, (ed. L. Weiskrantz), pp. 211–228. Oxford Univ. Press, Oxford.

Corkin, S. (1968). Acquisition of motor skill after bilateral medial temporal lobe excision. *Neuropsychologia*, **6**, 255–265.

Cowey, A. (1963). The basis of a method of perimetry with monkeys. *Q. J. exp. Psychol.*, 15, 81–90.

Cowey, A. (1967). Perimetric study of field defects in monkeys after cortical and retinal ablations. *Q. J. exp. Psychol.*, **19**, 232–245.

Cowey, A. and Stoerig, P. (1989). Projection patterns of surviving neurons in the dorsal lateral geniculate nucleus following discrete lesions of striate cortex: implications for residual vision. *Exp. Brain Res.*, **75**, 631–638.

Cowey, A. and Stoerig, P. (1991). The neurobiology of blindsight. *Trends Neurosci.*, **29**, 65–80.

Cowey, A. and Stoerig, P. (1992). Reflections on blindsight. In *The neuropsychology of consciousness*, (ed. D. Milner, and M.D. Rugg), pp. 11–37. Academic Press, London.

Cowey, A. and Stoerig, P. (1995). Blindsight in monkeys. *Nature, Lond.*, **373**, 247–249.

Cowey, A. and Weiskrantz, L. (1963). A perimetric study of visual field defects in monkeys. *Q. J. exp. Psychol.*, **15**, 91–115.

Cowey, A., Stoerig, P., and Perry, V.H. (1989). Transneuronal retrograde degeneration of retinal ganglion cells after damage to striate cortex in macaque monkeys: Selective loss of P-beta cells. *Neuroscience*, **29**, 65–80.

Crick, F. (1994). *The astonishing hypothesis. The scientific search for the soul.* Charles Scribner's Sons, New York.

Crick, F. and Koch, C. (1990). Towards a neurobiological theory of consciousness. *Seminars Neurosci.*, **2**, 263–275.

Crick, F. and Koch, C. (1995). Are we aware of neural activity in primary visual cortex? *Nature*, **375**, 121–123.

Damasio, A. (1994). *Descartes' error.* Picador, New York.

Damasio, A., Lima, A., and Damasio, H. (1975). Nervous function after right hemispherectomy. *Neurol.*, **25**, 89–93.

Darwin, C. (1871). *The descent of Man.* John Murray, London.

Dawkins, M.S. (1980). *Animal suffering: The science of animal welfare.* Chapman and Hall, London.

Dawkins, M.S. (1987). Minding and mattering. In *Mindwaves*, (ed. C. Blakemore and S. Greenfield), pp. 151–160. Basil Blackwell, Oxford.

Dawkins, M.S. (1990). From an animal's point of view: Motivation, fitness, and animal welfare. *Beh. Brain Sci.*, **13**, 1–61.

Dawkins, R. (1976). *The selfish gene.* Oxford Univ. Press, Oxford.

Davies, M. and Humphreys, G.W. (1993). *Consciousness. Psychological and philosophical essays.* Basil Blackwell, Oxford.

De Haan, E.H.F., Young, A.W., and Newcombe F. (1991). Covert and overt recognition in prosopagnosia. *Brain*, **114**, 2575–2591.

Delay, J. and Brion, S. (1969). *Le syndrome de Korsakoff*. Masson, Paris.

Dennett, D.C. (1991). *Consciousness explained*. Penguin Press, London.

Denny-Brown, D. and Chambers, R.A. (1955). Visuo-motor function in the cerebral cortex. *J. nerv. ment. Dis.*, **121**, 288–289.

Desimone, R. and Ungerleider, L.G. (1989). Neural mechanisms of visual processing in monkeys. In *Handbook of neuropsychology*, vol. 2, (ed. F. Boller and J. Grafman), pp. 267–299. Elsevier, Amsterdam.

Diamond, J., Valentine, T., Mayes, A.R., and Sandel, M. (1994). Evidence of covert recognition in a prosopagnosic patient. *Cortex*, **30**, 377–393.

Dickinson, A. (1988). Intentionality in animal conditioning. In *Thought without language,* (ed. L. Weiskrantz), pp. 305–325. Oxford Univ. Press, Oxford.

Edelman, G.M. (1989). *The remembered present: A biological theory of consciousness*. Basic Books, New York.

Eichenbaum, H., Otto, T., and Cohen, N.J. (1994). Two functional components of the hippocampal memory system. *Beh. Brain Sci.*, **17**, 449–518.

Farah, M.J. (1990). *Visual agnosia*. M.I.T. Press, Cambridge, MA.

Farah, M.J., O'Reilly, R.C., and Vercera, S.P. (1993). Dissociated overt and covert recognition as an emergent property of a lesioned neural network. *Psychol. Rev.*, **100**, 571–588.

Feinberg, T.E., Dyckes-Berke, D., Miner, C.R., and Roane, D.M. (1995). Knowledge, implicit knowledge and metaknowledge in visual agnosia and pure alexia. *Brain*, **118**, 789–800.

Felleman, D.J. and Van Essen, D.C. (1991). Distributed hierarchical processing in the primate cerebral cortex. *Cerebral Cortex*, **1**, 1–47.

Fendrich, R., Wessinger, C.M., and Gazzaniga, M.S. (1992). Residual vision in a scotoma; implications for blindsight. *Science*, **258**, 1489–1491.

ffytche, D.H., Guy, C.N., and Zeki, S. (1995). The parallel visual motion inputs into areas V1 and V5 of human cerebral cortex. *Brain*, **118**, 1375–1394.

Finlay, A.L., Jones, S.R., Morland, A.B., Ogilvie, J.A., and Ruddock, K.H. (1997). Movement elicits ipsilateral activity in the damaged hemisphere of a human hemianope. *Proc. R. Soc. Lond.*, **264**, 267–275.

Frederici, A.D. (1982). Syntactic and semantic processes in aphasic deficits: the availability of prepositions. *Brain and Language*, **15**, 245–258.

Fries, W. (1981). The projection from the lateral geniculate nucleus to the prestriate cortex of the macaque monkey. *Proc. Natl Acad. Sci., USA*, **213**, 73–80.

Gabrieli, J.D.E., Milberg, W., Keane, M.M., and Corkin, S. (1990). Intact priming of patterns despite impaired memory. *Neuropsychologia*, **28**, 417–428.

Gaffan, D. (1974). Recognition impaired and association intact in the memory of monkeys after transection of the fornix. *J. comp. physiol. Psychol.*, **86**, 1100–1109.

Gallows, B., Heywood, C.A., Popplewell, D.A., Roland, P., and Cowey, A. (1994). Visual form discrimination from color or motion cues: functional anatomy by positron emission tomography. *Proc. Natl Acad. Sci., USA*, **91**, 9965–9969.

Gazzaniga, M.S. (1966). Visuomotor integration in split-brain monkeys with other cerebral lesions. *Exp. Neurol.*, **16**, 289–298.

Gazzaniga, M.S., Fendrich, R., and Wessinger, C.M. (1994). Blindsight reconsidered. *Current Directions in Psychological Science*, **3**, 93–96.

Glisky, E.L. (1995). Computers in memory rehabilitation. In *Handbook of memory disorders*, (ed. A.D. Baddeley, B.A. Wilson, and F.N. Watts), pp. 557–575. Wiley, Chichester.

Glisky, E.L. and Schacter, D.L. (1988). Long-term retention of computer learning by patients with memory disorders. *Neuropsychologia*, **26**, 173–178.

Glisky, E.L., Schacter, D.L., and Tulving, E. (1986). Learning and retention of computer-related vocabulary in memory-impaired patients: Method of vanishing cues. *J. clin. exp. Neuropsychol.*, **8**, 292–312.

Goodale, M.A., Jakobson, L.S., and Keiller, J.M. (1994). Differences in the visual control of pantomimed and natural grasping movements. *Neuropsychologia*, **32**, 1159–1178.

Graf, P. and Schacter, D.L. (1985). Implicit and explicit memory for new associations in normal and amnesic subjects. *J. Expt. Psychol.: learn, mem., cog.*, **11**, 501–518.

Graf, P., Squire, L.R., and Mandler, G. (1984). The information that amnesic patients do not forget. *J. Expt. Psychol.: learn, mem, cog.*, **10**, 164–178.

Grasby, P., Frith, C.D., Friston, K.J., Bench, C., Frackowiak, R.S.J., and Dolan, R.J. (1993). Functional mapping of brain areas implicated in auditory-verbal memory function. *Brain*, **116**, 1–20.

Gray, C.M. and Singer, W. (1989). Stimulus-specific neuronal oscillation in orientation columns of cat visual cortex. *Proc. Natl. Acad. Sci., USA*, **86**, 1689–1702.

Gray, J.A. (1982). *The neuropsychology of anxiety*. Oxford Univ. Press, Oxford.

Gray, J.A. (1995). The contents of consciousness: A neuropsychological conjecture. *Beh. Brain Sci.*, **18**, 659–722.

Gross, C.G. (1991). Contribution of striate cortex and the superior colliculus to visual function in area MT, the superior temporal polysensory area, and inferior temporal cortex. *Neuropsychologia*, **29**, 497–515.

Gruber, H.E. (1974). *Darwin on man*. Wildwood House, London.

Hameroff, S. and Penrose, R. (1995). Orchestrated reduction of quantum coherence in brain microtubules: A model for consciousness. In *Scale in conscious experience: Is the brain too important to be left to specialists to study?*, (ed. J. King and K.H. Pribram), pp. 241–274. Erlbaum, Mahway, NJ.

Hayman, C.A., Macdonald, C.A., and Tulving, E. (1993). The role of repetition and associative interference in new semantic learning in amnesia: A case experiment. *J. cogn. Neurosci.*, **5**, 375–389.

Hernandez-Gonzalez, C.C. and Reinoso-Suarez, F. (1994). The lateral geniculate nucleus projects to the inferior temporal cortex in the macaque monkey. *Neuro. Rep.*, **5**, 2692–2696.

Hess R.F. and Pointer, J.S. (1989). Spatial and temporal contrast sensitivity in hemianopia. A comparative study of the sighted and blind hemifields. *Brain*, **112**, 871–894.

Heywood, C.A., Cowey, A., and Newcombe, F. (1991). Chromatic discrimination in a cortically colour blind observer. *Euro. J. Neurosci.*, **3**, 802–912.

Heywood, C.A., Gadotti, A., and Cowey, A. (1992). Cortical area V4 and its role in the perception of colour. *J. Neurosci.*, **12**, 4056–4065.

Heywood, C.A., Cowey, A., and Newcombe, F. (1994). On the role of parvocellular (P) and magnocellular (M) pathways in cerebral achromatopsia. *Brain*, **117**, 245–254.

Heywood, C.A., Gaffan, D., and Cowey, A. (1995). Cerebral achromatopsia in monkeys. *Euro. J. Neurosci.*, **7**, 1064–1073.

Hilgard, E.R. (1977). *Divided consciousness*. Wiley, New York.

Hobhouse, L.T. (1901). *Mind in evolution*. Macmillan, London.

Holmes, G. (1918). Disturbances of vision by cerebral lesions. *British Journal of Ophthalmology*, **2**, 353–384.

Hubel, D.H. and Wiesel, T.N. (1962). Receptive fields, binocular interaction and functional architecture in the cat's visual cortex. *J. Physiol.*, 160, 106–154.

Humphrey, N.K. (1970). What the frog's eye tells the monkey's brain. *Brain, Beh. Evol.*, **3**, 324–337.

Humphrey, N.K. (1974). Vision in a monkey without striate cortex: a case study. *Perception*, **3**, 241–255.

Humphrey, N. (1992). *A history of the mind*. Chatto & Windus, London.

Humphrey, N. and Weiskrantz, L. (1967). Vision in monkeys after removal of the striate cortex. *Nature, Lond.*, **215**, 595–597.

Hverta, M.F. and Harting, J.K. (1984). The mammalian superior colliculus: studies of its morphology and connections. In *Comparative neurology of the optic tectum*, (ed. H. Vanegas) pp. 687–773. Plenum Press, New York.

Ingle, D. (1967). Two visual mechanisms underlying the behavior of fish. *Psychol. Forsch.*, **31**, 44–51.

Jacoby, L.L. and Hollingshead, A. (1990). Toward a generate/recognize model of performance on direct and indirect tests of memory. *J. Memory Language*, **29**, 433–454.

Jacoby, L.L. and Kelley C. (1992). Unconscious influences of memory: dissociations and automaticity. In *The neuropsychology of consciousness,* (ed. A.D. Milner and M.D. Rugg), pp. 201–233. Academic Press, London.

James, Wm. (1890). *Principles of psychology*. Macmillan, London.

Jarrard, E.L. (1986). Selective hippocampal lesions and behavior: implications for current research and theorizing. In *The hippocampus* (2nd edn), (ed. R.L. Isaacson and K.H. Pribram), pp. 93–122. Plenum Press, New York.

Jarrard, E.L. (1993). On the role of the hippocampus in learning and memory in the rat. *Behav. Neur. Biol.*, **60**, 9–26.

Jason, G.W., Cowey, A., and Weiskrantz, L. (1984). Hemispheric asymmetry for a visuo-spatial task in monkeys. *Neuropsychologia*, **22**, 777–784.

Jennings, H.S. (1904). *Behavior of the lower organisms*. Indiana Univ. Press, Bloomington.

Kapur, N. (1995). Memory aids in the rehabilitation of memory disordered patients. In *Handbook of memory disorders*, (ed. A.D. Baddeley, B.A. Wilson, and F.N. Watts), pp.533–556. Wiley, Chichester.

Karten, H.J. and Shimizu, T. (1991). Are visual hierarchies in the brains of the beholders? Constancy and variability in the visual system of birds and mammals. In *The changing visual system*, (ed. P. Agnoli and W. Hodos), pp. 51–59. Plenum Press, New York.

Kasten, E. and Sabel, B.A. (1995). Visual field enlargement after computer training in brain-damaged patients with homonymous deficits: an open pilot trial. *Restor. Neurol. Neurosci.*, **8**, 113–127.

Keating, E.G. (1980). Residual spatial vision in the monkey after removal of striate and preoccipital cortex. *Brain Research,* **187**, 271–290.

Kentridge, R.W., Heywood, C.A., and Weiskrantz, L. (in press). Residual vision in multiple retinal locations within a scotoma: Implications for blindsight. *J. Cogn. Neurosci.*, **9**.

King, S.M., Azzopardi, P., Cowey, A., Oxbury, J., and Oxbury, S. (1996). The role of light scatter in the residual sensitivity of patients with cerebral hemispherectomy. *Vis. Neurosci.*, **13**, 1–13.

Kerkhoff, G., Munsinger, U., and Meier, E. (1994). Neurovisual rehabilitation in cerebral blindness. *Arch. Neurol.*, 51, 474–481.

Killackey, H., Snyder, M., and Diamond, I.T. (1971). Function of striate and temporal cortex in the tree shrew. *J. comp. physiol. Psychol.,* **74**: suppl. 2, 1–29.

Klüver, H. (1942). Functional significance of the geniculo-striate system. *Biol. Sympos*, **7**, 253–299.

Knowlton, B.J., Ramus, S.J., and Squire, L.R. (1992). Intact artificial grammar learning in amnesias: Dissociation of abstract knowledge and memory for specific instances. *Psychol. Sci.*, **3**, 172–179.

Kolb, F.C. and Braun, J. (1995). Blindsight in normal observers. *Nature, Lond.*, **377**, 336–338.

Ladavas, E., Paladini, R., and Cubelli, R. (1993). Implicit associative priming in a patient with left visual neglect. *Neuropsychologia*, **31**, 1307–1320.

Lashley, K.S. (1950). In search of the engram. *Symp. Soc. Exp. Biol.*, **4**, 454–482.

Latto, R. and Cowey, A. (1971). Visual field defects after frontal eye-field lesions in monkeys. *Brain Res.*, **30**, 1–24.

Lepore, R., Cardu, B., Rasmussen, T., and Malmo, R.B. (1975). Rod and cone sensitivity in destriate monkeys. *Brain Res.*, **93**, 203–221.

Levine, D.N. and Calvano, R. (1989). Prosopagnosia: A deficit in visual configural processing. *Brain Cognit.*, **10**, 149–170.

Linebarger, M.C., Schwartz, M.F., and Saffran, E.M. (1983). Sensitivity to grammatical structure in so-called agrammatic aphasics. *Cognition*, **13**, 361–392.

Locke, J. (1690). *An essay concerning human understanding*. J.M. Dent & Sons, Everyman's Library. (Page citations from 1971 edn.)

Luciani, L. (1884). On the sensorial localisations in the cortex cerebri. *Brain*, **7**, 145–160.

Luria, A.R. (1968). *The mind of a mnemonist*. Basic Books, New York.

McAndrews, M.P., Glisky, E.L., and Schacter, D.L. (1987). When priming persists: Long-lasting implicit memory for a single episode in amnesic patients. *Neuropsychologia*, **25**, 297–506.

McGlynn, S. and Schacter, D.L. (1989). Unawareness of deficits in neuropsychological syndromes. *J. clin. expt. Neuropsychol.*, **11**, 143–205.

McLeod, P., Dittrich, W., Driver, J., Perrett, D., and Zihl, J. (1996). Preserved and impaired detection of structure from motion by a 'motion-blind' patient. *Visual cognition*. **3**, 363–391.

Mair, W.G.P., Warrington, E.K., and Weiskrantz, L. (1979). Memory disorder in Korsakoff's psychosis. A neuropathological and neuropsychological investigation of two cases. *Brain*, **102**, 749–783.

Malmo, R.B. (1966). Effects of striate cortex ablation on intensity discrimination and spectral intensity distribution in the rhesus monkey. *Neuropsychologia*, **4**, 9–26.

Marcel, A.J. (1983a). Conscious and unconscious perception: experiments on visual masking and word recognition. *Cog. Psychol.*, **15**, 197–237.

Marcel, A.J. (1983b). Conscious and unconscious perception: an approach to the relations between phenomenal experience and perceptual processes. *Cog. Psychol.*, **15**, 238–300.

Marcel, A.J. (in press). Blindsight and shape perception: deficit of visual consciousness or of visual function? *Brain*.

Marcel, A.J. and Bisiach, E. (1988). *Consciousness in contemporary science*. Clarendon Press, Oxford.

Marr, D. (1982). *Vision*. Freeman, San Francisco.

Marquis, D.G. (1935). Phylogenetic interpretation of the functions of the visual cortex. *Arch. Neurol. Psychiatr.*, **33**, 807–815.

Marshall, J. and Halligan, P. (1988). Blindsight and insight in visuo-spatial neglect. *Nature, Lond.*, **336**, 766–777.

Marslen-Wilson, W.D. and Teuber, H-L. (1975). Memory for remote events in anterograde amnesia: recognition of public figures from newsphotographs. *Neuropsychologia*, **13**, 353–364.

Marzi, C.A., Tassinari, G., Aglioti, S., and Lutzemberger, L. (1986). Spatial summation across the vertical meridian in hemianopics: a test of blindsight. *Neuropsychologia*, **30**, 783–795.

Merzenich, M.M. and Kaas, J.H. (1980). Reorganization of mammalian somatosensory cortex following peripheral nerve injury. *Trends in Neurosci.*, **5**, 434–436.

Michel, F. and Peronnet, F. (1980). A case of cortical deafness: clinical and electrophysiological data. *Brain Lang.*, **10**, 367–377.

Miller, M., Pasik, P., and Pasik, T. (1980). Extrageniculate vision in the monkey. VII. Contrast sensitivity functions. *J. Neurophysiol.*, **43**, 1510–1526.

Milner, A.D. and Goodale, M.A. (1995). *The visual brain in action.* Oxford Univ. Press, Oxford.

Milner, A.D. and Rugg, M.D. (ed.) (1992). *Neuropsychology of consciousness.* Academic Press, London.

Milner, B., Corkin, S., and Teuber, H-L. (1968). Further analysis of the hippocampal amnesic syndrome: 14-year follow-up study of H.M. *Neuropsychologia*, **6**, 215–235.

Mishkin, M. (1954). Visual discrimination performance following ventral ablations of the temporal lobe: II. Ventral surface vs. hippocampus. *J. comp. physiol. Psychol.*, **47**, 187–196.

Mishkin, M. (1978). Memory in monkeys severely impaired by combined but not by separate removal of amygdala and hippocampus. *Nature, Lond.*, **273**, 297–298.

Mishkin, M. and Pribram, K. (1954). Visual discrimination performance following ventral ablations of the temporal lobe: I. Ventral vs. lateral. *J. comp. physiol. Psychol.*, **47**, 14–20.

Mohler, C.W. and Wurtz, R.H. (1977). Role of striate cortex and superior colliculus in visual guidance of saccadic eye movements in monkeys. *J. Neurophysiol.*, **43**, 74–94.

Mondadori, C. and Weiskrantz, L. (1991). Memory facilitation induced by N-methyl-D-aspartate blockade. In *Long-term potentiation. A debate and current issues,* (ed. M. Baudry and J.L. Davis), pp. 259–266. M.I.T. Press, Cambridge.

Moore, T., Rodman, H.R., Repp, A.B., and Gross, C.G. (1995). Localization of visual stimuli after striate cortex damage in monkeys: Parallels with human blindsight. *Proc. Natl Acad. Sci., USA*, **92**, 8215–8218.

Morgan, C. Lloyd (1890). *Animal life and intelligence.* Edward Arnold, London.

Morgan, C. Lloyd. (1900). *Animal behaviour.* Edward Arnold, London.

Morland, A.B., Ogilvie, J.A., Ruddock, K.H., and Wright, J.R. (1996). Orientation discrimination is impaired in the absence of the striate cortical contribution to human vision. *Proc. Roy. Soc. B*, **263**, 633–640.

Moscovitch, M. (1982). Multiple dissociations of function in amnesia. In *Human memory and amnesia*, (ed. L. Cermak), pp. 337–370. Erlbaum, Hillsdale, N.J.

Murray, E.A. (1996). What have ablation studies told us about the neural substrates of recognition memory? *Seminars Neurosci.*, **8**, 13–22.

Myers, R.E. (1956). Functions of the corpus callosum in interocular transfer. *Brain*, **57**, 358–363.

Nakamura, R.K. and Mishkin, M. (1980). Blindness in monkeys following non-visual cortical lesions. *Brain Res*, **188**, 572–577.

Nakamura, R.K. and Mishkin, M. (1982). Chronic blindness following nonvisual lesions in monkeys: Partial lesions and disconnection effects. *Soc. Neurosci. Abstr.*, **8**, 812.

Nakamura, R.K. and Mishkin, M. (1986). Chronic blindness following lesions of nonvisual cortex in the monkey. *Exp. Brain Res.*, **62**, 173–184.

Nakamura, R.K., Schein, S.J., and Desimone, R. (1986). Visual responses from cells in striate cortex of monkeys rendered chronically 'blind' by lesions of nonvisual cortex. *Exp. Brain Res.*, **63**, 185–190.

Nyberg, L., McIntosh, A.R., Cabeza, R., Habib, R., Houle, S., and Tulving, E. (1996). General and specific brain regions involved in encoding and retrieval of events: What, where, and when. *Proc. Natl. Acad. Sci., USA*, **93**, 11280–11285.

Oakley, D.A. (1981). Performance of decorticated rates in a two-choice visual discrimination apparatus. *Behav. Brain Res.*, **3**, 55–69.

Oakley, D.A. and Russell, I.S. (1977). Subcortical storage of Pavlovian conditioning in the rabbit. *Physiol. Behav.*, **18**, 931–937.

O'Boyle, V.J., Murray, E.A., and Mishkin, M. (1993). Effects of excitotoxic amygdalo-hippocampal lesions on visual recognition in rhesus monkeys. *Neurosci. Abstr.*, **19**, 438.

O'Keefe, J. and Nadel, L. (1978). *The hippocampus as a cognitive map.* Oxford Univ. Press, Oxford.

Olton, D.S. (1979). Mazes, maps, and memory. *Am. Psychol.*, **34**, 583–596.

Paillard, J. Michel, F., and Stelmach, G. (1983). Localization without content: a tactile analogue of 'blind sight'. *Arch. Neurol.*, **40**, 548–551.

Pasik, P. and Pasik, T. (1971). The visual world of monkeys deprived of visual cortex: effective stimulus parameters and the importance of the accessory optic system. In *Visual processes in vertebrates*, (ed. T. Shipley and J.E. Dowling). *Vision Research Supplement no. 3*, 419–435. Pergamon Press, Oxford.

Pasik, T. and Pasik, P. (1980). Extrageniculate vision in primates. In *Neuro-ophthalmology* vol. 1 (ed. S. Lessell and J.T.W. van Dalen), pp. 95–119. Elsevier North-Holland, Amsterdam.

Pasik, P. and Pasik, T. (1982). Visual functions in monkeys after total removal of visual cerebral cortex. *Contributions to sensory physiology*, **7**, 147–200.

Paus, T. (1996). Location and function of the human frontal eye-field: A selective review. *Neuropsychologia*, **34**, 475–483.

Pavlov, I.P. (1928). *Lectures on conditioned reflexes.* Translated by W.H. Gantt. International Publishers, New York.

Payne, B.R. (1994). System-wide repercussions of damage to the immature visual cortex. *Trends Neurosci.*, **17**, 126–130.

Penfield, W. and Milner, B. (1958). Memory deficits produced by bilateral lesions in the hippocampal zone. *Arch. Neurol. Psychiatr.*, **79**, 475–497.

Penrose, R. (1989). *The emperor's new mind.* Oxford Univ. Press, Oxford.

Penrose, R. (1994). *Shadows of the mind.* Oxford Univ. Press, Oxford.

Perenin, M.T. (1978). Visual function within the hemianopic field following cerebral hemidecortication in man. II. Pattern discrimination. *Neuropsychologia*, **16**, 696–708.

Perenin, M.T. (1991). Discrimination of motion direction in perimetrically blind fields. *NeuroReport*, **2**, 397–400.

Perenin, M.T. and Jeannerod, M. (1978). Visual function within the hemianopic field following early cerebral hemidecortication in man. I. Spatial localization. *Neuropsychologia*, **16**, 1–13.

Perenin, M.T. and Rossetti, Y. (1996). Grasping without form discrimination in a hemianopic field. *NeuroReport*, **7**, 793–797.

Perenin, M.T., Ruel, J., and Hécaen, H. (1980). Residual visual capacities in a case of cortical blindness. *Cortex*, **16**, 605–612.

Pizzamiglio, L., Antonucci, G., and Francia, A. (1984). Response of the cortically blind hemifields to a moving visual scene. *Cortex*, **20**, 89–99.

Pope, H.G. and Hudson, J.I. (1995). Can memories of childhood sexual abuse be repressed? *Psychol. Med.*, **25**, 121–126.

Pöppel, E. and Richards, W. (1974). Light sensitivity in cortical scotomata contralateral to small islands of blindness. *Exp. Brain Res.*, **21**, 125–130.

Pöppel E., Held R., and Frost D. (1973). Residual visual function after brain wounds involving the central visual pathways in man. *Nature, Lond.*, **243**, 295–296.

Poppelreuter, W. (1917). *Disturbances of lower and higher visual capacities caused by occipital damage* (Oxford Univ. Press, Oxford, 1990, translation of original German book).

Posner, M.I. and Rothbart, M.K. (1992). Attention mechanisms and conscious experience. In *Neuropsychology of consciousness*, (ed. A.D. Milner and M.D. Rugg), pp. 89–111. Academic Press, London.

Premack, D. (1988). Minds with and without language. In *Thought without language*, (ed. L. Weiskrantz), pp. 46–77. Oxford Univ. Press, Oxford.

Ptito, A., Lassonde, M., Lepore, F., and Ptito, M. (1987). Visual discrimination in hemispherectomized patients. *Neuropsychologia*, **25**, 869–879.

Ptito, A., Lepore, F., Ptito, M., and Lassonde, M. (1991). Target detection and movement discrimination in the blind field of hemispherectomized patients. *Brain*, **114**, 497–512.

Rafal, R., Smith, W., Krantz, J., Cohen, A., and Brennan, C. (1990). Extrageniculate vision in hemianopic humans: Saccade inhibition by signals in the blind field. *Science*, **250**, 118–121.

Ramachandran, V.S. (1993). Behavioural and MEG correlates of neural plasticity in the adult human brain. *Proc. Natl Acad. Sci., USA*, **90**, 10413–10420.

Reber, A.S. (1993). *Implicit learning and tacit knowledge*. Oxford Univ. Press, Oxford.

Richards, W. (1973). Visual processing in scotomata. *Exp. Brain Res.*, **17**, 333–347.

Riddoch, G. (1917). Dissociation of visual perceptions due to occipital injuries, with especial reference to appreciation of movement. *Brain*, **40**, 15–17.

Rodman H.T., Gross C.G., and Albright T.D. (1989). Afferent basis of visual response properties in area MT of the macaque. I. Effects of striate cortex removal. *J. Neurosci.*, **9**, 2033–2050.

Roediger, H.L. III and McDermott, K.B. (1993). Implicit memory in normal human subjects. In *Handbook of neuropsychology*, vol. 8, (ed. F. Boller and J. Grafman), pp. 63–131. Elsevier, New York.

Rolls, E.T., Baylis, G.C., and Hasselmo, M.E. (1987). The responses of neurons in the cortex in the superior temporal sulcus of the monkey to band-pass spatial frequency filtered faces. *Vis. Res.*, **27**, 311–326.

Romanes, G.J. (1882). *Animal intelligence.* Kegan Paul, Trench & Co., London.

Rosenthal, D. (1986). Two concepts of consciousness. *Phil. Studies*, **49**, 329–359.

Rosenthal, D. (1990). A theory of consciousness. *Report No. 40. Research Group on Mind and Brain. Perspectives in Theoretical Psychology and the Philosophy of Mind.* Univ. of Bielefeld, Bielefeld.

Rosenthal, D. (1993). Thinking that one thinks. In *Consciousness. Psychology and philosophical essays*, (ed. M. Davies and G.W. Humphreys), pp. 198–223. Blackwell, Oxford.

Rossetti, Y., Rode, G., and Boisson, D. (1995). Implicit processing of somaesthetic information: a dissociation between where and how? *NeuroReport*, **6**, 506–510.

Rossetti, Y., Rode, G., Perenin, M. and Boisson, D. (1996). No memory for implicit perception in blindsight and numbsense. Abstract of paper at conference, *Towards a science of consciousness 1996 'Tucson II'*, Arizona, held at Tucson, Arizona.

Sacks, Oliver. (1992). The last hippy. *N.Y. Review of Books*, **39** (March 26), 51–60.

Schacter, D.L. (1989). On the relation between memory and consciousness: Dissociable interactions and conscious experience. In *Varieties of memory and consciousness: Essays in honor of Endel Tulving*, (ed. H.L. Roediger III and F.I.M. Craik), pp. 355–389. Erlbaum, Hillsdale, NJ.

Schacter, D.L. (1992). Consciousness and awareness in memory and amnesia: critical issues. In *Neuropsychology of consciousness*, (ed. A.D. Milner and M.D. Rugg), pp. 179–200. Academic Press, London.

Schacter, D.L. (1993). Priming and multiple memory systems: Perceptual mechanisms of implicit memory. In *Memory systems 1994*, (ed. D.L. Schacter and D. Tulving). M.I.T. Press, Cambridge, MA.

Schacter, D.L. and Graf, P. (1986). Preserved learning in amnesic patients: persepectives from research on direct priming. *J. clin. expt. neuropsychol.*, **8**, 727–743.

Schacter, D.L., McAndrews, M.P., and Moscovitch, M. (1988). Access to consciousness: dissociations between implicit and explicit knowledge in neuropsychological syndromes. In *Thought without language,* (ed. L. Weiskrantz), pp. 242–278. Oxford Univ. Press, Oxford.

Schacter D.L., Cooper, L.A., Tharan, M., and Rubens, A. (1991). Preserved priming of novel objects in patients with memory disorders. *J. cogn. Neurosci.*, **3**, 118–131.

Schilder, P., Pasik, P., and Pasik, T. (1972). Extrageniculate vision in the monkey. III. Circle vs triangle and 'red vs green' discrimination. *Exp. Brain Res.*, **14**, 436–448.

Schneider, G.E. (1967). Contrasting visuomotor functions of tectum and cortex in the golden hamster. *Psychol. Forsch.*, **31**, 52–62.

Scoville, W.B. and Milner, B. (1957). Loss of recent memory after bilateral hippocampal lesions. *J. Neurol. Neurosurg. Psychiat.*, **20**, 11–21.

Searle, J. (1995). The mystery of consciousness. *The New York Review of Books.* Part I. November 2, pp. 50–66; Part II. November 16, pp. 54–61.

Sergent, J. and Poncet, M. (1990). From covert to overt recognition of faces in a prosopagnosic patient. *Brain*, **113**, 989–1004.

Shallice, T. (1988). *From neuropsychology to mental structure.* Cambridge Univ. Press, Cambridge.

Shallice, T. and Saffran, E. (1986). Lexical processing in the absence of explicit word identification: evidence from a letter-by-letter reader. *Cogn. Neuropsych.*, **3**, 429–458.

Shallice, T. and Warrington, E.K. (1970). Independent functioning of the verbal memory stores: A neuropsychological study. *Q. J. exp. Psychol.*, **22**, 261–273.

Shallice, T., Fletcher, P., Frith, C.D., Grasby, P.M., Frackowiak, R.S.J., and Dolan, R.J. (1994). Brain regions associated with acquisition and retrieval of verbal episodic memory. *Nature*, **368**, 633–635.

Shanks, D.R. and St. John, M.F. (1994). Characteristics of dissociable human learning systems. *Beh. Brain Sci.*, **17**, 367–447.

Sherrington, C.S. (1940). *Man on his nature.* Cambridge Univ. Press, Cambridge.

Sherrington, C.S. (1957). Spinal cord. *Encyclopaedia Britannica.*, **21**, 227–228.

Shimamura, A.P. (1986). Priming effects in amnesia: Evidence for a dissociable memory function. *Q. J. exp. Psychol.*, **38A**, 619–644.

Singer, W. (1993). Synchronization of cortical activity and its putative role in information processing and learning. *Ann. Rev. Physiol.*, **55**, 349–374.

Singer, W., Zihl, J., and Pöppel, E. (1977). Subcortical control of visual thresholds in humans: evidence for modality specific and retinotopically organized mechanisms of selective attention. *Exp. Brain Res.*, **29**, 173–190.

Snyder, M., Killackey, H., and Diamond, T. (1969). Color vision in the tree shrew after removal of posterior neocortex. *J. Neurophysiol.*, **32**, 554–563.

Spelke, E.S. (1988). The origins of physical knowledge. In *Thought without language*, (ed. L. Weiskrantz), pp. 168–184. Oxford Univ. Press, Oxford.

Sperry, R. (1969). A modified concept of consciousness. *Psychol. Rev.*, **76**, 532–536.

Sperry, R.W. (1974). Lateral specialization in the surgically separated hemispheres. In *The neurosciences: Third study program,* (ed. F.O. Schmitt and F.G. Worden). M.I.T. Press, Cambridge, MA.

Sperry, R.W., Myers, R.E., and Schrier, A.M. (1960). Perceptual capacity in the isolated visual cortex in the cat. *Q. J. exp. Psychol.*, **12**, 65–71.

Sprague, J.M. (1966). Interaction of cortex and superior colliculus in mediation of visually guided behavior in the cat. *Science*, **153**, 1544–1547.

Squire, L.R. (1987). *Memory and brain.* Oxford Univ. Press, New York.

Squire, L.R. and Cohen, N.J. (1984). Human memory and amnesia. In *Proceedings of the conference on the neurobiology of learning and memory*, (ed. J. McGaugh, G. Lynch, and N. Weinberger), pp. 3–64. Guilford Press, New York.

Squire, L.R. and Knowlton, B. (1995). Learning about categories in the absence of memory. *Proc. Natl Acad. Sci., USA*, **92**, 12470–12474.

Stoerig, P. (1987). Chromaticity and achromaticity: Evidence for a functional differentiation in visual field defects. *Brain*, **110**, 869–886.

Stoerig, P. and Cowey, A. (1989). Wavelength sensitivity in blindsight. *Nature*, **342**, 916–918.

Stoerig, P. and Cowey, A. (1991). Increment threshold spectral sensitivity in blindsight: Evidence for colour opponency. *Brain*, **114**, 1487–1512.

Stoerig, P. and Cowey, A. (1992). Wavelength sensitivity in blindsight. *Brain*, (1992), **115**, 425–444.

Stoerig, P. and Weiskrantz, L. (1993). Sources of blindsight. *Science*, **261**, 493–495.

Stoerig, P., Hubner, M., and Pöppel, E. (1985). Signal detection analysis of residual vision in a field defect due to a post-geniculate lesion. *Neuropsychologia*, **23**, 5809–599.

Stoerig, P., Faubert, J., Ptito, M., Diaconu, V., and Ptito, A. (1996). No blindsight following hemicortication in human subjects? *NeuroReport*, **7**, 1990–1994.

ter Braak, J.W., Schenk, V.W.D., and van Vliet, A.G.M. (1971). Visual reactions in a case of long-standing cortical blindness. *J. Neurol. Neurosurg. Psychiat.*, **34**, 140–147.

Tomaiuolo, F., Ptito, M., Marzi, C.A., Paus, T., and Ptito, A. (in press). Blindsight in hemispherectomized patients as revealed by spatial summation across the vertical meridian. *Brain.*

Torjussen, T. (1976). Residual function in cortically blind hemifields. *Scand. J. Psychol.*, **17**, 320–322.

Torjussen, T. (1978). Visual processing in cortically blind hemifields. *Neuropsychologia*, **16**, 15–21.

Tranel, D. and Damasio, A.R. (1985). Knowledge without awareness: an autonomic index of facial recognition by prosopagnosics. *Science*, **228**, 1453–1455.

Trevarthen, C.B. (1968). Two mechanisms of vision in primates. *Psychol. Forsch.*, **31**, 299–337.

Tulving, E. (1983). *Elements of episodic memory.* Oxford Univ. Press, Oxford.

Tulving, E., Hayman, C.A.G., and MacDonald, D. (1991). Long-lasting perceptual priming and semantic learning in amnesia: A case experiment. *J. Expt. Psychol.: learn, mem., Cog.*, **17**, 595–617.

Tyler, L.K. (1988). Spoken language comprehension in a fluent aphasic patient. *Cogn. Neuropsych.*, **5**, 375–400.

Tyler, L.K. (1992). The distinction between implicit and explicit language function: evidence from aphasia. In *The neuropsychology of consciousness,* (ed. A.D. Milner and M.D. Rugg), pp. 159–179. Academic Press, London.

Van Buren, K.M. (1963). *The retinal ganglion cell layer.* Charles Thomas, IL.

Verplanck, W.S. (1955). The control of the content of conservation: reinforcement of statements of opinion. *J. Abnorm. Soc. Psychol.*, **51**, 668–676.

Verplanck, W.S. (1956). The operant conditioning of human motor behavior. *Psychol. Bull.*, **53**, 70–83.

Verplanck, W.S. (1992). Verbal concept 'mediators' as simple operants. *Analysis of verbal behavior*, **10**, 45–68.

Ware, C.B., Diamond, I.T., and Casagrande, V.A. (1974). Effects of ablating the striate cortex on a successive pattern discrimination: further study of the visual system in the tree shrew (*Tupaia glis*). *Brain Beh. Evol.*, **9**, 264–279.

Warrington, E.K. and Duchen, L.W. (1992). A reappraisal of a case of persistent global amnesia following right temporal lobectomy—a clinicopathological study. *Neuropsychologia*, **30**, 437–450.

Warrington, E.K. and Shallice, T. (1969). The selective impairment of auditory verbal short-term memory. *Brain*, **92**, 885–896.

Warrington, E.K. and Weiskrantz, L. (1968a). New method of testing long-term retention with special reference to amnesic patients. *Nature*, **217**, 972–974.

Warrington, E.K. and Weiskrantz, L. (1968b). A study of learning and retention in amnesic patients. *Neuropsychologia*, **6**, 283–291.

Warrington, E.K. and Weiskrantz, L. (1971). Organisational aspects of memory in amnesic patients. *Neuropsychologia*, **9**, 67–73.

Warrington, E.K. and Weiskrantz, L. (1973). An analysis of short-term and long-term memory defects in man. In *The physiological basis of memory*, (ed. J.A. Deutsch), pp. 365–395. Academic Press, New York.

Warrington, E.K. and Weiskrantz, L. (1974). The effect of prior learning on subsequent retention in amnesic patients. *Neuropsychologia*, **12**, 419–428.

Warrington, E.K. and Weiskrantz, L. (1978). Further analysis of the prior learning effect in amnesic patients. *Neuropsychologia*, **16**, 169–177.

Warrington, E.K. and Weiskrantz, L. (1982). Amnesia: A disconnection syndrome? *Neuropsychologia*, **20**, 233–248.

Webster, M.J., Bachevalier, J., and Ungerleider, L.G. (1993). Subcortical connections of inferior temporal areas TE and TEO in macaque monkeys. *J. Comp. Neurol.*, **33**, 73–91.

Weiskrantz, L. (1961). Encephalisation and the scotoma. In *Current problems in animal behaviour*, (ed. W.H. Thorpe and O.L. Zangwill), pp. 30–58. Cambridge Univ. Press, Cambridge.

Weiskrantz, L. (1968). Some traps and pontifications. In *Analysis of behavioral change*, (ed. L. Weiskrantz), pp. 415–429. Harper and Row, New York.

Weiskrantz, L. (1972). Behavioural analysis of the monkey's visual nervous system. *Proc. Roy. Soc. Lond. B*, **182**, 427–455.

Weiskrantz, L. (1977). Trying to bridge some neuropsychological gaps between monkey and man. *British Journal of Psychology*, **68**, 431–445.

Weiskrantz, L. (1978). Some aspects of visual capacity in monkeys and man following striate cortex lesions. *Arch. Ital. Biol.*, **116**, 318–323.

Weiskrantz, L. (1980). Varieties of residual experience. (Eighth Sir Frederick Bartlett Lecture.) *Q. J. exp. Psychol.*, **32**, 365–386.

Weiskrantz, L. (1983). Evidence and scotomata. *Beh. Brain Sci.*, **6**, 464–467.

Weiskrantz, L. (1985). On issues and theories of the human amnesic syndrome. In *Memory systems of the brain: Animal and human cognitive processes,* (ed. N.M. Weinberger, J.L. McGaugh and G. Lynch), pp. 380–415. Guilford Press, New York.

Weiskrantz, L. (1986). *Blindsight. A case study and implications.* Oxford Univ. Press, Oxford.

Weiskrantz, L. (1987a). Residual vision in a scotoma: a follow-up study of 'form' discrimination. *Brain*, **110**, 77–92.

Weiskrantz, L. (1987b). Neuroanatomy of memory and amnesia: A case for multiple memory systems. *Human neurobiol.*, **6**, 93–105.

Weiskrantz, L. (1987c). Neuropsychology and the nature of consciousness. In *Mindwaves*, (ed. C. Blakemore and S. Greenfield), pp. 307–320. Blackwell, Oxford.

Weiskrantz, L. (ed.) (1988). *Thought without language.* Oxford Univ. Press, Oxford.

Weiskrantz, L. (1989). Remembering dissociations. In: *Varieties of memory and consciousness: Papers in honour of Endel Tulving*, (ed. F. Craik and H. Roediger), pp. 101–120. Erlbaum, Hillsdale, NJ.

Weiskrantz, L. (1990a). Problems of learning and memory: one or multiple systems? *Phil. Trans. R. Soc.*, **329B**, 99–108.

Weiskrantz L. (1990b). Outlooks for blindsight: explicit methodologies for implicit processes. (The Ferrier Lecture.) *Proc. Roy. Soc. Lond. B.*, **B239**, 247–278.

Weiskrantz, L. (1991a). Disconnected awareness for detecting, processing, and remembering in neurological patients. *J. Roy. Soc. Med.*, **84**, 466–470.

Weiskrantz, L. (1991b). Dissociations and associates in neuropsychology. In *Perspectives on cognitive neuropsychology*, (ed. R.G. Lister and H.J. Weingartner), pp. 157–164. Oxford Univ. Press, Oxford.

Weiskrantz, L. (1995). Blindsight: Not an island unto itself. *Curr. Dir. Psychol. Sci.*, **4**, 146–151.

Weiskrantz, L. (1996). Blindsight revisited. *Current opinion in neurobiology*, **6**, 215–220.

Weiskrantz L. and Cowey, A. (1970). Filling in the scotoma: a study of residual vision after striate cortex lesions in monkeys. In *Progress in physiological psychology*, vol. 3, (ed. E. Stellar and J.M. Sprague), pp. 237–260. Academic Press, New York.

Weiskrantz, L. and Warrington, E.K. (1970). Verbal learning and retention by amnesic patients using partial information. *Psychon. Sci.*, **20**, 210–211.

Weiskrantz, L. and Warrington, E.K. (1979). Conditioning in amnesic patients. *Neuropsychologia*, **17**, 187–194.

Weiskrantz, L., Mihailovic, Lj., and Gross, C.G. (1962). Effects of stimulation of frontal cortex and hippocampus on behaviour in the monkey. *Brain*, **85**, 487–505.

Weiskrantz, L., Warrington, E.K., Sanders, M.D., and Marshall, J. (1974). Visual capacity in the hemianopic field following a restricted occipital ablation. *Brain*, **97**, 709–728.

Weiskrantz, L., Cowey, A., and Passingham, C. (1977). Spatial responses to brief stimuli by monkeys with striate cortex ablations, *Brain*, **100**, 655–670.

Weiskrantz, L., Harlow, A., and Barbur, J.L. (1991). Factors affecting visual sensitivity in a hemianopic subject. *Brain*, **114**, 2269–2282.

Weiskrantz, L., Barbur, J.L., and Sahraie, A. (1995). Parameters affecting conscious versus unconscious visual discrimination without V1. *Proc. Natl Acad. Sci., USA*, **92**, 6122–6126.

Werth, R. (1983). 'Blindsight': some conceptual considerations. *Beh. Brain Sci.*, **6**, 467–468.

Wilson, B.A. (1995). Management and remediation of memory problems in brain-injured adults. In *Handbook of memory disorders*, (ed. A.D. Baddeley, B.A. Wilson, and F.N. Watts), pp. 451–479.

Winocur, G. and Weiskrantz, L. (1976). An investigation of paired-associate learning in amnesic patients. *Neuropsychologia*, **14**, 97–110.

Wittgenstein, L. (1922). *Tractatus logico-philophicus*. Routledge and Kegan Paul, London.

Wood, F., Ebert, V. and Kinsbourne, M. (1982). The episodic-semantic memory distinction in memory and amnesia: Clinical and experimental observations. In *Human memory and amnesia,* (ed. L. Cermak). Erlbaum, Hillsdale, NJ.

Yapko, M.D. (1994). *Suggestions of abuse*. Simon and Schuster, New York.

Young, A.W. (1988). Functional organization of visual recognition. In *Thought without language,* (ed. L. Weiskrantz), pp. 78–107. Oxford Univ. Press, Oxford.

Young, A.W. (1994). Conscious and unconscious recognition of familiar faces. In *Attention and performance XV*, (ed. C. Umulta and M. Moscovitch, pp. 153–178. M.I.T. Press, Cambridge, MA.

Young, A.W. and De Haan, E.H.F. (1992). Face recognition and awareness after brain injury. In *The neuropsychology of consciousness*, (ed. A.D. Milner and M. D. Rugg), pp. 69–90. Academic Press, London.

Young, A.W., De Haan, E.H.F., and Newcombe, F. (1990). Unawareness of impaired face recognition. *Brain Cogn.*, **14**, 1–18.

Young, A.W., Humphreys, G.W., Riddoch, M.J., Hellawell, D.J., and De Haan, E.H.F. (1994). Recognition impairments and face imagery. *Neuropsychologia*, **32**, 693–702.

Young, M.P. (1992). Objective analysis of the topological organization of the primate cortical visual system. *Nature*, **358**, 152–155.

Young, M.P. (1993). The organization of neural systems in the primate cerebral cortex. *Proc. R. Soc. Lond. B*, **252**, 13–18.

Yukie, M. and Iwai, E. (1981). Direct projection from dorsal lateral geniculate nucleus to the prestriate cortex in macaque monkeys. *J. Comp. Neurol.*, **201**, 81–97.

Zeki, S. (1978). Functional specialization in the visual cortex of the rhesus monkey. *Nature, Lond.*, **274**, 423–428.

Zeki, S. (1981). The mapping of visual functions in the cerebral cortex. In *Brain mechanisms of sensation*, (ed. Y. Katsuki, R. Notgren, and M. Sato), pp. 105–128. Wiley, New York.

Zeki, S. (1993). *A vision of the brain*. Blackwell Scientific Publications, Oxford.

Zihl, J. (1980). 'Blindsight': improvement of visually guided eye movements by systematic practice in patients with cerebral blindness. *Neuropsychologia*, **18**, 71–77.

Zihl, J. (1981). Recovery of visual functions in patients with cerebral blindness. *Exp. Brain Res.*, **44**, 159–169.

Zihl, J. and von Cramon, D. (1979). Restitution of visual function in patients with cerebral blindness. *J. Neurol. Neurosurg. Psychiat.*, **42**, 312–322.

Zihl, J. and von Cramon, D. (1980). Registration of light stimuli in the cortically blind hemifield and its effect on localization. *Beh. Brain Res.*, **1**, 287–298.

Zihl, J. and von Cramon, D. (1985). Visual field recovery from scotoma in patients with postgeniculate damage: a review of 55 cases. *Brain*, **108**, 335–365.

Zihl, J. and Werth, R. (1984a). Contributions to the study of 'blindsight' -I. Can stray light account for saccadic localization in patients with postgeniculate field defects? *Neuropsychologia*, **22**, 1–11.

Zihl, J. and Werth, R. (1984b). Contributions to the study of 'blindsight' -II. The role of specific practice for saccadic localization in patients with postgeniculate visual field defects. *Neuropsychologia*, **22**, 13–22.

Zihl, J., Tretter, F., and Singer, W. (1980). Phasic electrodermal responses after visual stimulation in the cortically blind hemifield. *Behav. Brain Res.*, **1**, 197–203.

Zihl, J., von Cramon, D., and Mai, N. (1983). Selective disturbance of movement vision after bilateral brain damage. *Brain*, **106**, 313–340.

Author index

Subject index